In the Footsteps of Genghis Khan

In the Footsteps of

Genghis Khan

JOHN DeFRANCIS

A KOLOWALU BOOK  UNIVERSITY OF HAWAII PRESS

HONOLULU

951.7
D

Library of Congress Cataloging-in-Publication Data

DeFrancis, John, 1911–
    In the footsteps of Genghis Khan / John DeFrancis.
      p.   cm.
    "A Kolowalu Book."
    ISBN 0–8248–1493–2 (alk. paper)
    1. Inner Mongolia (China)—Description and travel. 2. Kansu
Province (China)—Description and travel. I. Title.
DS793.M7D37   1993
951'.77—dc20   92-36542
                                                     CIP

Designed by Kenneth Miyamoto

FOR

CAMELEER ZHOU

and even
CAMELEER XIAO and MANAGER GUO and
ADMIRAL CHEN

and of course
MARTIN and GEORG and TORGNY

and especially
KAY

Contents

Maps

Acknowledgments

All the photographs of the travels narrated in this book were taken by H. Desmond Martin. Unfortunately, neither he nor I thought to include him among the subjects to be photographed. As a result, the only photographic record of his participation in the journey is his shadow in the picture he took of the Xinjiang caravan in chapter 10.

The drawings in this book were made by Myra Taketa, a multitalented secretary in the Department of East Asian Languages and Literatures at the University of Hawaii, whose sunny disposition increased the pleasure of our collaboration in the production of these light sketches.

1 / You Can't Do
That Anymore

We dodged warring armies by stealing twelve hundred miles down the bandit-infested Yellow River on an inflated sheepskin raft. You can't do that anymore. You can't repeat our thousand-mile camel trek across the Gobi Desert in the footsteps of Genghis Khan. You can't sit at a camel-dung campfire in the very heart of that huge desert and listen to a Mongol narrate how the Great Khan was castrated by a captured Tangut beauty he tried to take to bed. Neither can you visit the oasis, then one of the most remote places in the world, where we met a Mongol princess descended from survivors of the most horrendous mass migration in human history. Nor can you barge into the preserve of a churlish Muslim warlord and become a prisoner in his fortress town.

There's lots more we did then that you can't do anymore, for a variety of reasons. For one thing, many areas of China that challenged the adventuresome in the good old bad old days were declared off-limits more than a half-century ago. Since then, the barriers have been removed (though sometimes replaced) in most of the country, including even Tibet, but not in the heart of the Gobi Desert, not in sensitive border areas, which have become even more inaccessible today than they were then.

In recent years quite a few tourists have gotten to the fringes of that forbidden expanse. I have joined them, in my mind's eye, like a starveling out of Dickens gazing hollow-eyed into a bakeshop window. But even though the view from the outside is now obscured, it is still possible, for a discerning eye, to make out something of the veiled interior.

It's easy enough to get to a few vantage points where you can try to

1

peek in. You could start by boarding a train at Peking, which the Chinese have browbeaten most of us into calling Beijing, though there is no more reason to do so than to change Rome to Roma or Moscow to Moskva. From Peking you go about five hundred miles northwest to the capital of the Inner Mongolia Autonomous Region at Hohhot, which was called Guihua when I visited it back then. (I'm talking about the year 1935, and I'm going to give you the names of places then and now, in the presently preferred spelling, so that you can follow me on the map.)

Don't assume that you've now reached the land of Genghis Khan. You're still a long way from there. In Hohhot, Mongols are to Chinese as hare is to horse in a cacciatore rabbit stew containing one of each. That was true even then, as it is now. And also, don't be taken in by the hyped-up travelogues of minor Munchhausens who make a big thing of being escorted a few miles off the railway. What they actually see in such vetted tours is even more ersatz than the Wild West marketed at a dude ranch.

In our mid-thirties travels, we left the train at Guihua (Hohhot), rather than continue a bit farther to the end of the line at Baotou, because it was the starting point for most of the caravans going west toward central Asia. Arriving too late in the caravan season to join up with one there, we went by car a hundred miles north to a major caravan outpost called the Temple of the Larks. It was not until we got three-quarters of the way there, some seventy miles away from the railroad, that we reached honest-to-goodness Mongol territory.

Most of the area in between had been gobbled up by land-hungry Chinese spilling north beyond the Great Wall. In displacing the Mongols they had turned good grassland into marginal farmland, a process that in some places ended up as bad desert. Some Mongols, too, had taken to farming. They were hardly distinguishable from Chinese. In that intermediary area near the railroad we met with only a few Mongols who were still clinging to their old way of life.

Because no outsiders have reported on conditions in the area since our long-distant visit, there is no way of knowing where the dividing line is today between steppe and sown, or what the relations between Mongols and Chinese are really like now. They were going from bad to worse to worst then.

Even more shrouded in obscurity is the part of Mongolia that we covered by camel after leaving the Temple of the Larks. From that caravan outpost we started out on the first leg of our camel trip, a thirty-eight-day trek of six hundred miles into the heart of the Gobi Desert. For some of that distance we skirted the border between Inner and Outer Mongolia—

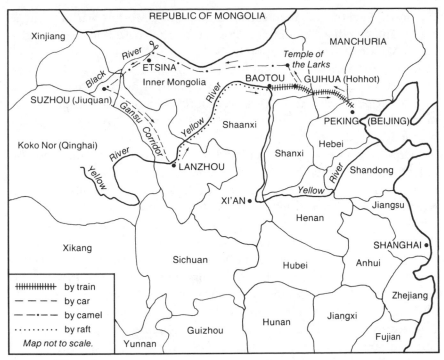

Route of Travel

what we should more formally call the border between the People's Republic of China and the Republic of Mongolia, until recently known as the Mongolian People's Republic. It was an ill-defined border then, and it is still in dispute. As a sensitive military zone it has long been hermetically sealed off from prying eyes.

The same appears to be true of the second leg of our camel trip. That involved trekking another four hundred miles along the elongated riverine oasis known to the Mongols as the Etsin Gol, or River of the Emperor, and to the Chinese as the Hei Ho, or Black River. We had reached that oasis in the vicinity of two salt lakes, close to the border with Outer Mongolia, where the river gives up its attempt to push through the desert. It was then one of the most isolated spots on earth. From there we followed the north-flowing river upstream, with the desolate waste of the Gobi Desert closely hemming in the river on both sides.

Our camel trip ended at a decrepit walled town called Suzhou, later renamed Jiuquan or Wine Spring, that has metamorphosed into an industrial metropolis, thanks to the railroad built along the old Silk Road through the Gansu Corridor between Tibet on the south and Mongolia on the north. Suzhou was then the stronghold of a Muslim warlord named Ma, meaning "horse," a common Muslim surname based on the first syllable of Mahomet. He was unpopularly called Big Horse, as were several other Muslim warlords, including an older brother we encountered later. Our Suzhou Big Horse was peevishly affronted at our trespassing on his private property. The result was an enforced stay there of more than a month instead of the two or three days on which we had originally planned.

Sharp-eyed observers can get some tantalizing glimpses into the two bits of terra incognita that mark the beginning and end of our travels in the Gobi. They note the existence of two little-known spur lines, both of which run north from trunk rail lines, all the product of frenetic railway construction in the past few decades. One spur goes north from near Baotou. The other goes north from near Suzhou.

The spur from Baotou goes about a hundred miles to a place named Bayan Obo, which translates as something like Rich Cairn. In Mongolia cairns are heaps of stones that serve as landmarks for travelers. But obviously no one builds a railroad just so people can gawk at a pile of stones. One possibility is that the spur was planned as a dagger pointing up at the soft underbelly of the vast but sparsely populated Republic of Mongolia. Another purpose may have been to feed the Baotou industrial complex with coal that I remember being reported in the area. But no one on the outside knows precisely what's going on in that part of Mongolia.

Marco Polo was a more observant traveler than a lot of our present-day visitors to China. On reporting his journey through Suzhou and points east, that remarkable Venetian gave a brief but accurate account of the Black River route, the same route we had taken in the footsteps of Genghis Khan, for he had recognized that it was a major means of access between the center of Mongol power in the north and the territories Genghis had set out to conquer in the south. A few recent travelers have reported on visits to Suzhou and the nearby western end of the Great Wall, but no one seems to have thought of looking north to that corridor of conquest. If they had, they might have wondered why the Chinese have built a spur line from near Suzhou north several hundred miles along the river almost to the border of Outer Mongolia. This looks like another dagger aimed at that bulging belly of the Republic of Mongolia.

Or does the spur have an economic significance that we missed? Perhaps the Chinese built it to exploit the riches of a mountain sacred to the Mongols called Bayan Bogdo, or Rich God. Although we never learned why the Mongols call it that, one can be pretty sure it's not because of the material riches found in the mountain. That wealth consists of mineral deposits discovered by a group of Swedish explorers only a short time before we visited the area. "The whole of the south side" they reported, "is pure ore, iron and manganese. The ore-bearing horizon stretches right up to the monastery of Tsagan-Obo-Sume." Have the Chinese profaned the sacred mountain by digging into it? If so, did the Mongols react like the lamas we were told about in the east, who furiously objected to violating the spirits of the earth by mining for coal?

Questions, questions, but no answers, for no one has gone there to ask them.

It would be nice if visitors to China with a taste for something different would attempt, hopefully with more success than I have had, to make some forays into forbidden territory, to start with, by taking a little ride on those two spur lines. Even if these are only workaday railroads hauling a lot of minerals, they probably go through some pretty interesting—perhaps even spectacular—countryside. But in case there's more to be seen from your railroad coach than mines and scenery, be sure your passport is in order and that you get permission to travel on those lines or elsewhere off the beaten track. You wouldn't want anyone to think you're trying to ferret out military secrets.

If you do succeed in obtaining such permission, I hope you will make better use of it than some tourists who have repeated other portions of our trip. Take the route we did through the Gansu Corridor from Suzhou east to Lanzhou, the main city in the province, a stretch that we covered under military escort on a truck belonging to the inhospitable Big Horse. That trip over what then passed for a motor road, on a vehicle driven by what passed for an experienced driver, didn't leave much to be undesired, but it did have the great advantage of letting us see a lot of the countryside and hobnob with a fair assortment of the local population.

Now, however, people whisk through the Corridor by plane or train, sometimes making a quick stop in Lanzhou and another in Suzhou, but not bothering to look at anything in between. That's a pity, for the whole Gansu Corridor is dotted with ancient walled towns containing historic temples and pagodas, as well as excavated archaeological sites where cultural relics of timeless artistry have been found. The view from a speeding conveyance is unlikely either to reveal these artifacts of the past or to provide understanding of why Gansu has been one of the most turbulent provinces in Chinese history.

To be sure, some of these places along the Corridor may not be accessible to outside visitors for one reason or another, including the perhaps

deserved reputation foreigners have of being too effete to endure the living conditions to which ordinary Chinese are accustomed. But even if
foreigners were willing and able to follow the when-in-Rome precept,
they would not be able to repeat the next phase of our travels. At that
time, on arriving at Lanzhou we found that the normal way back to
Peking via Xi'an (bus from Lanzhou and train from Xi'an) was blocked by
fighting between Chinese Muslim forces allied with Chiang Kai-shek's
regime and Chinese Communist forces under Mao Zedong nearing the
end of their Long March.

There were only two alternatives. One was to fly over the fighting in a
plane operated by a German-run airline. The other was to dodge around
it by hiring an inflated sheepskin raft to carry us down the river to
Baotou, from which we could take our old train back to Guihua and then
on to Peking. The latter provided more opportunity for new experiences,
so that's what we did. It took us two weeks to cover the tortuous course
of the river in its almost twelve hundred miles from Lanzhou to the railhead.

You can't do that anymore for the simple reason that the Yellow River
is now blocked by a dam constructed in 1967 near Yinchuan, a city for-
merly called Ningxia, now the capital of the Ningxia Hui Autonomous
Region. *Hui* is a term meaning "Muslim" derived from the word "returned" that supposedly refers to those who had returned to the true
faith. *Ningxia* is the old provincial term for the region. The area has now
been set aside for one of China's fifty-five "national minorities," in this
case one that is distinguished only in religion from non-Muslim Chinese,
who are called "Han" after the great Han Dynasty (206 B.C. to A.D. 220).
But that "only" actually covers a world of difference, given the all-
encompassing nature of Islam. It has made for a relationship that over the
years has ranged from uneasy accommodation to mutual butchery.

Although that area is no longer accessible by raft, it is now served by a
railroad extending all the way from Lanzhou to Baotou. Like the line from
Lanzhou to Suzhou and points west, that from Lanzhou to Baotou
involves remarkable feats of engineering through terrible terrain.

Not many people have taken the train along this stretch of the Yellow
River. Fewer still have stopped off anywhere along the way and written
about what the situation is like there now. Those few are almost all of
Chinese ancestry—some citizens of Hong Kong, others "overseas Chi-
nese." People with the wrong genes ride through on the train between
Lanzhou and Baotou without much chance of getting off to look around.

That situation reminds me of my return to the States from China in

1936 by way of Korea and Japan. On my train journey through Korea, then part of the empire of the Rising Sun, a Japanese soldier insisted on pulling down the window shades to prevent my prying eyes from seeing the landscape.

The shades are not drawn on the Chinese train, but fleeting glimpses of the countryside won't tell you much about present conditions in what used to be one of the worst hellholes of China. Even if, like the favored few of Chinese ancestry, you manage to get off and look around, you won't see much in a few specially selected sites. You might be permitted the touristy thrill of a perfectly safe ride on a raft for a few miles in a designated area. You might also get to look at some interesting desert-control undertakings and wander around the mosque-filled city of Yinchuan. But such experiences are likely to leave you, as they have obviously left most recent Chinese visitors, with limited understanding of their significance. What is lacking is a sense of the past that can inform the present.

When we were trekking through the desert, I filled my journal with descriptions of the fascinating, ever-changing landscape, but my ignorance of geology limited my understanding of what I was seeing. In similar fashion, ignorance of the past also impedes understanding of the human landscape. Henry Ford was wrong. History is not bunk.

Here is a bit of personal history, based mainly on journal notes now yellowed with age, which can be read as both a tale of high adventure in the wild west of China and as prelude to the present in that tortured land.

MAYBE FORD WAS CITING 'SELECTIVE HISTORY'

2 / Martin and the
Ides of May

‡‡‡‡‡‡‡

Before Martin's death in 1973, he had achieved his lifetime goal of writing a book about Genghis Khan's conquest of China. That was years after we had gone our separate ways. Our paths crossed for only a few months (we couldn't stand each other for longer than that). Or, more literally, it was only for a few months that we walked the same road in the footsteps of Genghis Khan.

‡‡‡‡‡‡‡

Martin's coat of arms might well have been a stiff upper lip rampant on a field of whiskey and sodas. Actually, that second-hand witticism only came to mind later, when a lawyer friend of mine referred to him as a fellow member of the bar—the one in the Hotel du Nord watering hole frequented by Peking's most indefatigable elbow-benders. My main impression on first encounter was that he faintly recalled the stereotype of upper-class British.

I was alone in the dining hall of the school hostel having an early dinner so that I could put a miserable cold to bed. A stranger appeared at the doorway. He hesitated a moment, then came up to my table.

"May I?"

I nodded, pointed to the chair opposite, and blew my nose again.

We exchanged introductions. He handed me his card: H. Desmond Martin, Esq. A Canadian. Not tall, about five nine. Slim figure, well groomed, but not in a way that would draw attention. He sat erect, seemed a bit stiff and formal. His speech was direct and slightly clipped, with just a hint of pedantic precision.

"Your name, DeFrancis, is it French?"

"No, Italian. It was originally DeFrancesco."

"Why did you change it?"

"I didn't. My father did. He gave up hope of ever getting Americans to pronounce it right. So he changed his name from Francesco DeFrancesco to Frank DeFrancis."

"Sounds aristocratic."

I laughed. "Hardly. My folks were peasants."

Something in the emanations from Martin aroused a perverse desire to rub in the difference between us.

"My mother was illiterate, but my father knew how to read."

"Oh."

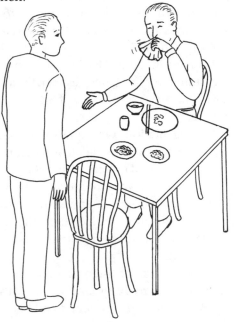

"Yeah. He was just a laborer, but people called him *Il Professore*. That was only because they considered him very sharp. His education was actually quite limited. So I was told. He died when I was very young, so I have hardly any direct memories of him."

Martin was less forthcoming about himself. His family went back some way in England, but he himself had come to China from Canada. He was a graduate of McGill University in Montreal, class of 1934.

Humph. A slow learner. He was twenty-five years old, he said, two years older than I was, but hadn't graduated until a year after me. But I was wrong. He had taken time out to travel a lot. Where to? Oh, various places. And he read a lot too. It was just that he was in no hurry. Not like me. I was anxious to get on with life.

He asked about my schooling.

"Yale 1933."

There was only a slight lifting of an eyebrow, but he might as well have blurted out the question. How had a member of the lower classes managed that?

"Scholarships, and luck."

Especially luck. First a well-paying steel-mill job in the summer between high school and college. Then even greater luck—a long-lasting job as night dispatcher for the AAA. Yes, I occasionally nodded off in class, but that job had enabled me to pay all my college expenses and accumulate a nice nest egg that I used to finance my trip to China.

"Why China?"

I was resigned to Martin's question. People seemed to think that anyone immersed in China, especially anyone deeply involved in the language, must be something of a freak. In my case the answer was embarrassing.

"Miscalculation. Oh, things have worked out pretty well so far, but I started out with a miscalculation that might have proved disastrous."

Martin wanted to hear all about it.

In my senior year in college, I said, I had happened to room next to what China hands call a missionary brat. He was Winston Pettus, whose father ran a school called the College of Chinese Studies in Peking. He regaled me with tales about China. Ah, the Exotic East. It beckoned. I responded.

In the course of listening to Win's wondrous tales I concocted a brilliant plan for my future. At home, with the Great Depression still raging, my B.A. degree in economics and history was not worth much more than the five-cent apples the unemployed were selling on almost every street corner. So I conceived a plan to go to China, learn Chinese, and present myself there to a company like Standard Oil, saying "Hire me! I'm one up on the other guys because I know Chinese."

The only thing wrong with this plan, I belatedly discovered, was that it was all wrong. Not the least of my oversights was the fact that Standard Oil did its hiring in New York, not in the field. And the tongue-tied tycoons who run our business enterprises (into the ground, it often seems) could hardly care less whether or not their underlings could handle the language of the country they worked in: the natives were expected to know English.

"That must have been a blow," said Martin.

Not until I got to China, I told him. Win said he could arrange for me to have a job as library assistant in his father's school, which would take care of most of my expenses. So I decided to seek my fortune by heeding the old call "Go West, young man!"—and I would heed it so faithfully that I would end up in the East.

My westward trek to the East got me to China at the end of the summer following graduation. I went by car from New Haven to San Diego in five days of driving day and night with three classmates. Then I took a slow boat to China—a month-long trip by a Dutch freighter that went nonstop from San Diego to Shanghai.

My education began immediately on arrival. Shipboard friends invited me to tag along when they went to a restaurant for dinner as guests of a fellow American, the local representative of Standard Oil, or some such concern. At the end of the evening our host presented a tip by taking out a Chinese banknote, tearing it in half, and throwing it at the waiter's feet.

I gaped. We representatives of the Master Race strode out past a row of bowing servitors.

The next day I took a train to Peking.

"So here I am," I concluded.

Martin asked about the school.

"It's run with an iron hand by Old Man Pettus. Most of the students are missionaries. The language program is grueling—some five to six hours of teacher-student contact a day, much of it on a one-on-one basis in a tiny cubicle with a series of teachers who push you to your limit. I recommend it as a good way to start, with its emphasis on learning to speak. But it's limited academically."

Martin asked who the nonmissionaries studying Chinese were. I told him there were only two or three, all older people, not in the regular program. They seemed to be friends of Pettus, staying in the hostel, dabbling a bit in Chinese.

"No younger people?"

"Not here. There are a few studying on their own elsewhere. I understand it doesn't cost much to hire a Chinese tutor. A friend of mine, Haldore Hanson, tells me he's just hired one of the American Legation teachers for only ten dollars Mex a month."

"Did you say 'ten dollars Mex'? What's that?"

"Oh, that's the usual way of citing the cost of things in the local currency. It seems that some time ago Mexican silver dollars were imported into China in large quantities and soon became the main medium of exchange in most of the country. Right now a dollar Mex is equal to US forty cents. So Hal's teacher costs him only ten dollars Mex, or four U.S. dollars, a month. I can put you in touch with Hal if you want more information about hiring a teacher."

Martin didn't seem too keen to learn more about the program at the school or about studying on one's own.

"What else do you do besides study?"

I told him about my library job. It was actually a sinecure. I felt like a kid in a candy store. Routine work like checking out books left me with plenty of opportunity to gorge on the cornucopia of enticing things displayed on the shelves.

"What about social life?"

I didn't think we'd be moving in the same circles, but I told him that for me Peking offered a satisfying amount of social life made all the pleasanter by the fact that, for some unaccountable but eminently happy reason, young bachelors were in short supply.

"Do you have a girlfriend?"

"No, but I'm working on one. I'm trying to overcome a bad start."

"How was that?"

"Actually, I only half-remember the episode. She—her name's Kay Wilson—embarrassed me by telling about it when we bumped into each other again at a party at the Legation. As she tells it, she comes to the library one day and spies me seated at the checkout desk bent over a book. 'I know him.' she says. 'He was at Val Shooligan's party the other day.' So she waltzes up and says cheerily: 'Oh, hello. Do you have Juliet Bredon's *Peking?*' I look up, scowling, and say, 'Have you checked the card catalogue?' At that point Mr. Wang, the librarian, comes over and asks if he can help. He finds the book for her, suggests other reading, climbs up the ladder to get a couple more books. She leaves gnashing her teeth and muttering, 'Aren't the Chinese the *nicest* people.' That's how she tells it."

"What's she like?"

"Hal Hanson describes her as a vivacious blonde from India. Not really blonde, though. That's his way of saying she was born in India of missionary parents. Five feet two and a quarter inches tall. She insists on that quarter-inch. Smart, soft on the outside, but with a good firm backbone. Resourceful. She was passing through Peking with a tour group, fell in love with the city, scrounged around, and, the day before her group was slated to leave, landed a job teaching English and typing and shorthand in a commercial school, keeping just one step ahead of her classes. The students love her. She's a very caring person."

"Are you making any progress?"

"I don't know yet."

Martin asked me if I had given up the idea of a career in business.

"Yes. It isn't just that I made a mistake about corporate hiring practices. I don't like what I've seen of the American business community here. Narrow. No long-range vision, no serious interest in trying to understand the Chinese and their problems. I'm fascinated by everything about the country—its language, its writing system, the grandeur of its past, the terrible problems of the present. But I'm frankly coasting along right now. Don't know where I'm heading."

I asked Martin whether he had come here to study Chinese.

"Well, I've just arrived, and I'm sort of scouting around."

In later meetings Martin gradually opened up. He loved to talk, and could chatter on and on, on all sorts of topics, for he was unquestionably well read. He enjoyed hearing himself talk and paid no mind to whether his audience shared the enjoyment.

His main interest, it transpired, was military history, to which the conversation, or rather his monologues, somehow always returned. On that subject he waxed especially prolix, if not exactly eloquent, telling you more than you wanted to know about the campaigns of great military leaders like Napoleon. He had tramped over some of the historic battlefields in Europe, and roamed over all of them in his mind. If you asked him a question about this battle or that, he would whip out a piece of paper, sketch the disposition of the opposing forces, and expound on how the victor had moved troops around to take advantage of the terrain, the weather, and the weaknesses of the enemy. He never seemed to notice my eyes glazing over.

Martin had a special interest in the Mongols and their military exploits. I ventured a remark about the fear the Mongols engendered by their horrendous massacres. He chided me for not viewing the matter in proper perspective.

"Europeans expressed horror at the massacres but conveniently forgot the blood-letting they engaged in against each other, as well as against anyone blocking the advance of Western civilization. Why, in 1291 Edward I of England slew something like eight thousand of the people of Berwick. No, the Mongols were not exceptionally cruel. Their massacres were just on a bigger scale because the places they overran were generally larger and more populated."

Genghis Khan was Martin's greatest hero.

"My ambition in life is to write a history of the Mongol conquest of China in the thirteenth century."

"It hasn't been done already?"

"Only in part. I've read just about everything that's been written about the Mongols in English. Now I'd like to tap Chinese and Mongolian sources to make a detailed study of how Genghis carried out his campaigns against China."

"You have your work cut out for you. Learning those two languages should keep you busy for a while."

"Actually, I'm not very good at languages. I'll have to rely on others for assistance."

"Isn't that pretty risky? And expensive? How can you be sure that assistants won't overlook something of importance? Or misunderstand the material? Or commit other errors? You'll have to assume responsibility for any mistakes, you know."

Martin acknowledged the risks but said he would try to minimize them by hiring the best assistants available.

"What about the expense?"

"Fortunately," he said, "I can afford it."

The next time I saw Martin my cold had progressed down to my chest. I had a hacking cough.

"That's quite a bark you have there," said Martin. "You sound like a seal."

"My bite's worse."

"What you need is a vacation. I understand you've been studying for a year and a half without a break, and that you've had colds all winter long. You're run-down. You should take a break, get out of Peking, bask in the sun."

The next day I felt even worse. Martin came to my room as I was propped up in bed doggedly reviewing my character cards for the day— small slips about two inches square with a Chinese character or phrase on one side and its transcription and meaning on the other.

"About that vacation," he said, as if we were continuing yesterday's conversation. "I have an idea."

"Yeah?"

"Yes. You need a vacation; I need to travel with someone who can speak Chinese. Let's join forces on a trip retracing the footsteps of Genghis Khan."

"Look, Martin," I said, with more than a hint of irritation. "I haven't the foggiest notion of what that means. Of course you're right about my needing a vacation. But to be brutally frank, I don't see how our different life-styles can accommodate a trip together. I have to watch my pennies so they'll last long enough to get me back to the States."

Martin tried to interrupt, but I pressed on.

"And that's not all. If I did make any sort of trip, I would want to live as much like the Chinese as possible. Here in Peking we're isolated from the life of ordinary Chinese. I need to acquire a gut feeling for at least some aspects of Chinese life, and I won't get that by burying my nose in a book or staying in places that cater to foreigners."

"But that's exactly what I need, too. You don't understand. Yes, I don't have to pinch pennies. Even so, I want to get a firsthand grasp of the conditions facing the Mongols when they invaded China."

I thought that over. Perhaps I was doing Martin an injustice. Certainly he was not flaunting the difference between us. Was I being overly sensitive about the matter? Maybe there was a basis for doing something together after all. Despite what seemed to be his standoffishness, perhaps he really would be willing, for his own reasons, to come down to the level at which I had to operate out of necessity. There was a great deal to be said, too, for traveling with someone who was a walking encyclopedia of the area we would be covering, even if that knowledge was largely bookish. And I was beginning to realize how much I needed to climb out of the rut I was in, practice my Chinese in a real-life situation, get somewhere where I could stick out my elbows without poking a zillion Chinese in the ribs.

I looked at him hard. "Do you really mean that about getting a firsthand grasp of what conditions may have been like earlier?"

"I most certainly do. I'm quite prepared to forgo first-class travel, accommodations catering to foreigners, and all that sort of thing."

"Well. . . ."

"Yes, I want to experience Chinese life as close as possible to that of the thirteenth century."

Little did he realize how close to that century he was actually to get.

Martin took a map from his pocket and spread it out over the bedspread.

"Look. Here's our itinerary. First we go from Peking to Xi'an by train."

"That's easy."

"Then we take a bus from Xi'an to Lanzhou in Gansu province."

"On the Old Silk Road?"

"Yes. Then we take another bus along that road through the Gansu Corridor. That's the route that Marco Polo took into China, you know.

We get to Suzhou, a town known to Marco Polo as Sicciu, and from there make a little jaunt about twenty miles farther west to the end of the Great Wall."

"That's nice. Most people only get to see the eastern end near Peking."

"Then we return to Suzhou. This part I'm not too sure about. The situation in that area is unclear, but it might be possible to go a bit north along the Black River. Maybe even as far as the Black City, Marco Polo's Etsina. That's the reverse of the route that Genghis Khan took. He led his invasion forces south along the river to Suzhou, then east along the Corridor."

"How would we cover the stretch along the river?"

"We'll have to check it out at Suzhou. Perhaps we can arrange some sort of motor transport. Or perhaps we can do part of it on horseback or camel."

"I don't know about the horse and camel bit. I really don't know how to ride."

"Let's worry about that later. We can take it easy in the river area. Maybe we can do a spot of camping and hiking there. You can soak up a lot of sun and get rid of your persistent colds."

I was growing more and more interested. Nice to have a vacation that was a bit adventuresome and out of the ordinary. The train trip would be routine, but I liked the idea of going by bus along the romantic Silk Road, encountering the ghost of Marco Polo in his travels of almost seven hundred years ago. And I liked even better the prospect of camping at the Black River—basking in the sun, hiking along the river, swimming in its cool water.

"Well?" asked Martin. "Agreed?"

"Well . . . oh, hell, yes! Agreed!"

And so the die was cast. We were to retrace the footsteps of Genghis Khan. It was the first day of April. Old Man Pettus would have said it was a singularly appropriate date.

"What do we do to get ready?" I asked. "How long before we start?"

"Leave the details to me. I'll find out just what has to be done. We'd better get started right away on some things that will take time."

"Like having a pair of hiking boots made for me. No chance of finding a ready-made pair to fit my long narrow feet."

"Let's give ourselves about three weeks," said Martin.

One of the tasks that needed to be done was to get internal visas from the Chinese authorities granting us permission to travel in the back country. Martin expected no problem for himself, since he had a good friend in the British Legation who could handle the paperwork for him. After a wait of several weeks, however, he was informed that travel was restricted to the main cities along the railroads. Gansu was off-limits.

The American Legation was of even less help to me. The bureaucrats there even urged me to abandon the trip. I tried to bypass them by approaching the American Consulate in the nearby port city of Tientsin, hoping the officials there would not check with those in the legation. The ploy worked, more or less. Mostly less. My passport was returned in the record time of four days, stamped with permission to travel along the railways. It had an addition that must have been made by a Chinese bureaucrat with a puckish sense of humor I was in no mood to appreciate. Permission was granted to travel in the Tibetan-inhabited province of Koko Nor or Qinghai, which I had not asked for, but was specifically withheld from Gansu, a necessary transit area to get to Koko Nor.

Martin and I glumly held a council of war. I was particularly disappointed. "There goes my nice pipe dream of taking a dip in the Black River and sunning myself on the riverbank."

I halfheartedly suggested going to Xi'an and just trying our luck at getting into Gansu. Martin shot that one down immediately. He had already suggested the idea to his legation friend, but the latter had cited several specific cases of people being turned back unless they were traveling on necessary business. And "necessary business" did not include the deal I had worked out with Dr. Feng, a parasitologist at Peking Union Medical College who was a specialist on malaria-carrying mosquitoes. His information on the Northwest being practically nil, Dr. Feng was anxious to obtain specimens from that area and arranged for me to catch mosquitoes for him. He gave me the necessary equipment, together with a lesson in catching and preserving mosquitoes. As Chief of Mosquito-Catching Operations in northwest China, I was also provided with an impressive-looking document informing those whom it might concern that in the interests of science I should be shown all possible courtesies. Unfortunately, I was the only one impressed by the document. Martin's friend merely laughed when told about this scheme for passing ourselves off as a scientific expedition.

Martin at least had obtained a better idea of what lay behind the difficulty in securing permission to travel where we wanted to go. He said he had recently met Georg Söderbom, a young Swede who was born in the Northwest, and had had some long talks with him. Besides possessing a native's knowledge of the area, Georg had participated in several expeditions led by Sven Hedin, the famous Central Asian explorer, and had traveled over the area we wanted to visit.

It seems that most of the region was under the control of Muslim Chinese warlords, including three brothers who had divided the province of Gansu among themselves. The authority of the central government under Chiang Kai-shek simply did not extend into that area. The Chiang regime could not admit that, of course, so it claimed that travel there was dangerous. This may have been true, but it wasn't the primary reason for refusing permission to travel in the region.

"I'm really disappointed," I said. "I had my heart set on camping along the river for a week or two."

"Well, Georg suggested a possible alternative, but I don't know if it will be acceptable to you. It would take longer than the four or five weeks we had originally planned on."

"Let's hear it."

"We begin by taking a train from Peking to Guihua. That's the terminus of the major caravan route to Central Asia. Georg says he has a friend there, a fellow Swede called Torgny Oberg, who can put us up and help us get camels and a camel driver. He can also help us arrange to join up with a caravan leaving Guihua for the west."

"What would be our exact route?"

"From Guihua we go north about a hundred miles to a place called the Temple of the Larks. Along the way we pass from Chinese-controlled territory to that under Mongol administration. Getting by the checkpoint may be a problem, but Georg says he has some ideas as to how that can be managed."

"Then what?"

"Then we go west, skirting the border with Outer Mongolia, for about six hundred miles to the Black River oasis."

"Six hundred miles!"

"I'm afraid that isn't all. We go another four hundred miles along the river, changing back again from Mongol to Chinese territory and arriving finally at Suzhou."

"Over a thousand miles by camel! You're crazy! That's out of the question. You know I don't know how to ride."

"But I'm told this is different. You don't ride astride. Caravan camels carry a load that makes a nice, flat platform. You sit on the load with your legs stretched out. It's very comfortable. All you feel is a gentle rocking motion. It lulls you to sleep."

A likely story. But Martin insisted that he had pressed Georg carefully about the matter, since he didn't have any experience with camels either.

"Well," I said, "after our thousand-mile nap on a camel, then what?"

"At Suzhou we have a choice. We can either continue to Lanzhou by camel or take a bus. In any case it's just going in the reverse direction of the route we had originally planned on from Peking to Suzhou. From the Black River on, we'll be *following* the footsteps of Genghis Khan instead of *retracing* them."

"But how are we going to handle the fact that we don't have permission to travel in Gansu?"

"That's the cleverest part of Georg's plan. When we get to Suzhou, we'll be thrown out of the province, but that'll be toward the east, which is our way home anyway."

"In other words, we're to circle around and sneak in by the back door."

"That's it."

All this was a lot more than I had bargained for. Instead of a simple journey by train and bus, we would be making a much longer trip, a large part of it by camel. That upped the stakes in a decision that was already going to cost me a lot, since, in addition to my half of expenses, it meant giving up my cushy library job.

When I had first mentioned the possibility of making a trip into the Northwest, Old Man Pettus had gently advised against it by pointing out the difficulties, not to mention the dangers. From persuasion he soon went to command: no trip. My decision to go anyway meant burning a rather substantial bridge behind me. I tried not to worry too much about the uncertainty of what lay on the other side of it. Only later did I come to realize what a turning point it was to be in my life. At the time I felt mainly anticipation, and an occasional qualm at my rashness.

I asked Martin how he felt about it.

"Of course I'm all for making the trip. Our original plan would only have enabled me to go over the Black River invasion route. Now I'll also be able to check on some other routes that Genghis and his forces followed. They made additional thrusts toward Guihua."

I told Martin that, apart from my doubts about travel by camel, the main problem for me was the extra time and expense. The caravan route would add several weeks to our original plan.

"True, but that doesn't mean extra cost at the same rate as the rest of the trip. I've been told that caravan travel is very inexpensive. It eliminates stopping at inns and eating in restaurants. Transportation shouldn't be a big factor either. When we're through with our camels, we can probably sell them for not much less than the original cost to us."

That settled it for me. I'd gotten so keyed up about taking a break in the great open spaces of the Northwest that I couldn't bear the thought of giving in and continuing in the same old rut. I swallowed hard.

"OK," I said. "Let's go."

"Fine! But we'll have to act fast. We've lost a lot of time. It's almost the middle of May. The caravan season is drawing to a close. We'd better get to Guihua as soon as possible if we're to join a caravan headed west."

"I've been ready for weeks."

"Then let's plan to leave on the fifteenth."

There should have been a Roman soothsayer to warn us against the ides of May.

3 / The City "Returned to Civilization"

‡ ‡ ‡ ‡ ‡ ‡ ‡ ‡

For centuries the Mongols had had to put up with the vainglorious Chinese name Guihua, meaning "Returned to Civilization." After 1949 the Chinese Communists, perhaps prodded by Mongols allied to them in their rise to power, renamed the city Hohhot, a name reflecting the modern pronunciation of what the Mongols in their glory years called Kuku Khoto or Koko Khoto, The Blue City. A minor but not insignificant change among the cataclysmic changes that have convulsed China in the past few decades. Unremarked by Western visitors. Like much else.

‡ ‡ ‡ ‡ ‡ ‡ ‡ ‡

We left Peking by the overnight train for Guihua in a third-class compartment we shared with four Chinese men. They were all dressed in long gowns that came down to their ankles and were fastened with frogs on the right side. This attire, the equivalent of a westerner's coat and tie, immediately set them apart from pants-wearing members of the lower class. All turned out to be representatives of business firms based in Tientsin.

We had hardly gotten ourselves settled and completed our mutual introductions, with me interpreting for Martin, when one of the men seated beside me put me in my place, evolutionarily speaking, by plucking at the hair on my arm and exclaiming to his smooth-skinned compatriots: "Look! So hairy!" The others crowded around. Martin was similarly honored with their attention. We felt like performing for them by squatting down and scratching under our armpits.

21

Our clothes also came in for considerable attention. One of the men, who said he dealt in shoes, looked critically at my hobnailed boots. These were objects of pride to me. I felt they had transformed me, as if by the flick of a magician's wand, from a Milquetoast librarian's assistant to an intrepid desert explorer. The dealer in shoes shook his head over them. How could feet be happy in such overweighted encumbrances when they might be cozily encased in the daintier cloth shoes worn by both sexes in China?

All four men complained about the hard times. The Great Depression had affected China, too, reaching the Far East a few years after it had started in the United States. On top of this, there was the perennial uncertainty of the political situation, plus the usual difficulties involving extortion and squeeze. It was impossible to do business without paying people off.

One of the men represented a rug-making firm that bought wool in Guihua, the main mart for wool obtained from Mongolian sheepherders that was destined in part for the carpet mills of America. One of his main complaints was that the train personnel had to be bribed to take care of the merchandise and see that it went through safely.

We all sighed lugubriously.

Whatever the problems of transporting merchandise, transporting people seemed to be reasonably well handled. The train was in good condition, efficiently enough run, and as clean as could be expected, to damn with faint expectations.

About thirty miles out of Peking we passed through the Great Wall at Nan Kou, or "Southern Pass," where tourists are taken to see the Great Wall at Badaling. Through here, successive invaders breached China's defensive barrier to establish themselves as new masters of the Middle Kingdom.

At one of the stops, a small station near the Great Wall, we saw a statue with a plaque informing us that the railroad had been designed and built by China's first construction engineer. He was a Yale man, I was happy to note, one of the first Chinese to graduate from an American university.

"Look!" I said to our Chinese fellow travelers. "He and I were schoolmates."

This gave me a good deal of face in their eyes. One of the men had heard of "Yelu" University. And they were very proud of the railroad. All said they traveled over it frequently. The railroad was a commendable feat of engineering, especially in the area of the steep mountains that led up the Mongolian plateau. For a considerable distance along the way we passed work gangs engaged in building barriers and channels to guard the tracks from being washed away.

We chatted for several more hours. Martin soon lost interest in our conversation and spent most of the time reading. Eventually we all got tired and turned in for the night.

The arrangements in our "hard sleeper" compartment were adequate, if austere. The wooden bunks were entirely bare. We slept in our clothes, with part of our luggage as head-rests and a couple of blankets to cover us. That is actually to oversimplify the matter. Any position I tried to sleep in revealed how little padding there was on my frame. It occurred to me for the first time that friends who considered me underweight might have been literally correct when they described me as just a bundle of skin and bones.

On arriving in Guihua early in the afternoon, we were subjected to still another passport check, the third in our trip of less than five hundred miles, again by a military officer sporting a gun at his hip and accompanied by a soldier armed with a rifle. The officer checked our papers carefully, asked who the friends were whom we said we had come to visit, and washed his hands of us when someone arrived to lead us off to the Oberg home.

Torgny and his wife, Brita, were a friendly young couple who immediately made us feel welcome. Their home was a sprawling house in the usual Chinese style, with several courtyards separating various wings. It was also a base of operations for Georg Söderbom, who was absent when we arrived, having gone up north a few days before in the hope of selling one of his cars to a Mongol prince there.

The Obergs were waited on by a number of servants, mostly Chinese, but including—as Torgny's specialist on camels—a Mongol named Arash, who Torgny said was a "tent lama." This is the name applied to a monk who leaves a monastery, abandons his vows of celibacy, and sets up his own tent with a wife, although she is not socially recognized as such and does not put up her hair in the style of a married woman.

The Chinese were smooth-skinned, bland, uniformly dressed servants who went about their business with quiet efficiency. Arash stood out from them as a distinct personality. His face was darker, more rough-hewn, the brows constantly knitted, as if set by a lifetime of squinting at the desert sun. He wore trousers tucked into high Mongol boots and a shirt buttoned down the middle with frogs. Sleeves rolled up above the elbows gave the impression of a no-nonsense worker about to tackle a job requiring special skill. A length of dark cloth wrapped around his

head as a sort of turban ended on the right side of his brow in a sideways tailpiece that flopped down around his shoulder. It gave him a slightly swashbuckling air that added to the general impression of a status somewhere between servant and friend in the Oberg household.

As soon as we had settled in, Martin suggested going out for a ride to see the sights and to start conditioning ourselves for the trip. I didn't get to see many of the sights, as I had to concentrate my attention on trying not to part company with the horse assigned to me. This allegedly gentle three-year-old mare was fairly easy to manage so long as we proceeded at a nice sedate pace. But when we accelerated a bit to what Martin said was a slow trot, I bounced around to such an extent as to arouse the open-mouthed wonder of the populace, especially other riders, all of whom rode as if they had been born in the saddle. I seemed to be the only inept rider in a population much of which bustled about on horseback. Most of the people were Chinese. They seemed to be as adept riders as the few Mongols among them.

The mare was considerate enough to select a freshly ploughed field in which to tender me a bill of divorcement. I landed without injury except to my pride. We rode back at a pace that I heard Martin mutter was a funeral march.

Martin estimated the distance of our ride at five to six miles. That, of course, applied only to himself. The distance for me was appreciably greater if we apply the Chinese method of reckoning distance in hilly country. They consider that the uphill distance from A to B is greater than the downhill distance from B to A, for the eminently sensible reason that it requires more effort to go uphill than downhill. Applying this energy-expenditure yardstick, I estimated that while Martin was riding his paltry five to six miles, I had accompanied him for no less than twenty to twenty-five. Not bad for a beginner!

The ride gave me a better feel for Guihua as a frontier settlement. Martin helped fill in the historical background.

The city is situated in a plain in the area where the Yellow River, after a long run in a northerly direction, bumps into the barrier of the Mongolian plateau and is forced east for a while before making another turn toward the south. Early records indicate that it is located on the site of a military post that goes far back in history. It had become an important center by the time of Marco Polo, who referred to it as Tenduc, a name perhaps related to that of some nearby ruins known as Tokoto. That keen observer noted that already in his time wool, and especially camel wool, was a major product of this area. He remarked that the people made fine-quality fabrics "of camel hair very good and every color. And they live on flocks and on the fruit which they take from the land, with which they do great business, and some trade is done there and handicraft."

In the sixteenth century the city became the center of power of Altan Khan, the "Golden Khan." This last great leader of the Mongols appears, in his early years, to have fitted the stereotype of the marauding Mongol. For several decades he ravaged North China, at times coming close to capturing Peking.

The Chinese bought him off by making large payments, which he used to build the city into a place of splendor famous throughout Central Asia. It also became a major Mongol trading center. Nomads came from afar to what they called The Blue City, a name that some sources say they gave it because of the blue-glazed tiles that first caught their eyes as they approached the city from the mountains on the north.

Like an ordinary mortal, at one time the Golden Khan came down with an attack of gout, a throbbing inflammation of his left big toe. He who loved the feel of his feet in the stirrups of a hard-running horse suffered the indignity of having to sit with his foot propped up on a cushioned stool.

The shamans invoked the help of the gods to heal their ruler. Wait for a night when the moon is full, they were told, and assemble to chant the successive steps of the treatment. Shorn of the magic words that guaranteed success, the steps were as follows:

> Place young male supine before seated Khan.
> Disembowel youth.
> Place gouty foot in warm abdominal cavity.
> Continue treatment until body cools.

This medical practice was discontinued when the khan got religion, a gentler religion that frowned on killing. As a devout follower of Buddha, he had many scriptures translated into Mongolian in the monasteries under his control.

The Golden Khan eventually yielded to the Chinese. In 1571 he submitted to the emperor, who gratefully enfeoffed him with a title meaning "The-Yielding-to-Righteousness King." And the Chinese changed the name of the ceded Blue City to Guihua, meaning "Restored to Civilization."

These names resonate with the insufferable superiority flaunted by the Chinese toward those beyond the pale, especially those beyond the Great Wall that encloses the center of civilization called the Middle Kingdom. Never mind that the Chinese had their share of barbarism. Even in their weakness they were incapable of viewing outsiders as other than inferiors.

The erstwhile Blue City continued to flourish as a frontier outpost where Chinese and Mongols met. In the nineteenth century a Russian traveler described it as having two hundred tea shops, five theaters, fifteen temples, and six Mongol monasteries. In the twentieth century it still retained its dual role as trading center and garrison city. It became the headquarters of General Fu Zuoyi, the military governor of the area when we were there, and was also the main terminus for caravan trade across the desert. Some of the great merchant houses of the city proudly traced their origins back to beginnings in the seventeenth century.

Guihua actually consisted of two parts. Some three centuries ago the Manchu rulers of China set up beside the Old City of Guihua proper a New City garrisoned by their own people. They called this new addition Suiyuan, a name with the literal and pointed meaning "Pacify Remote Regions." Chiang Kai-shek's regime, continuing the insensitive practice of its predecessors, also applied the name to the province of which the city was the administrative center. The names Guihua and Suiyuan properly referred only to the old and the new cities, respectively, but they were often applied loosely to the combination of the two. Sticklers for accuracy used the portmanteau name Guisui.

Old City had once been enclosed by walls, but these had been torn down, except at the North Gate, to make way for progress. New City was still walled about in the traditional manner and boasted an impressive gate tower. The combined population totaled about one hundred twenty thousand people. Chinese comprised the vast majority of the population. This was generally true of the cities lying in the border region between China proper and the Mongol-inhabited areas to the north.

Guihua was very much a frontier city that owed much of its vitality to the caravan trade. This was almost entirely controlled by Chinese trading firms that engaged in buying and selling with the Mongols and looked to them as the main supply of camels.

The morning after our arrival, Torgny, accompanied by Arash, took us to the main camel market. This was normally a huge affair, thronged with some of the seventy-five hundred camels owned by Guihua firms. To our dismay, we found no activity there. We had arrived too late. The market had just been shut down only a day or two before, ushering in the off-season for camels.

"Ordinarily," Torgny explained, "the camel market is very busy. Most of the buying and selling of camels takes place here. But when the hot weather starts, the camels are sent out to pasture and the market shuts down."

Torgny added that dealing in camels required the same degree of expertise as dealing in horses. He himself was not particularly expert in that area, but Arash was positively first-rate, and Torgny relied heavily on him to size up the camels and engage in the bargaining.

The actual dickering was carried on inside the crowded and clamorous marketplace in the midst of buyers and sellers who were anxious to find out the exact prices that others were offering or accepting. Old hands like Arash had their work cut out for them to carry on their negotiations in secret even though under constant scrutiny by competitors. Arash always went to the camel market wearing a shirt with long, loose sleeves that could be extended beyond the ends of his fingers. Others intent on serious negotiations came in similar apparel. When ready to make a specific bid, a prospective buyer thrust his hand up the sleeve of the prospective seller. Thus out of sight, the hands of the two negotiators touched out a series of signals: "M$60" . . . "No, M$75." And so it went, until either the deal was made, or it fell through and the two tried their luck elsewhere.

Martin and I agreed that all this was very interesting, but we were upset to have arrived in Guihua too late for the camel auctions.

"Don't give up," Torgny said. "I do business with an establishment that might have a few camels it would be willing to sell. You won't have the selection that's available in this market, though. Let's go right over there. If you hurry, you still have a chance of catching up with a caravan that has already started out and joining up with it for your trip west."

Torgny then took us to call on the Chinese trading house that he mainly dealt with. This concern was one of the smaller companies involved in trading with the Mongols. It had only two hundred camels and thirty employees. Its absentee owner, who lived in the neighboring province of Shanxi, left the job of running the concern to a manager named Guo.

We were greeted by Manager Guo with the Chinese equivalent of Rotary Club heartiness. Soberly dressed in a long gown of good material, a short jacket buttoned down the middle, and a two-toned skullcap that looked almost like a crown, he exuded success and well-being as he welcomed Torgny as an old friend and Martin and me as honored guests.

Before getting around to our own business, we first had to engage in some polite chitchat. We learned that Manager Guo's firm dealt chiefly with the Mongols and that most of its dealings took the form of bartering Chinese goods, such as cloth and tea, for hides and furs and wool and other products of the grassland and desert areas.

A major export from this area was sheep intestines. These were carried to Guihua by camel caravan from Xinjiang and intervening grazing areas. From here they were shipped to Tientsin and then abroad, chiefly to the United States and Europe, where they were used as sausage skins or casings.

We were shown a huge collection of furs that we were told were now a drag on the market. Normally furs were an important export item and brought in much desperately needed foreign exchange. Some furs were bought in the area right around Guihua, but most were collected by agents who traded with the Mongols at a greater distance. The furs were stockpiled in Guihua for shipment abroad.

The depression in the United States was a major factor in the depressed state of the market. Manager Guo, like most other merchants who dealt in furs, had bought at relatively high prices, and all were now faced with enormous losses. Fox, wolf, and lynx skins were available at prices that averaged four to six dollars Mex.

Torgny interposed to note that business dealings were based on actual silver dollars. This was especially true in unsettled areas, where many people simply refused to accept the various kinds of paper currency that warlords of dubious fiscal solvency attempted to foist on them. In the frontier areas most travelers had to carry metal coinage.

"You'll have to do the same," Torgny told us.

There was, of course, considerable risk in carrying cash around, or even in transmitting it. Guo told us of an ingenious scheme that some business houses based in Shanxi, Shandong, and other provinces resorted to in order to get around the problem. They sold goods, such as cloth, on credit throughout the year to people in the area, arranging for payments to fall due in the summertime. During the summer, representatives of the company were sent around to collect the money that was due. The silver dollars so collected were used on the spot to buy horses, which were then driven back to the home province and sold. A double profit was realized and the danger and expense of transmitting cash was obviated.

Finally turning to the main matter of concern to us, Manager Guo said that all his camels had been sent north, where grazing was better and cheaper, as it was approaching the summer season when the camels were taken off caravan work and allowed to recover during the hot weather. His company's last caravan directed to the Black River had left May 8, a week before. He professed not to know whether some other company was still planning to send out a caravan west to which we might attach ourselves.

After considerable parleying, Guo agreed to sell us some camels and to provide what foreigners variously call a cameleer, or camel driver or camel puller, to guide us. We asked for one camel driver and three camels, one for each of us.

"It would be best," said Manager Guo, "if you took five camels and two camel drivers."

We insisted that one camel driver would be enough, as we expected to share fully in all the tasks connected with our journey, even the most menial. We also thought that three camels would suffice. Torgny convinced us that it would be safer to have a reserve animal, so we finally compromised on four camels. There would, however, be some delay in delivery, as the camels would have to be brought down from the north, where they had been sent for summer grazing.

All this discussion was carried on between Torgny and Guo, for I found, to my consternation, that the local dialect was difficult for me to follow. This worried me a great deal, as I was supposed to be the interpreter on the trip.

"Don't worry about it," said Torgny. "You'll catch on before long. Most of the differences are in pronunciation."

He added that the Peking dialect, which was essentially equivalent to Standard Mandarin, differed from the various local dialects in northwest China in a more or less regular way. For example, some people in the Northwest confused initial *f* and *h,* initial *l* and *n,* and final *n* and *ng.* So one might hear *fuzhao* for *huzhao,* "passport," and *Lanjin* for *Nanjing,* the capital of the country. However, Torgny again assured me, I would soon catch on.

I later found that this was indeed the case, though the differences were not as simple and regular as Torgny made them out to be. Though I became able to cope, I was never fully comfortable with the various kinds of Northwestern Mandarin that we encountered. It was always restful for my ears to hear the familiar sounds of the Peking dialect.

In the days that followed I tried to get as much practice as possible in speaking with local people. Martin and I made daily trips to see Manager Guo and press him impatiently about our camels. He invariably was on the verge of having news for us. And he invariably urged us to give further thought to the need for a second camel driver and a fifth camel.

As the days succeeded each other in this fashion, we worked off some of our frustration by following a program that would get us into better physical shape. Martin was already in good condition, but I was still plagued by colds. Early on we decided that some walking would do me good.

Our first excursion took us in the direction of the Da Qing Shan, or Great Blue Mountains, lying north of the city. On the outskirts we passed an encampment of some three thousand soldiers belonging to General Fu Zuoyi. Martin thought that the hills formed a pretty background for the encampment, with its rows of white tents and masses of soldiers parading on the drill ground. As he prepared to take a picture, a soldier ran up to ask gruffly what we were up to. I replied that we were impressed by the beautiful scene and would like to photograph it, especially if he would stand at attention precisely in the center of the entrance gate with his fine-looking rifle. The soldier struck a pose, Martin took the picture, and we continued on.

About six miles out we passed a roadside stand run by a pleasant-looking couple who chatted with us while serving us tea and cakes. Then we undertook a short climb into the foothills. From the striking blue color of these hills it was easy to see the derivation that some sources claim for the Mongol name for Guihua—Kuku Khoto, or Blue City.

On the way back we again passed the encampment and stopped for another look through the gate. This time there was a different guard on duty. He peremptorily shooed us away. Martin said that the troops we had briefly glimpsed drilling in the camp seemed better than most Chinese soldiers he had seen, and that Fu Zuoyi himself had the reputation of being one of the more able Chinese military leaders.

We returned home after a fifteen-mile hike that ended with my legs creaking in protest at every step. That evening my muscles cramped taut like violin strings that had been tightened to the breaking point. Torgny said he could play a tune on them. He proceeded to demonstrate by pouring on some liniment and plucking away to the accompaniment of my discordant yelps.

A few days later I met Georg for the first time when he returned from the north after failing to sell his car. A blue-eyed, fair-haired giant of a man, he topped my six feet by a good four or five inches and outgirthed me by several times that amount. He wore a rumpled suit that looked as if he had slept in it, as, according to Brita, he most likely had.

Georg was a dynamo of pent-up energy that expressed itself in abrupt movements and perpetual motion. He made frequent trips between Peking and his ranch, with intermediate stops in Guihua and the Temple of the Larks. And when not dashing about he was constantly occupied with some task or other, for he abhorred inaction the way nature abhors a vacuum. His speech was explosive and expansive, his appetite for food and drink and talk gargantuan.

When we told him about the apparent runaround we were getting from Manager Guo, Georg immediately suggested a plan to ferret out the exact situation. He invited all of us to dinner the next day with the understanding that we would try to drink Guo under the table in the hope of getting the truth out of him.

Georg started things rolling by having each of us select a favorite dish from the restaurant's extensive menu. To accompany our feast he ordered several bottles of vintage *bai gar,* or "white dry." The name suggests, but feebly, a dry martini—very dry, with the vermouth reduced to a soundless whisper and the gin replaced with liquid fire. Tossed down in tiny jiggers, white dry burns its way down the gullet like molten lava.

While we waited for the first course, Georg suggested I start things going by playing "guess-fingers" with our guest of honor, since I was already familiar with this popular game of forfeits. I explained to Martin

that two contestants simultaneously extend one to five fingers, or a clenched fist for none, while shouting out their guesses as to the total number of fingers that would be extended by the two locked in convivial combat. The loser drinks, and the object of the game is to see who can last the longest.

On the first go I extended four fingers while calling out "Six!" Guo simultaneously extended three fingers while crying "Seven!" I lost and had to drink. My wily opponent outguessed me in the first three tries, and it was not until the fourth that I was able to force a drink on him.

Just as I was beginning to panic, Georg took over, and then the others took turns playing the game with Guo. While they all did better than I had, none of them succeeded in gaining a majority of wins. Guo was very pleased with himself at having outwitted all the foreign devils. However, in his euphoria at beating each of us individually, he overlooked the fact that he had lost to us collectively.

When Guo's face began to reach what Georg judged to be the right shade of red, he called a halt while we attacked a few more dishes and engaged in desultory talk that we kept bringing around to the matter of our camels.

Guo again raised the subject of our taking on a second camel driver. The one he had in mind, he said, was first-rate, one of the best in the firm, Xiao by name. This peerless veteran of many desert crossings had made the Black River trip several times and so was thoroughly familiar with the route. When I asked why this paragon could not be our one and only camel driver, Guo let slip that Xiao would be able to go no farther than the Black River, where he was to check on the company outpost and relieve one of the men due for rotation. He would therefore not be able to accompany us to Suzhou and beyond. Now the reason for Guo's insistence on a second man was clear. Xiao had to go to the Black River anyway on company business, so why not arrange for him to be paid for the trip by the two gullible foreigners?

Georg signaled to me to keep my cool. There was more to come.

Guo went on to say that Xiao, together with the camels intended for us, was reported to be somewhere in the vicinity of the Temple of the Larks. He had circled the place to avoid the tax on camels and been on his way south to Guihua when he was discovered and forced to return. With luck, he might be able to get out of his tax-evasion caper simply by paying the regular tariff. Otherwise he might be fined and even held a while for tax evasion. It all depended on what he would be able to negotiate. Yes, there was a possibility that it might take several weeks to settle the matter. These delicate matters take time, you know.

At a morose breakfast the next morning, Georg hesitatingly suggested an alternative to our waiting indefinitely for Guo's camels to be brought down to us in Guihua. At his ranch about a hundred miles from the Temple of the Larks he had a herd of sixty camels, some of which had been on Sven Hedin's expeditions. We could take our pick of them at US$24 per camel, a fair enough price. The main problem was finding an experienced camel driver who could take us across the desert. There was a small Chinese community near the temple where one might be found hanging about. At best, however, it was a gamble, as without someone to vouch for him there would be no way of knowing if he was really reliable. If we wanted, we could go up north with him, because he intended to return there soon for another try at selling his car.

Martin and I spent the morning discussing the pros and cons of the two alternatives. Guo helped us decide by appearing a little before noon with another vague promise that the camels were on their way but without any reference to the revelations he had made the previous evening. When he again raised the subject of our taking on a second camel puller, we brusquely dismissed the matter by saying that under no circumstances would we agree to the added expense.

We decided that there was nothing to be lost in taking up Georg's offer to drive up to the Temple of the Larks with him and trying our luck there. As we were to leave the next day, we spent the afternoon repacking our things. A few of the less bulky items we could take in the car. The remainder, consisting of several boxes, bags of flour, and miscellaneous equipment, would be sent up to us by camel. We were told the shipment would arrive in five days. By that time we hoped to have found camels and a camel driver for our trip.

4 / By Bedbug
to Larkland

‡‡‡‡‡‡‡‡

In recent years some tourists have reported on the guided tours they've been permitted to take a few miles upland from the railroad city of Hohhot. Their accounts show that they saw little and understood less.

My Japanese friend Fujiko Osono also saw little but understood more when she was permitted to make a one-day round-trip journey in 1972 over the route it took us more than a day to accomplish in one direction. She made the trip in the company of Owen Lattimore, the leading American expert on Mongolia, who was able to compare conditions he saw then with his earlier visits to the area.

The road is "not at all bad" now, according to Fujiko. What used to be a checkpoint between Chinese and Mongolian jurisdiction no longer serves as such and hasn't changed much over the years. One occasionally sees motorcycles where horses used to be. Many Mongols now place their tents on wooden platforms instead of on the ground.

More important, Fujiko reported a huge influx of Chinese into the area. And most important of all, in the year of their visit, when the Cultural Revolution and Chinese chauvinism were at fever pitch, the Mongols were so guarded in their speech that Lattimore didn't even dare talk to them in their own language in the company of the Chinese cadres.

The more things change. . . .

‡‡‡‡‡‡‡‡

We drove from Guihua to the Temple of the Larks in a jalopy that Georg affectionately called The Bedbug. The name suggests both its size and its condition.

The car was a two-seater that when fresh off the assembly line must have been a teenager's dream. Since then it had led a life of automotive debauchery that included coming off second best in a brawl with a Chinese freight train. It was now reduced to a state of decrepitude kept just short of total disintegration only by the wizardry of Georg and a Chinese helper.

The Bedbug's retractable roof had long since disintegrated and had been removed so as to meet a more urgent need than protection against the elements. All the space to the rear of the scat was filled with spare parts, luggage, and miscellaneous goods. On this mountainous heap Georg's helper found a precarious perch. Georg himself occupied half of the seating area in front. Martin and I split the other half evenly between us.

We drove off with a warm exchange of hand-wavings between ourselves and the Obergs. A passageway through streets crowded with riders, carts, and pedestrians was speedily cleared for us because The Bedbug, long since shorn of its muffler, signaled our coming well in advance.

About five miles out from the city we entered the Great Blue Mountains at the opening of a valley appropriately called the Mouth of the Pass. Our road followed the partially dried course of a river, quite wide and strewn with stones and boulders. In times of heavy rain the river swells up to fill the whole bed and becomes impassable. Now there was only a shallow stream that we crossed and recrossed in low gear, slowly and with caution. The Bedbug had been denuded of its fenders. It avenged this indignity by splashing mud and water all over the car, the luggage, and the passengers.

For a dozen or so miles our road went up without too steep an incline. Then came a sharp ascent leading to a crest called Centipede Pass.

"This is the best pass through the mountains," said Georg. "There are many other passes from the plain to the back country. That's what the local people call the Mongolian plateau we're heading for. But those passes can't accommodate carts, much less cars. Even camels have difficulty negotiating them."

"That leaves horses," said Martin, very pleased to have a chance to expound on his favorite subject. "Genghis Khan sent his cavalry through those passes. The Chinese couldn't mount a strong defense of every one of them. The Mongols used the tactic of splitting up into small detachments. They probed for weak spots, then quickly concentrated their forces to overrun a weak defense. Mobility was the key to their success."

Martin's admiration for the Mongols centered on their military strategy and tactics. Mine was at a lower level. As a nonrider, I felt a kind of awe at the riding ability that enabled Mongols to spend long hours in the saddle, dash about all over the landscape, and thunder down these valleys en masse, aiming arrows at the terrified defenders. I cowered in my seat.

Part way up the pass, The Bedbug began to sputter and buck. Georg ordered the three of us to jump out and help push the car. This worked for a while. Then the car gave a final gasp and shuddered to a halt.

A check under the hood revealed trouble with the carburetor. This was taken apart and cleaned before a transfixed audience of villagers from nearby and a passing audience of carters leading their horse- and donkey-drawn vehicles up and down the pass. The carters smirked.

At long last the carburetor was put back into working order. Georg drove on alone in low gear while we jogged behind in a cloud of dust churned up by the car and the rest of the traffic in the heavily traveled pass. Occasionally The Bedbug sputtered and showed signs of stalling again. Then the three of us bent far over to push with outthrust hands against the back of the low-slung car. Georg helped with encouraging yells.

In the area near the summit, where the pass was narrowest, the explosions made by the mufflerless Bedbug were magnified as they reverberated against the mountainsides. The din was such that horses reared up, donkeys shied, pigs ran off, and chickens flapped their way to safety. Guihua-bound carters contributed to the bedlam as they frantically sought to slow the headlong descent of their heavily loaded vehicles by bearing down hard on hand brakes pressed against the wheels. These screeched like misheld chalksticks drawn across an endless blackboard. The carters impartially bellowed a choice stream of invective both at their terrified draft animals and at us.

With a heave and a ho and a loud curse for carburetors, we finally shoved The Bedbug over the top of the pass. There we paused to gasp for breath with lungs that were functioning at only half capacity, since the other half was completely clogged with dust. George asked if we had made up our faces for a minstrel show.

Our descent on the other side of Centipede Pass was much easier because the slope was less pronounced. On the northern side of the mountain range we dropped only slightly onto the Mongolian plateau. This stood between one and two thousand feet above the Guihua plain, itself at an elevation of two thousand to twenty-five hundred feet.

We were following another mountain stream down the other side of the pass when a sudden downpour overtook us. To escape a drenching in the topless Bedbug, we took shelter in a nearby inn. This was simply a single, low-raftered room with two high *kang,* the typical brick-bed of North China—a raised platform warmed by flues connected with a stove. One of the platforms was occupied by three heavy-lidded Chinese stretched out next to opium pipes, upon which they sucked with sodden pleasure. We appropriated the other brick-bed and had some much appreciated tea that finally washed the dust out of our air passages.

The opium smokers were too far gone in their dreams to pay any attention to us.

"They're probably carters," said Georg. "Opium's cheap here. Most people can afford to smoke it, and a lot of them do. Not many Mongols, though. Their problem is drink."

"Home brew?" Martin asked.

"Yes, but that's not too bad. The worst is the stuff the Chinese traders get them to drink in their barter deals."

After the downpour we continued by driving onto a rolling plain over a road that was hard and fairly smooth. It consisted of several parallel trails made across the open country by carts and motor vehicles.

This soon brought us to a settlement known to the Mongols as Kuku Irghen, or Blue Cloth, a name that recalled the origins of the town as a trading center. The Mongol character of the area was now largely lost. This region had been opened up for Chinese colonization and the town had become a Chinese garrison post guarding the northern approach to Centipede Pass and hence to Guihua. It was also a toll station and major checkpoint where travelers between Chinese and Mongol territory could expect to undergo particularly careful scrutiny.

Martin and I approached the checkpoint with guilty consciences. Only Georg's passport was completely in order. Martin's was good for a limited part of the area. Mine expressly restricted travel to towns served by a rail-road. We were at the mercy of officials of notoriously ill-repute—servile toward the strong, overbearing toward the weak, venal toward all.

Georg had carefully rehearsed us for this crucial encounter. The day before, when Georg and Torgny were telling us about travel in the area, I had mentioned having a letter of introduction to the paramount leader among the Mongols, Prince De, who was occasionally to be found at the Temple of the Larks. It had been given to me by Major Constant, the military attaché in the American Legation.

By a nicely timed stroke of luck, I had met the major shortly before our leaving Peking at a party given by his popular young daughter. It turned out that he believed in learning about China at first hand and had met the prince while traveling in Mongolia. Alone among those attached to the legation, he had encouraged me to make the trip. Helping me get permission from the Chinese to travel in the Northwest was not in his jurisdiction. He had done the best he could by giving me the letter of introduction.

Georg wanted to know what it said.

"Nothing much. Apart from a few stereotyped phrases, it merely introduces 'De Fanke' (that's me, DeFrancis) and 'Ma Ding' (that's Martin) to Prince De. It's signed 'Kang Shidan' (that's Constant). The most impressive part is the envelope. It has 'The Honorable Prince De' in big black characters, and, in red characters, 'Office of the Military Attaché at the American Legation.' "

Georg had asked to borrow the letter before we approached the checkpoint. Now we anxiously trailed behind him.

Georg strode up to a group of officials lounging in the area of passport control. He stopped before one of the group and, after a curt greeting, placed the letter and the three passports on the table, with mine at the bottom and his opened on top. The envelope of the letter from Major Constant was prominently exposed so that the big black characters for "Prince De" were plainly visible. Pointing back toward us, he said "They're with me." As if that was all that needed to be said, he beckoned to us to follow him and extended his hand for the passports. The official had had time only to glance at Georg's passport and the envelope addressed to Prince De. He meekly returned the documents to Georg and politely waved us on.

Once we had returned to the car and were able to draw a breath of relief, Georg told us what lay behind our getting through the checkpoint with such unexpected ease. Some weeks before, he had traveled through here in the company of a senior Mongol prince. The official who had waved us through today headed the group on duty at that time. One of those snotty small fry who believed that the lowest Chinese official was superior to any Mongol, even a prince, he had behaved with more than usual insolence. The prince was infuriated and lodged a bitter complaint with the man's superiors, who professed to be exceeding wroth at their subordinates. They probably were, though not for the same reason as the prince. In any case, they decided that their underlings were expendable.

The errant official was punished with a severe beating, and those on duty at the time were ordered to make a public apology to the prince. Georg was present at these proceedings and so gained enormous face. He had been through the checkpoint several times since then and had been treated with unwonted courtesy each time, even when a different group of officials was on duty. Clearly, Georg had achieved fame as someone to be treated gingerly. We were lucky to be able to get through on the coat-tails of his notoriety.

"Well," said Martin. "Now we're in Mongolia, out of the clutches of the Chinese."

"I wouldn't say that," Georg said. "The Chinese have a long reach. Or rather, someone might make a grab for you at any time. This is uncertain country. You have to feel your way."

"Simple," I said. "You just have to know how."

Our next stop was a social call. We dropped in at the home of Arash, Torgny's expert on camels, who was still in Guihua, just to say hello to his family. We were greeted by his wife, Sereji, and seven- or eight-year-old daughter, Kongkhor. The child gave a shriek of joy on seeing Georg. She jumped into his arms and gave him a big hug, brought over a little mat to sit beside him, and engaged him in animated conversation that was punctuated by his laughter and her giggles. I felt a twinge of envy at Georg's ability to establish such a warm relationship with this family. Kongkhor, especially, made me wish I had a kid sister like her to be protective toward.

When we saw her on that visit, Kongkhor was a vivacious little thing who showed promise of growing into a beautiful woman. We heard later that she contracted smallpox and nearly died before Georg was able to persuade the family to let him take her to Guihua for treatment. She might have recovered unscathed if Arash's mother had not become worried about this truck with foreign shamans. At his mother's insistence, Arash brought Kongkhor back before she was fully cured. As a result, she became badly scarred and lost the sight in one eye.

We were welcomed with some coarse bread and the inevitable brick tea. This was Mongol style, made with the addition of a creamy sort of cheese that dissolved to make a delicious drink. I had a couple of bowlfuls and asked Georg if it would be in order to extend compliments to the cook. Sereji looked surprised, then beamed. Kongkhor giggled. I had some more tea.

Arash's home was what some foreigners refer to as a Mongol tent and others call a yurt, following the Russian term *yurta,* which derives from a Turkish word for a dwelling. The Mongols themselves use the term *ger.*

A Mongol yurt, to use the most common name, is a circular domed structure made of sheets of heavy felt stretched over a collapsible lattice framework and lashed down by horsehair ropes. It is so constructed that it can be quickly taken apart, transported on two or three camels, and reassembled at some other spot. Such mobility is required by nomads, who follow their herds from summer highland grazing areas to winter lowland pastures. The curved lines of the yurts provide the further advantage that they can better withstand the strong winds of grassland and desert than can angular Western-style tents.

In the center of the yurt is a fire pit set in a square hearth measuring two to three feet on each side. From the fire pit the smoke rises to a hole in the center of the domed roof. This is equipped on the outside with a movable piece of felt to regulate the draft. The floor consists of pounded earth covered with several sheets of felt matting. There are no chairs. Everyone sits on the floor on small rugs, unless they are too poor to afford them. The host sits on the right side of the door. As guests we sat on the left, on some finely woven saddle rugs with white and tan patterns against a blue background.

Mongols usually sit either cross-legged or on one knee, with the other knee up. Chinese prefer to sit on their haunches. Martin and I never managed to be comfortable for long in either the Chinese or the one-knee position, so we contented ourselves with sitting cross-legged on the mats that Kongkhor had spread out for us.

Arash's yurt seemed to be well supplied with at least the basic necessities. It contained a wooden rack with an assortment of cooking utensils on the right side of the hearth, rolls of bedding pushed up against the wall, and several gaily painted wooden chests that were used to hold ordinary family possessions such as clothing. Some had the additional function of displaying various religious images, including one in a figured silver case, and several small brass butter lamps and offering bowls. There was also an altar with a small statue of Buddha that shone like gold in the light of the fire.

The yurt was located near a monastery called Shirit Cho in an area inhabited by a group of Mongols who had taken to farming and had inter-married with the Chinese, so that they were rapidly losing their identity. The monastery itself possessed a domain of about ten miles square. It was under the jurisdiction of the church, not of the Mongol princes. This ecclesiastical rule reminded me of the Catholic feudatories in Europe's Middle Ages.

In Mongolia, as in medieval Europe, the monasteries were economic as well as religious entities. They owned great herds of animals tended by poor monks who were often little better than serfs. High lamas also had their own private herds. The monasteries functioned as credit institutions as well.

In setting himself up as a "tent lama," Arash had succeeded in acquiring independence from these feudal monasteries. He was lucky to be em-ployed by a foreigner. That provided an unusual opportunity to change his way of life.

After our pleasant social interlude, we resumed our journey in weather that, in typical fashion for this area, was undergoing a rapid change in mood. Near sunset the temperature fell considerably and the sky was darkened by a cloud cover that dropped a bit of rain and threatened to release a heavy downpour. By this time it was so late that we could not have reached the Temple of the Larks before darkness set in. Martin and I were for going on anyway. Georg's helper put forward a number of argu-ments against night travel. One was the danger of being bitten by Mongol dogs. That sounded pretty specious to us.

"Actually," Georg said, "the dogs are pretty vicious. They've been trained to suspect, with good reason, that anyone going about on foot at night is up to no good. They're not really a danger to us so long as we don't get out of the car."

I imagined us being pursued by ravening dogs, as in those pictures of Siberian sleighs with drivers madly lashing their horses to outrun a pack of wolves.

"But" Georg added, "there's a real danger of being shot at by trigger-happy people on guard against marauders. They can't imagine that respectable people might choose to travel at night."

That decided us to stop for the night near a cluster of mud buildings that made up the tiny village called Tsatsa. We put up at a Chinese trading post that rented out a room or two as a sideline. The Bedbug was safely ensconced in a walled courtyard. The four of us were assigned a dark room about half-occupied by an assortment of goods and half-filled by a large brick-bed. For bedding we decided to make do with one big sheep-skin coat and a few blankets that happened to be readily accessible. It was too much bother to unload everything in order to gain access to things we had not anticipated needing until the end of a supposedly short run by car.

Our lodgings for the night turned out to deserve multiple star rating. To everyone's surprise, we did not have to share our quarters with the hordes of minuscule creatures that ordinarily snuggle up to the warmth of hapless travelers.

We started off again shortly after dawn. The three of us sardined behind the windshield wrapped ourselves in blankets. The Chinese helper on his windswept perch was more warmly encased in his sheepskin coat.

About seventy miles from Guihua we reached the farthest limit of Chinese cultivation. Occasionally we passed an abandoned village. Georg said that colonization had receded in recent years, in part because of banditry and fighting among warlords. Another reason was the blowing away of topsoil that should never have been put under the plow.

It was a pleasure to make the transition into the rolling grasslands of Mongolia. Large herds of horses and camels that had been peacefully nibbling away at the ample forage first jerked up their heads in startled alarm and then stampeded in terror at our noisy approach. In short stretches we were able to hit speeds of forty to fifty miles per hour. Occasionally we encountered patches of coarse sand that we had to negotiate at slow speed.

About seven miles from our destination we ran into the edge of a rainstorm but had to push on through it. Since The Bedbug had no windshield wiper, Georg drove with his head stuck out to the left, I helped by peering out on the right, and the Chinese called out further navigational advice from the vantage point of his elevated perch. We soon emerged from the storm and stopped for a moment to clean off the windshield before going on.

Off in the distance we spotted the almost black outline of the hills that rim the little plain which was our destination. As we approached it, the first thing to strike our eyes was a group of white buildings in the Tibetan style of temple architecture on the far side of a dry riverbed. On the near side we passed a group of mud buildings that Georg said housed a colony of Chinese merchants. Farther along the plain we crossed the dry bed of the river several times as we aimed toward a cluster of three yurts that we espied in the distance. In front of them someone was hopping up and down with a great waving of arms. Georg drew up near our boisterous welcomer before one of the yurts that he said was his and announced that we had arrived. We had come 105 miles from Guihua to this junction of several great caravan routes.

5 / The Temple of the Larks

✝✝✝✝✝✝✝✝

The summer after our trip together Martin went back to the Temple of the Larks to check out suggestions that there might be ruins of ancient cities in the area. He discovered quite a few ruins but, because of the disorder that was soon to erupt into open warfare, was able only to make a hasty survey. He had the satisfaction, though, of publishing a brief report of his explorations.

Martin found many sites of towns and villages that may have functioned as agricultural and commercial centers. In addition, he discovered the remains of an outer section of the Great Wall that lay far north of the main wall. He also found new evidence that long before this area fell under the influence of Tibetan Buddhism its inhabitants had been adherents of Nestorian Christianity.

In the years since Martin's return visit hardly any outsiders have been allowed into the area. And neither the Chinese nor the Mongols appear to have done any further explorations there.

As for the temple itself, my Japanese friend Fujiko Osono has informed me that it was burned down, for the second time in its history, in the course of the fighting that broke out the year after we were there. At the time of her visit in 1972 the population had grown to seven thousand people, all Chinese, who were operating factories in the area behind the ruins of the temple and engaging in other activities unknown in earlier years.

✝✝✝✝✝✝✝✝

Georg introduced our frenetic greeter as Manfred Bökencamp, a German friend who had also been on several of the Hedin expeditions into Central Asia. He was staying here in order to save money while waiting for a chance to join another expedition.

45

Yurts belonging to Georg and Gonzell

"Room and board are cheap," he said cheerfully. "I'm a nonpaying guest in Georg's yurt. I keep my food bill down by hunting. There's lots of game in this area."

The other two yurts belonged to a missionary by the name of Gonzell. He was a jovial man of the cloth who had a peculiar shaking laughter that reminded me of the good-natured villains in the Mickey Mouse movies. We were all invited to be his guests at an enormous Western-style breakfast in his nicely appointed yurt. It even boasted a table, where we showed ourselves to be formidable trenchermen.

After breakfast Martin and I decided to take a long walk so that we could get a better idea of the area. Georg left his helper behind to tinker with the car while he accompanied us as our guide.

"This area is the western end of the grasslands," he told us. "Beyond here it gets harder and harder to find good pasture. Since this is so close to Guihua, it's a favorite place to pasture camels when they rest up during the summer months. This is also a crossroads of several caravan routes. One leads east to Manchuria, another south to Guihua, a third west to the Black River, Xinjiang, and finally the Soviet border. At one time there was also a caravan route north to the capital of Outer Mongolia. No more."

We walked to the southern ridge of the hills that rim the plain. From there the Temple of the Larks lay spread out before us.

The plain was cut by a river, now dry, that Georg said was called Aibagh-in Gol. (*Gol* is the Mongolian word for "river.") He pointed out some mud buildings on the near approach to the river. They housed a colony of Chinese merchants and a radio station run by the Chinese for the Mongols. This was one of several stations located at the headquarters of various princes for rapid communication among themselves and with the Chinese authorities throughout the border region. Private individuals were also permitted to transmit messages if they were on good terms with those in control of the facilities.

Some of the mud buildings in the Chinese section served as warehouses for goods bought and sold in the trade with the Mongols. Others served as dwellings for the hundred or so people who comprised the Chinese section of the local population. Apart from the merchants, there were also a few hangers-on, mainly camel drivers awaiting the resumption of the caravan season; we hoped they might include one who could guide us to the Black River. The merchants were representatives of firms like that of Manager Guo in Guihua. They dealt with the Mongols largely by barter, receiving wool, skins, furs, and animals and giving in exchange mainly cloth, tobacco, flour, and tea—and spirits, the undoing of many Mongols.

Beyond the cluster of mud huts the landscape was dotted with scattered yurts belonging to the several hundred Mongols living in the area. The number fluctuated as the Mongols shifted back and forth between their summer and winter pastures. These, plus the inhabitants in the temple, made for a total Mongol population of somewhat less than two thousand. Not far beyond the Mongol yurts was the temple itself.

"At breakfast," said Martin, "I noticed that Gonzell referred to the temple as a monastery, whereas everyone else I've read calls it a lamasery. What's the correct label?"

"Strictly speaking, the temple should be called a monastery, because it houses both lamas, who teach and may marry, and monks, who don't teach and are not supposed to marry. And the religion should be called 'Tibetan Buddhism', not 'Lamaism.' But you're right, most people don't use the appropriate terms."

"How big is the monastery?"

"At full strength it has about fifteen hundred lamas and monks. Sometimes they're down to a few hundred. The rest scatter to beg for alms."

"How did the temple get the Chinese name Bailing Miao?" I asked. "I know it means Lark Temple or Temple of the Larks. But how come?"

"The whole area here is known to the Chinese as Bailing Di, meaning Larkland or Land of the Larks. The reason is that there are actually many larks in the area. They're not just ordinary larks either. These are a species noted for their fine singing. They have a remarkable ability to mock the

The Temple of the Larks

songs of other birds, and even the meow of a cat. They're much in demand among Chinese bird-fanciers throughout North China."

I already knew that the Chinese were great fanciers of birds. One of the pleasanter sights in Peking was that of Chinese men, especially gray-beards, each with a little cage containing a bird that hopped gaily about inside and sometimes burst into song. Some of the cages were works of art. The owners cleaned and changed the red sand at the bottom of the cage every day. Many took their birds for a walk the way Western city dwellers walk their dogs on a leash. They strolled sedately along, gently swinging a cage, occasionally holding it up daintily, the better to hear the song of the sweet-toned pet. Sometimes men gathered in twos or in little groups to debate the relative merits of their prize possessions.

Georg said that some of the finest of those birds came from right here in Larkland. The Mongolian larks made their nests in the ground. Droves of Chinese would descend on the nearby plain in early summer, before the nestlings learned to fly, and garner them for sale at the large bird market in Guihua. Some merchants trading in the area used part of their locally derived profits to acquire larks to take back to China, as other merchants did with horses, in order to avoid the danger of transmitting cash.

Fledglings whose quality of voice had yet to be determined fetched a relatively low price, as they represented something of a gamble. Master singers—the term is used advisedly, since only males are considered to have good voices—were sometimes paired with mediocre fledglings to provide them with a model to improve their singing. Mature birds with proven beauty of song were avidly sought by connoisseurs, who were willing to pay the equivalent of two months of an average person's income for one such bird. The very best songbirds cost more than a horse.

After returning from our walk we went from birds to other fauna of the area as Bökencamp kept up a running commentary of his hunting exploits while he prepared to serve us a meal of antelope meat. This was not only our lunch but our dinner as well, and both were feasts even if the menu was a bit restricted. Bökencamp had shot several antelope, which he served in big chunks grilled to perfection over the fire in Georg's yurt.

We ate Mongol style, holding a chunk up to our mouths with one hand and cutting off a bite at a time with the other. We used a knife from our knife-and-chopsticks set contained in a bamboo holder. These were similar to the ones that all Mongols carry at their belts along with a wooden bowl tucked into the bosom of their belted gowns. They are thus always ready to accept an invitation to dinner.

Mongol knife-and-chopstick sets are typically contained in a section of hollow bamboo about nine inches long. Into these fit a pair of ivory chopsticks and a long-bladed knife whose handle protrudes a few inches above the bamboo sheath. At the top this has a little ring, through which passes a cord that is tied to the belt around the waist. The sets are often little works of art, with jeweled tips on the hilt of the knife and similarly jeweled clasps around the bamboo case. Carnelian, turquoise, and jade are the preferred jewels of the better sets. Ours were inexpensive ones that had a bit of ivory at the hilt of the knife and at the bottom of the bamboo sheath.

Georg said Mongols like to warn foreigners against eating meat in the native fashion. They share the Chinese view that we are all Da Bizi, or "Big-Noses," and that our proboscises must surely interfere with efficient eating and are in danger of being lopped off. I had particular reason to take the warning to heart, but happily joined the others in braving the danger.

Just before turning in for the night Georg entertained us with several Mongol songs. One was a lively courting song that went

> Hey, you flower of the grasslands there!
> There's a new tent going up for me in camp.
> Would you like to light the fire in it?

Georg sang in a low voice against the background of the wind battering against the yurt. He said that's the way Mongols sing in the privacy of their yurts.

We went to bed replete with antelope meat and warmed by the fire in a yurt that proved its worth against the unseasonable weather outside. The rain that had started in the afternoon changed to hail that pattered against the felt. The temperature dropped into the thirties and the wind howled around the yurt where we lay snug in our sleeping bags. At long last we were in the land of Genghis Khan.

We awakened to find that the surrounding hills, normally a bleak expanse of treeless brown earth, had been transformed into a beautiful landscape by a thin blanket of snow. This disappeared soon after the sun came up.

After breakfast Georg decided to take advantage of the good weather by driving up to his ranch about a hundred miles away, where he had the camels that he could supply us. He also had to check on a car that needed to be repaired and driven back to Guihua to show to a Mongol prince who might be interested in buying it. On the way he planned to stop at the Chinese settlement to check on the availability of a camel driver to take us to the Black River. Bökencamp and the Chinese helper were to accompany him. That meant that there was room for only one other passenger in The Bedbug.

Martin and I tossed a coin to see which of us could accompany Georg. He won. After a moment's thought, he generously insisted I should go. "I'm sure I'll be making other visits to this area. You probably won't have another opportunity." But on further thought it seemed advisable for me to remain behind, in case the things that we had asked Torgny to send up by camel arrived and presented a problem that needed to be dealt with.

After they left I occupied myself with bringing my journal up to date and delving into the material—books, articles, and typewritten and handwritten notes—dealing with this area that Martin had brought along. Some of it was boring detail about military matters, but there was also some that was of greater interest to me.

Late in the day a messenger arrived from the wireless station with a note from Martin written on the back of a radiogram from Torgny that they had picked up in the morning on their stop at the Chinese settlement. His wire was brief but electrifying: "Camels arrived Guihua." So the camels promised by Manager Guo had finally arrived! We must have passed them on our way up, perhaps in Centipede Pass. If we had only had the patience to wait just one more day in Guihua, we would now be united with our camels, ready to start our travels. Instead we were again separated by a hundred miles, with our positions reversed at the two ends. To make matters worse, I now had no idea where the baggage we had asked Torgny to send up to us from Guihua when we left was.

Martin's note said Georg thought it would be safer to accept Guo's camels and camel driver rather than gamble on finding a reliable guide here in the Chinese settlement. So they had fired off a wire to Torgny asking him to send the man and the four camels up to us here immediately. That certainly was the right decision, but it still left a lot of loose ends.

Not long after dark I got into my sleeping bag in the hope of forgetting my frustrations in sleep. Although Gonzell was only two doors away in his own yurt, I felt awfully alone in the vast expanse of Mongolia. Outside the wind howled and moaned. I felt like howling back.

The next morning, right after breakfast, Gonzell went to visit a Mongol family a couple of miles away, leaving me alone with my thoughts. These transformed me momentarily into another Connecticut Yankee in King Arthur's Court, as a thunderous pounding of hooves prompted me to look up in time to see a knight clad cap-à-pie in black armor charging full tilt past the yurt with lance lowered at the ready straight out before him. My medieval knight turned out to be a Mongol dressed in black with a conical hat who was trying to lasso one of the horses in a small herd in full flight before him. His equipment was a rawhide noose at the end of a slender fifteen to twenty-foot pole that I had mistaken for a lance.

The pole-and-noose device of the Mongols requires as much skill as the lariat favored by American cowboys. Mongols train their steeds to recognize which horse in a herd is to be lassoed. They give chase by riding without touching the reins, using both hands to guide the pole so that the noose lands over the horse's head. The most skilled of the men do not drape the noose around the neck of the horse; instead they adroitly maneuver it across the throat and up between the ears. When a horse has been lassoed, the rider's steed abruptly slackens its speed and braces itself against the sudden jerk of the other horse. The rider, too, braces himself in a maneuver requiring tremendous strength and dexterity to hold the lassoed horse, for these Mongol cowboys have no saddle horn to absorb

the first shock, only the strength of their arms. With fine-tuned coordination, rider and steed together pull the horse up short very quickly.

During Gonzell's absence I had the dubious pleasure of taking his place in receiving some visitors of distinction. These were three lamas, who approached the yurts on splendid mounts that they rode at a brisk trot across the plain.

I was struck again by what a fine figure Mongols cut when mounted. They ride with short stirrups, saddle well forward on the horse, and they seem almost fused to their mounts, like equestrian statues magically endowed with life. Dismounted, however, they clump along in a stiff and ungainly bowlegged waddle, leaning a bit forward as if still in the saddle. They wear high boots that are picturesquely turned up at the toes but are not much good for walking—which Mongols loathe anyway—for the boots are cumbersomely made of stout leather, with the added encumbrance of a pocket attached at the top to accommodate odds and ends like a man's pipe or a woman's accessories.

The lamas dismounted and approached the yurt where I was sitting in the doorway. We bowed to each other. I bid them welcome in Chinese but was disconcerted to find they were as ignorant of that language as I was of theirs. All I was able to say was a brief "Sain baino!" that I hoped was the appropriate greeting in this situation. So we all sat cross-legged, smiling inanely at each other. As proxy host, I was especially uncomfortable at my inability to perform the function expected of me.

One of the lamas handed me a card with an inscription in Mongolian on one side and some Chinese characters on the other. From the latter I discovered that the most distinguished-looking of my visitors was a Khutukhtu, or Living Buddha.

This was indeed a visitor of distinction. In the religion of Mongolia, a Khutukhtu is a reincarnation only a few steps below the Dalai Lama and other great incarnations in Tibet. There were many Living Buddhas in the Mongol pantheon. All of them were reincarnations of long-dead Tibetan saints who periodically came to life in the bodies of Mongol lamas. The Khutukhtus were highly venerated by Mongols of all ranks, for they were believed to have great powers of healing and foretelling the future. Their power was not only spiritual. They also headed monasteries housing hundreds and even thousands of lamas and monks, the latter often little more than serfs, and controlled extensive areas of land and herds of animals.

I was able to learn more about my distinguished visitor when Gonzell's English-speaking teacher finally appeared to interpret for us. He was the head of a lamasery about thirty-five miles west of Baotou, had been here at the Temple of the Larks for almost three weeks attending a conclave of princes and religious leaders, and was visiting our camp in the hope of being treated for some sores. I was not so indelicate as to ask what those sores might be. We chatted for a while about other matters. At long last Gonzell returned and took the visitors to his yurt for a private medical consultation.

The next morning Gonzell was again preoccupied with visits to nearby Mongol yurts. Left to myself, but undisturbed this time, I spent the morning in the yurt reviewing my Chinese character-cards and putting them in some semblance of order. In the afternoon I walked the two miles to the wireless station, returning empty-handed and exhausted by a wind so strong that I had to battle my way back.

During the evening the gang returned from their trip to the ranch, but without the Chinese helper, who had been left behind to do some more repair work on a car. Martin pronounced the trip a particular success because en route they had visited an important monastery and the palace of the prince who headed a local group of Mongols called Durbets, where, thanks to Georg, they had been able to meet the prince and his family, including several of his illegitimate sons.

Bedbug and the Durbet prince's youngest
illegitimate son

Georg and Bökencamp planned to leave the next day to return to
Guihua. It had earlier been agreed that before they left we would all sit
down together and review our trip to the Black River and beyond. Everyone was so tired, however, that we put off the matter till next morning.

After breakfast, Georg and Bökencamp gave us their frank assessment
of our situation. Because of the unsettled conditions throughout the area,
especially the perennial risk of bandits, they thought it likely that anyone
sent to us by Manager Guo would take the northernmost route, through
the heart of the desert.

"That's the preferred route now," said Georg. It's pretty much the same
as what my brother Gustav first explored a few years ago. It's safer from
bandits because it goes through the worst part of the desert. They're not
likely to bother you there."

But the very badness of the terrain made it harder for camels, not to mention people. Moreover, because of the delays we had encountered, we would be hitting the worst part of the desert in the worst part of the summer, with camels that would be in the worst condition owing to their continued use when they should be resting. And it was now much too late for us to hope for the security of joining a big caravan. We would have to risk it on our own.

"From what you're saying," said Martin, "we'll apparently be taking a route even farther north than the one you followed a few years ago on the Hedin expedition. Didn't your brother actually cross the border into Outer Mongolia for a short stretch?"

"That's right. But he did it by car, fast, to avoid a bad stretch of sand. Don't try it by camel. They'll be sure to catch you. Stay a few miles south of the border. Guo's man will know enough to do that."

"There doesn't seem to be much difference between these routes," Martin said, "except maybe for trucks. I understand you lost 100 out of the 250 camels that you had on leaving the Temple of the Larks."

"We also had trouble with bandits. You may be able to avoid that problem, but it's going to be hard on you and the camels. You have to be very careful with them."

Both Georg and Bökencamp said quite forthrightly that they did not envy us making the trip at this time. Georg quoted the saying of veteran camel drivers that they would not send their worst enemies across the Gobi in midsummer. Coming from such old hands at desert travel, these opinions were something to give us pause.

But we both took note that neither Georg nor Bökencamp was urging us to abandon the trip. Had they done so, we might have been inclined to follow their advice. But they spoke only of difficulties, not of impossibilities, and we felt challenged. For Martin, perhaps the additional difficulties and risks were even to be welcomed. They presented an opportunity to experience conditions that might even more closely approximate those which others had had to endure in earlier centuries. We both flatly said that we were going ahead with our plans but wanted a clearer idea of the difficulties confronting us and how to cope with them.

"The first problem," said Georg, "is your camels. I hope Guo sends you some good ones. The best are geldings. Stallions are too hard to handle. As for females, I have an axiom that a female camel is only half a camel."

We had, on Arash's advice, asked Manager Guo for geldings, but were told he wasn't sure what was available and might have to give us some females. Georg said that on their way down to Guihua, they might pass our camels, which should be easy to identify; for just as no one but mad dogs and Englishmen go out in the noonday sun, so no one in his right mind would have a camel driver and four camels start out on a trip at this time of year. If possible, they would examine the camels and wire us about their condition. In any case, he said that if we were stuck with some female camels, he doubted that they would last the whole trip to the Black River and back. He was glad we had followed Torgny's advice to take along a reserve camel and suggested we spare all of them as much as possible by not riding them all the time.

"The second major problem is what route you should take back. On leaving here you'll head west through what is called the Great Gobi to the Black River. You'll have to hole up a while there to rest your camels. Then you'll go southwest along the river to Maomu, the first Chinese town you'll come to about a hundred miles north of Suzhou. From there you have two choices."

One alternative was to stay outside the Great Wall and trek parallel to it in what is called the Little Gobi. That would take us to another desert area, called the Alashan, west of the Yellow River, which we could follow until we came to Baotou. This was a physically demanding route for both animals and men. It was also less interesting, since we would already have experienced desert travel in the Great Gobi. But there was rumor of a ruined city somewhere north of the Great Wall that we might try to locate and explore.

The second alternative was to go right down to Suzhou and then back via the Silk Road. This had the disadvantage of being more expensive and more subject to hassles with warlords. It had the advantage of enabling us to see more things of interest and to have the option of returning more quickly from Suzhou by bus, though service on that line was inclined to be erratic.

"There's no need to make a decision now between these alternatives. You can do that when you reach Maomu. There are a lot of variables involved. Your experience up to that point will put you in a better position to consider the matter. And I'll give you a letter of introduction to a friend of mine in Maomu who can help you with information on local conditions."

After discussing further details of our trip, we all had lunch together before Georg and Bökencamp took off for Guihua. I said goodbye with the feeling that a sort of umbilical cord had been cut.

Martin accompanied them as far as the wireless station and returned with a radiogram from Torgny saying that our camels had started out. It was a relief to know that they were on their way to us. But we wondered if Georg and Bökencamp would miss them on the drive toward Guihua, as we had done on the drive up from there.

Bökencamp had left Gonzell with a good supply of antelope meat, as well as a bustard he had shot on the way back from the ranch. This bird is somewhat bigger than a turkey and is supposed to have a similar taste. It was hard to tell. We had to rest our jaws between mouthfuls. Bustards are said to live for sixty or seventy years. Ours must have been a centenarian.

We went to bed early because Martin had arranged to leave at 5:00 A.M. with Gonzell's teacher to visit a ruined city some twenty to twenty-five miles away. He invited me to go along, but I declined, as it seemed the better part of wisdom not to subject myself to a horseback ride of forty to fifty miles.

Martin returned in late afternoon, quite tired out but tremendously pleased with the results of his trip. Ordinarily he had a rather deliberate manner of speaking. Now the words fairly tumbled out of him as he told of his visit to the ruins and related them to things he had read.

The ruins had been found just a few years before by Owen Lattimore, who in 1934 published an article about his find in the *Geographical Journal* under the title "A Ruined Nestorian City in Inner Mongolia." Martin had a copy of the article, along with a great many notes that he had taken during the course of his extensive reading and research. His trip to the ruined city, together with what he had read about it, had whetted his appetite to return here later in the hope of discovering other ruins. "I'm convinced there are more in the area. They're just waiting for someone to find them."

The ruins belonged to a group of people called Onguts who, in the thirteenth and fourteenth centuries, inhabited the area known to Marco Polo as Tenduc, his name also for its chief center, near the present Guihua. The Onguts were located between the nomadic pastoral Mongols to the north and the settled agricultural Chinese to the south. Like other intermediate peoples, they had some of the features of both groups. Marco Polo said of them, "The people get their living by their cattle and tillage, as well as by trade and handicraft."

Such mixed peoples sometimes sided with the nomads to the north, sometimes with the agriculturalists to the south. In the case of the Onguts, they chose to throw in their lot with the Mongols. As Martin noted at considerable length, this opened up an invasion route, perhaps the very one we had taken from Guihua, that some of Genghis Khan's forces followed in the conquest of North China. The closeness of the relationship is indicated by the fact, noted by Marco Polo, that successive rulers of the Ongut kingdom obtained wives from the family of the Great Khan.

The Ongut story contradicted the usual superficial view of Chinese history as a struggle between advanced agriculturalists and barbaric nomadic invaders. The existence of an intermediate group of people between the two main contestants revealed the frontier problem as much more complex than most people had thought, particularly Americans with their cowboys-and-Indians concept of civilization confronted by barbarism.

The intermediate position of the Onguts, especially their physical location athwart the caravan routes from Central Asia to China, helps to explain their adherence to Nestorian Christianity, relics of which Lattimore had found in his exploration of their ruined city. This was a Christian sect whose adherents believed in the separateness of the divine and human nature of Christ. Nestorianism originated in Asia Minor in the fifth century, spread eastward through Central Asia, and became established in China in the Tang Dynasty (A.D. 618–906) and later in the court of the Great Khan.

Ongut Nestorianism was a rival of Catholicism as represented by John of Montecorvino, first archbishop of Cambaluc or Peking, a contemporary of Marco Polo and fellow Italian. This great Franciscan missionary was permitted to practice his faith freely under the liberal religious policy of the Mongol rulers, especially Kublai Khan, who decreed in Xanadu a pleasure dome of the mind where all were permitted to expound their creeds and beliefs.

An Ongut ruler was converted to Catholicism by the archbishop, who baptized him with the name George. But then came reverses. In a letter dated January 8, 1305, the archbishop narrated the sad fate of his proselytizing activities in the following words:

> A certain king of this part of the world, by name George, belonging to the sect of the Nestorian Christians, . . . in the first year of my arrival here [about 1295] attached himself to me, and, after he had been converted by me to the verity of the Catholic faith, took the Lesser Orders, and when I celebrated mass used to attend me wearing his royal robes. Certain others of the Nestorians on this account accused him of apostasy, but he brought over a great part of his people with him to the true Catholic faith, and built a church of royal magnificence in honor of our God, of the Holy Trinity, and of our Lord, the Pope, giving it the name of *the Roman Church*. This King George, six years ago, departed to the Lord, a true Christian, leaving

as his heir a son scarcely out of the cradle, and who is now nine years old. And after King George's death, his brothers, perfidious followers of the errors of Nestorius, perverted again all those whom he had brought over to the Church, and carried them back to their original schismatic creed. And being all alone, and not able to leave His Majesty the Khan, I could not go to visit the church above-mentioned, which is twenty days' journey distant. The King's son is called John, after my name, and I hope to God that he will follow in the footsteps of his father.

The twenty-day journey that the archbishop could not take to the domain of Prince John, who actually died too young to fulfill the prelate's hope, was the one we had covered in less than that many hours in our train ride from Peking to Guihua.

If transportation had improved on that route, it appeared that there had not been much change since his time on the road from Guihua to the Temple of the Larks. In reviewing our situation the morning after Martin's return from his trip, we estimated that our camels had left Guihua seven or eight days before. And still they had not arrived. Nor was there any word from Georg and Bökencamp, which meant that they must have missed the camels on their drive back to Guihua. We were edgy with frustration.

There didn't seem to be anything we could do about it, however, so to occupy ourselves we walked over to have a look at the temple. This particular monastery was one of the largest in Mongolia. From a distance we had been impressed with how vividly the white and black and gold of the buildings stood out against the drab background of their surroundings. The temple looked new. It was.

A little over two decades earlier, marauding Chinese soldiers had looted the old temple and burned it to the ground. The Chinese government, anxious to defuse the anger of the Mongols at this sacrilege to one of their holiest edifices, had provided the funds to rebuild it.

The temple rose in terraced steps in a hollow on the southern slope of a small ridge. It was so constructed that all the main buildings faced toward the holy city of Lhasa. From a distance the temple as a whole appeared as a dazzling white-walled complex comprising a mixture of flat-roofed buildings in the Tibetan style and multistoried edifices in the Chinese style of architecture, colorful in red and gold with majestic upsweeping roofs. The nine main buildings rising one above the other on the gentle slope were surrounded by a warren of low, white boxlike structures containing cells for fifteen hundred lamas and monks.

A closer look showed that, in contrast to the layout of the Chinese temples, there were only a few of the spacious courtyards to which we had become accustomed. Many of the buildings, especially the living quarters, were crowded close to each other. The larger courtyards, Gonzell told us, served as arenas for the performance of dazzling religious spectacles later in the summer. These occasions were marked by electric excitement, as huge crowds gathered to witness the dancing of diabolically masked figures accompanied by the din of clashing cymbals, clamoring bells, booming drums, and bassoonlike blasts from gigantic Tibetan trumpets.

We wandered about the now eerily silent courtyards, occasionally peering into the dark interiors of deserted buildings, in one of which we saw a huge hexagonal barrel that we recognized as what Gonzell called a Tibetan prayer wheel. It seems the lamas of Tibet and Mongolia had devised a way of speeding up their orisons by using prayer wheels of various sizes. All were based on the common principle of piercing a cylindrical container with an axial rod around which was wrapped a continuous roll of paper inscribed with religious texts. By turning or twirling the rods, believers gained as much merit with each revolution as they would have by actually reciting the inscription.

Whole sutras, and even the complete set of holy scriptures, could be contained in the larger prayer wheels. Some of these had even been mechanized by placing them on top of buildings so that they could be kept in constant motion by the power of the wind. There were also portable prayer wheels the size of a small tin can with a rod protruding through the lid that contained only the ancient Buddhist prayer *Om mani padme hum,* "Om, the indivisibility of the jewel and the lotus."

The entrance to each building was from a sort of open porch. On each of the walls adjacent to the entryway were large murals in the Tibetan style. Neither Martin nor I knew enough about the motifs of this religious art to make much of what we saw. The artwork seemed to both of us to be of inferior quality.

In our wanderings we finally came across a monk who could speak Chinese. He was a slack-jawed creature in a filthy red gown who continued to twirl a hand prayer wheel even while I attempted to engage him in conversation. We tried to get some information from him about the murals and about the temple in general, but he turned out to be astonishingly ignorant about it all, and about other matters as well.

"Are you Japanese?" he asked.

No doubt if we had been better informed about Tibetan Buddhism ourselves, we would have gotten much more out of our visit. As it was, we were depressed by the contrast between the outer magnificence of the temple architecture and the inner rot of a religion that Georg, and even more strongly Gonzell, said was ravaging the whole structure of Mongol society. Both tended to look at this religion in terms of its every-day reality rather than what it professed. Our extensive discussions with them led us to adopt a similar perspective. I, even more than Martin, came to have a decidedly negative feeling toward it.

6 / The Swedish
Connection

·

‡ ‡ ‡ ‡ ‡ ‡ ‡ ‡

The shortest distance between two points in Mongolia used to be via Sweden. That's only in a manner of speaking, of course. It's a way of saying that travel "Beyond the Wall" was facilitated if you had the help of a blond native of the area who had the foresight to be born there of missionary parents.

For four hundred years, starting with Catholics in the seventeenth century and continuing with Protestants in the nineteenth, missionaries spent their lives in China trying to win converts to Christianity. The Communists put an end to that after 1949, for they looked upon the missionaries, who sometimes advocated reform but always opposed revolution, as allies of foreign imperialists and native reactionaries.

‡ ‡ ‡ ‡ ‡ ‡ ‡ ‡

I asked Gonzell one day about the strong Swedish presence in Mongolia, which seemed to make a greater impression in the area than did the other foreigners in the regions where they tended to congregate.

It all appears to have begun toward the end of the last century when some Americans of Swedish origin felt the call to bring God's word to Mongolia. What inspired them initially was a book by an English missionary who had labored for ten years among the Mongols without making a single convert. Here was a challenge worthy of the Vikings' heirs! They founded a society to carry out missionary work and called for volunteers from Scandinavia as well as America.

Those who answered the call staked out Mongolia north of the railroad as their sphere of operations. The wrong side of the tracks, the social cesspool where Mongols and Chinese scrabbled for nature's leftovers in the big bend of the Yellow River, became the domain of Belgian Catholics, who sheltered their flock in fortified missions.

Within a decade of the beginnings in 1892, the majority of the forty-five Swedish missionaries in place were massacred in an antiforeign outburst that was fanned by the crumbling Manchu regime to divert attention from its own misrule. In one place of carnage a search party found only a child's shoe and a plait of fair hair. This martyrdom, as Gonzell called it, failed to dampen the missionaries' zeal. Others came. More children were born to them.

Georg was born in 1906, Torgny within a year or two of him. Both were born "Beyond the Wall."

"I was brought up in an orphanage," Torgny had told us one day at dinner in Guihua. Brita looked pained. A wife who had heard her husband's joke too many times. "His parents founded it," she added.

Georg and Torgny grew up with three native languages: they spoke Swedish with their parents and Chinese and Mongolian with their playmates. English they added later. When we were visiting them, Torgny would address Brita in Swedish, give a servant orders in Chinese, discuss camels with Arash in Mongolian, and tell the two of us what was going on in the only language that we could handle with ease. His command of Chinese was unrivaled even by many of the self-styled Black-Haired People. Some who had never seen a foreigner before took him to be a native with blond hair. He had such a finely tuned ear that he could often pinpoint a speaker not just to a district but even to a specific village.

It seemed to me that Swedish offspring like Georg and Torgny adapted themselves to the life of the natives around them to a greater degree than did the progeny of American and British missionaries. In any case, apart from their command of the local forms of speech, Georg and Torgny were just as sensitively attuned to other aspects of life about them. From their repeated crisscrossing of the border region they had acquired a first-hand knowledge of the lay of the land, including the human terrain in all its intricate detail. Both were masters at sizing up people and situations. Throughout the border region virtually the only law was the law of the jungle. In their dealings with Mongols and Chinese, their livelihood and their very lives depended upon their ability to cope with this reality.

Despite the somewhat flamboyant nature of their way of life, which contrasted with the more sedate existence of most missionaries and their offspring, both Georg and Torgny worked hard for a living. In addition to the usual ups and downs of business life, they had also to contend with a pervasive military presence that exercised the real power, with a civil bureaucracy known neither for efficiency nor probity, and with Chinese business associates who, like most of their kind, were honest in their own fashion but quite prepared to squeeze a bit of extra profit from anyone so unwary as not to read the fine print of agreements seldom reduced to writing.

The home of Torgny and Brita, and the general style of life they enjoyed, although comfortable by most standards, did not place them in the category of the truly rich. At a time when the usual monthly pay for a servant was equivalent to about six American dollars, it was easy for any-one with access to foreign currency to live relatively high on the hog. For them, as for most foreigners, this was a time that George Kates, another member of our fraternity of light-pursed students, aptly characterized by entitling a book about his China experience *The Years That Were Fat.*

Torgny, like Georg, made his living by engaging in a number of differ-ent enterprises. However, unlike Georg, who seemed to be constantly flitting all over the area, he was a bit more solidly anchored to Guihua. Resourceful though both were, Georg seemed particularly adept at turn-ing his hand to almost anything, from doctoring a camel to fixing a car with improvised parts in the middle of the desert. This made him a valued member of the Hedin expeditions. His exploits were noted in the ac-counts of the expeditions published by that famous explorer.

Sven Hedin did a great deal to arouse Swedish interest in Mongolia and Central Asia through a series of explorations that started around the turn of the century. In addition to producing scientifically valuable reports on his explorations, he also recounted them in some half-dozen books writ-ten in a rather florid style that gave him a wide readership. Martin's travel-ing library included several of these works.

Hedin naturally turned to local Swedes for help in his explorations. Just a year before, Georg had accompanied him on an expedition financed by the central government in Nanking to seek out a possible motor route across the desert. Georg's brother Gustav, who at that time was in his third year of detention in Xinjiang after running afoul of the warlord there, had pioneered that route even before Hedin. He had bought a decrepit Cadillac from the retiring American Minister to China, fixed it up for desert travel, and with a single Mongol companion had suc-ceeded in getting through the desert, avoiding some of the worst obsta-cles, the sandy areas, by making a dash through a forbidden section of Outer Mongolia. He had gotten through safely to Xinjiang and on his return from there found another way of avoiding the sandy stretch while remaining on the safe side of the frontier. It was on still another trip to Xinjiang that he had gotten caught up in the disturbance there and ended up in a warlord prison.

Georg said the purpose of the motor road through the desert was to forge an economic link with China's westernmost province of Xinjiang. I expressed doubt about the economic value of such a road. Martin could see military value in it.

"Hasn't there been constant danger of Xinjiang breaking away from central government control? And with the Gansu Corridor in the hands of Muslim warlords, Nanking certainly needs an alternate route to its western territories."

Martin launched into an interminable monologue on the military aspects of the road. I finally managed to steer the talk to the best-known Swede in Mongolia: Frans August Larson, who called himself Larson, Duke of Mongolia. Georg, of course, knew him well. They had both been on Hedin's latest expedition.

Larson had come out from Sweden in 1893, in one of the first waves of missionaries. He was best known, though, for the dude ranch he had recently established farther east in Mongolia.

"In a way," said Georg, "that ranch is a kind of missionary work too. He's introducing foreigners to Mongolia. He didn't have much success as a regular missionary."

Nobody did. But he tried. He traveled all over Mongolia preaching and handing out Bibles. In a book narrating his life among the Mongols, Larson tells of being in Urga, the capital of Outer Mongolia, before it fell under Soviet influence and acquired the new name of Ulan Bator, or Red Hero. There he became friends with the then current reincarnation of the Urga Living Buddha, the third highest dignitary in the Tibetan Buddhist church, who ranked next after the Dalai and Panchen Lamas. The Mongols worshiped him as a god. They elevated him to a position described by Larson as that of emperor.

"His fun-loving personality," says Larson, "captured the hearts of the fun-loving Mongols." And also of the fun-loving missionary.

One day Larson found himself in the middle of a vast crowd near the palace. "You can imagine my surprise," he says, "when a window in the upper story of the palace was flung open and a jolly man, dressed in a gown of glittering gold, appeared and flung out a lady's corset." The crowd snatched for it. A big bottle of perfume followed. It hit the ground and broke. Then came a shower of watches, "good watches of Swiss

manufacture." More perfume. Ladies' dresses. An evening gown of silver lace. Then shoes. And hats. "Both men and women put these on over their own headgear. The Living Buddha even tried one,—a concoction of straw and ostrich feathers,—and thrust his head through the window for the admiration of the crowd before he threw it down." More things followed. The jolly prelate ended the afternoon's jollity by scattering around hundreds of horns and whistles and some Christmas tinsel.

The Living Buddha loved all things Western, including champagne. He received catalogues from New York, Paris, London, Rome, Berlin, and Stockholm, and ordered one of everything. Then, to make room, once a year he threw out the previous year's accumulation to the crowd below.

Not all Mongols were fun-loving. When the Living Buddha died in 1924, "worn out," the historians say, "by spirits and syphilis," the humorless spoilsports who headed the new regime practiced religious birth control by decreeing an end to further reincarnations of the Living Buddha. But not before he had made Larson a member of the Mongolian peerage. Larson's dukedom was the dude ranch that he developed to give tourists a taste of life in the grasslands of Mongolia.

I was of two minds about Georg's view of Larson as a missionary introducing foreigners to the Mongolian way of life. There was some merit to that view, but considering what was omitted, Larson was actually operating a Mongolian Potemkin village, where the problems besetting the people were swept under the gaily colored mats set out for visitors. There was a mawkish quality to his whole approach.

There is no doubt, though, that Larson, through his own colorful life and popular writing about Mongolia, helped arouse interest in the area among Swedes and other foreigners. He appears to be second only to Hedin in his contribution along this line.

A more limited contribution is that of another Swede, Bernhard Karlgren, who pioneered the historical study of the sounds of Chinese on the basis of modern linguistic science. Between 1915 and 1926 he published several influential works that reconstructed the pronunciation of early Chinese, using a novel analysis of the phonetic aspects of the traditional characters, though some scholars fault Karlgren's approach as skewed toward a bookish language that probably never reflected any real spoken form of Chinese. (I was to criticize him later for contributing to popular misconceptions about the Chinese system of writing.) Karlgren's extensive publications, together with those of Hedin and a few other Swedes, have enabled Sweden to make a contribution to knowledge about China that is out of all proportion to the size of its population.

In contrast to Karlgren's dry scholarship, Hedin's flowery prose, and Larson's sentimental puffery, Gonzell's account of his work among the Mongols provided a perspective that was at once more insightful and more filled with human interest. For three days I was alone with him during Martin's trips to Georg's ranch and to the Nestorian ruins. He seemed happy to have company and pleased at my interest in his work.

Gonzell said that he had been ordained in the Baptist sect and was carrying on his work under the auspices of the Scandinavian Alliance Mission. He had learned Mongolian well enough to preach in that language, as I myself observed one Sunday. I joined him and his assistant, who was also his language teacher, in his second yurt for a service that was conducted entirely in the language of the half-dozen Mongol soldiers in attendance.

"This is an unusually low turnout," Gonzell said. "The yurt is generally filled on Sundays."

The service opened with several songs. These sounded vaguely familiar, though the words were completely incomprehensible. Then came a prayer, more songs, and a long talk by Gonzell. All I could make out was an occasional "Jesus." The soldiers sat stolidly with crossed legs, taking no part in the service.

One of the soldiers was an old veteran with a lined, weather-beaten, and pathetically ugly face. Its most outstanding feature was a peculiarly twisted mouth that gave him the appearance of an abashed and repentant sinner. I expected him to start weeping at any moment. Maybe his face did not really mirror his state of mind, but it might well have done so, given his actual physical state, for he stayed on after the service to be treated for syphilis and an assortment of other ailments.

I stayed on, too, in order to observe the goings-on, and also in the hope that refreshments would be served. Georg had cynically remarked that the Mongols came to Sunday service only to enjoy these goodies. If these were at all comparable to the breakfast spread that Gonzell had lavished on us when we first arrived, they must have gone well beyond the humdrum cookies and cakes of ordinary church functions. But we were all disappointed. Perhaps word had leaked out to the regular congregation that there would be no refreshments.

Gonzell said that he had few converts. "The princes and lamas are basically hostile toward my work. They tolerate it mainly because I provide some medical services." He also said that he had not received any formal training in this area. Like many missionaries, he had acquired some rudimentary knowledge of the subject, which was useful only because of the otherwise total lack of anything approaching modern medicine in the whole of the surrounding region.

I asked what the major medical problems were. "Venereal diseases. Gonorrhea and syphilis are rampant among the Mongols. It's a major factor preventing an increase in population."

Syphilis was especially virulent, bringing him many patients whose sores were resistant to his primitive remedies. Venereal diseases were endemic in both the general population and that large segment of it which was directly tied to the church as priests and monks and nuns.

Gonzell had little interest in the tenets of the religion that the Mongols had borrowed from the Tibetans some four centuries before. He had

even less patience toward those westerners who were infatuated with the religion as a manifestation of Eastern mysticism. What interested him was not religious theory but its application in everyday life. The life he had devoted himself to in this isolated corner of Mongolia said much about his own religious outlook.

Gonzell was caustic in his comments on the religious conduct of the Mongols as he saw it in actual practice. More than a third of the population belonged to the religious establishment, most of them from infancy, in any case before their eighth year. Almost half of these resided in monasteries. Monks were supposed to be celibate, but few of them were. They had sexual relations indiscriminatingly with all sorts of women, married and unmarried, including nuns, many of whom bore children. A similar situation prevailed among the population as a whole. Apart from what little help missionaries like himself could provide, Gonzell said the only other factor that offered hope in this generally gloomy situation was the beginning of a movement among the more enlightened princes to root out some of the evils of the religion.

It seemed to me a rather discouraging prospect. But Gonzell was clearly committed to his calling and was fully immersed in coping with things as he found them here. In any case, there seemed to be little enough to distract him from his work.

He did have one hobby, though. That was looking for flowers and sending specimens to the United States. He expressed the wistful hope of discovering a hitherto unknown kind of flower that would be named after him. As we walked out together toward the nearby hills, Gonzell kept up a running commentary on the flowers he had found, their relationship to flowers that grew in the States, and how he prepared his finds for shipment to places where they could be authoritatively identified. I was surprised, seeing with Gonzell's eyes, to discover how many flowers there were in what seemed like barren country. Purple iris and yellow pea blossoms were especially plentiful.

"You know," said Gonzell, "the Mongols have a charming name for the iris: *little daughter-in-law*. It's a term of endearment that suggests a nice, loving relationship in the Mongolian family. Not like English *mother-in-law's tongue* for the sword-shaped sansevieria."

In a short period of time we collected more than two dozen kinds of flowers. I hoped that we could find a new one and had planned how to handle it should it be my fortune to do so. I would call him over to identify a nearby plant so that he could not fail to spy the new flower. But I was disappointed in my hope of helping Gonzell to immortalize his name.

7 / My Namesake,
Prince Virtue

‡‡‡‡‡‡‡

The prince collaborated with everyone except the Communists. And of course they were the ones who won out in the end.

He started by aligning himself with Chiang Kai-shek in the hope that the Central Government would help to counter the threat posed by borderland warlords encroaching on Mongol territory and self-rule. But Nanking was unwilling, and in any case unable, to help the Mongols attain any significant degree of autonomy.

On the eve of the all-out Japanese attack on China in 1937, following their seizure of Manchuria in 1931, he went over to the side of the invaders. They set him up as head of Mengjiang or Mongolian Borderland, a truncated portion of western Inner Mongolia. His puppet regime adopted a new flag and a new calendar, with chronology reckoned from the reign of Genghis Khan.

Then, with the defeat of Japan, he switched back to the side of the Central Government and turned his tattered forces against the Communists in the ensuing civil war.

After the Communists came to power, they imprisoned him for collaborating with the enemy. He was pardoned in 1963 and given a job teaching at Inner Mongolia University in Hohhot, the capital of the Inner Mongolia Autonomous Region.

There is undoubtedly a great difference between the autonomy he was seeking earlier and the autonomy later granted by the Communists.

‡‡‡‡‡‡‡

The Chinese love to play games with the characters that make up their system of writing. There was a time when they took advantage of Western ignorance of their writing by giving unsuspecting foreigners names with bad connotations. (So did the Vietnamese, who slyly presented a hated French governor-general with a name that, in polite translation, means "to copulate with one's mother.") Fortunately the Chinese had abandoned that method of needling foreigners by the time I got to China. So it came about that I was given a name that I delighted in showing off at every opportunity.

I'll have you know that the Chinese called me Mr. Virtue. Honesty compels me to add that this was not because they recognized that sterling quality in me. The fact is that they gave me the name merely because the Chinese syllable *de,* meaning "virtue," sounds more or less like the first syllable of my last name. The Chinese prefer surnames of one syllable. So when they encountered a Mongol prince called Demchukdonggrub, they naturally shortened his name to De too.

My namesake, Prince De or Prince Virtue, was a thirtieth-generation direct descendent of Genghis Khan. He ranked first among the numerous princes in Inner Mongolia. My letter of introduction to him from Major Constant had helped ease our way through the checkpoint on the way to the Temple of the Larks. Now that we were actually there, I hoped to be able to deliver the letter to him personally and get his help in our further travels through Mongol territory. But there was considerable question as to whether we would be able to catch up with him.

"You've just missed him." Gonzell told us shortly after our arrival. "I understand he's left for Peking to see Chiang's Minister of War. No one knows when he'll be back."

The prince seemed to be continually dashing back and forth, negotiating with his fellow princes, with borderland warlords like Fu Zuoyi, and with representatives of Chiang Kai-shek's central government. Both Gonzell and Georg were well informed about these goings-on, adding to what was public knowledge their own firsthand observations from the perspective of the Mongols. Their accounts of his maneuvers evoked in my mind a nightmare spectacle of Prince De as the beleaguered quarry of a pack of wolves. To the south were Chinese warlords in loose alliance with Chiang Kai-shek; to the east were the Japanese occupiers in Manchuria; to the north were pro-Soviet Mongols in Outer Mongolia; and entangling his feet were backward elements among his own people.

The Chinese, with their ingrained feeling of superiority relative to the Mongols, adopted policies that were at best paternalistic and at worst genocidal. The Japanese sought to reduce the Mongols to the status of puppets. The Mongols to the north had almost completely eliminated the power of the priests and the princes. All three were to be feared.

The immediate problem was how to maneuver between the Japanese and the Chinese. Recently the former had demanded that Prince De move the capital of the group of princes that he headed from the Temple of the Larks to an area closer to Manchuria, and hence more easily accessible to their influence. He was further requested to agree to the establishment of an air base and the quartering of troops in his territory, force being threatened if he refused to acquiesce. All this was part of a Japanese attempt to push south and west from their base in Manchuria.

If what I saw was any indication, Prince De did not have much of a military force to counter the Japanese. On one of my solitary walks to the wireless station I stopped to watch about a hundred Mongol soldiers practicing some drills. They were dressed in dull gray uniforms, baggy in appearance and of doubtful cleanliness. Their drilling was as sloppy as their appearance. They were out of step, in broken ranks, and they did not even stand up straight when at attention. The soldiers attempted a kind of goose step that evoked the spectacle of an army of Charley Chaplin's caricaturing the German parade step.

Martin was surprised when I told him about it. "It's common knowledge," he said, though it was news to me, "that General von Seekt and other Nazi advisers are helping to train Chiang Kai-shek's troops. But I can't imagine that they're responsible for that bit of stupidity." We both lamented the decline from Genghis Khan's fierce mounted warriors to these ham-footed buffoons.

Georg told us that Prince De's present visit to Peking was aimed at gaining more support to resist the Japanese. "There's not much hope that he'll succeed, though. Chiang's policy is to give way before the Japanese while trying to consolidate his internal position. That means coping with various military rivals, and most especially wiping out the Communists." Georg said that Prince De had also been unsuccessful when he made a similar attempt following the initial Japanese invasion of Manchuria in 1931. The small delegation he headed was virtually ignored in Nanking. They left after issuing an angry protest that alarmed the government to the point where it asked the Panchen Lama to smooth things over. He actually sided with the Mongols, but did not succeed in getting them any help either.

Mongol resentment was compounded by Chinese encouragement of migration by peasants, a policy that often turned good grassland into poor farmland and then into poorer wasteland. It was further inflamed by the divide-and-rule policy that I knew to be as old as the earliest empire but could now label with a new term I had learned from Kay shortly before leaving Peking when she told me about a sort of skeleton in the family closet.

Kay's full name was Katharine Gerry Wilson. She said that Elbridge Gerry, on her mother's side, had signed the Declaration of Independence, but he was also a shady politician who in 1812, as governor of Massachusetts, had pushed through a law redrawing the boundaries of the senatorial districts so as to favor his party. His outraged opponents said the outline of one of these districts looked like a salamander, and they coined the term "gerrymander" to refer to his underhanded procedure.

The crooked politicos in the Chinese Central Government had gerrymandered the area preponderantly inhabited by Mongols—namely, the long band along the border with Outer Mongolia—into eight Chinese-style provinces, with a weak Mongol minority in the border area and a more powerful Chinese majority closer to China proper. One of the chief demands of the Mongols was recognition of their traditional division into several "leagues" and dozens of "banners" and the right to group these into a single administrative unit having some measure of autonomy.

As a champion of the Mongols, Georg was very critical of Chinese policy. "Fu Zuoyi is even worse than Chiang Kai-shek," he said, "if for no other reason than the fact that he's the one in effective control here. He makes no bones about his contempt for the Mongols. To him they're an inferior order of human beings. And he undercuts Prince De's authority wherever he can. The Chinese attitude toward the Mongols is appalling. Their policies are stupid. If the Chinese aren't careful, they'll give the Mongols no alternative but to go over to the Japanese. Already the Japanese are using Manchuria as a springboard to push farther into Mongol territory. They've been infiltrating agents closer and closer to this area."

Georg admired Prince De as the leader of a nationalist group known as the Young Mongols. These were better educated, more modern Mongols who sought both to reform Mongol society and to preserve it from being overwhelmed from the outside. As the acknowledged leader of this group, Prince De had also favorably impressed the few westerners who took an interest in the Mongols. They considered him the most outstanding leader among the various princes, dukes, and other nobles of the Mongol hierarchy.

Some of these were still living in the Middle Ages. Georg told of shepherding a group of old Mongol princes to Peking as their guide and interpreter. During a visit to the Peking Hotel, the princes derived hilarious pleasure from flushing the toilets and turning on the taps in the wash-

basins until they flooded over. They spent hours riding up and down in the elevators and holding imaginary conversations on the telephones. In the evening they wandered out onto the rooftop dance floor and peered down the cleavages of the shameless hussies dancing in the arms of their paramours.

So taken were they by the wonders they had seen that several princes insisted on Georg delivering some toilets to them, despite the reminder that these really should be connected to running water. The porcelain eye-catchers were placed outside the entrances of their tents, already made special by Chinese-style doorways, as status symbols of unparalleled distinction.

Besides these backward princes, the lamas presented another major problem. In the activities aimed at curbing the power of the priests, Gonzell saw Prince De in a less favorable light than did supporters like Georg and Major Constant. I had a long talk with him about this one day when Martin went to look at the Nestorian ruins.

"Prince De's brother," he pointed out, "is the head lama in Inner Mongolia. That's one reason he's so much under the influence of the lamas. He's too cautious in dealing with them, and too fearful of upsetting the status quo."

"Don't you think, though, that he has to be cautious? From what you tell me I gather that the lamas are awfully powerful. The whole situation seems to me to be pretty delicate."

Gonzell grudgingly admitted that something might be said for this point of view, but he still felt that the prince was proceeding much too slowly in promoting change. This was desperately needed in virtually all spheres of Mongolian society, including the religious as well as the political and economic.

A few of the more enlightened princes, Gonzell said, were trying to root out some of the evils of their religion. They sought to remove from the temples all those who were unable to read and write and to explain the fundamentals of their beliefs. Given the widespread ignorance of most lamas and monks, if such a move were actually carried out it would largely depopulate the monasteries and change the composition of the population as a whole. The effect would be drastic locally, for out of the total Mongol population of some two thousand people, fully half to three-quarters were attached to the temple itself, though many absented themselves from it for long periods of time, chiefly to go around begging alms.

Gonzell said the lamas were fiercely resisting this and other moves aimed at renovating Mongol society. He cited a recent episode in which an assembly of princes deliberated on the possibility of exploiting some outcroppings of coal that had been discovered in the vicinity. The lamas intervened and refused permission to mine the coal on the ground that it would disturb the spirits of the earth. Opposition included use of a malignant form of black magic for which the priests at the Temple of the Larks were especially notorious. They brought down curses upon their victims by reciting certain Tibetan incantations, and they worked themselves into such a frenzy that they became really dangerous. In some cases they resorted to poison in dealing with persons they had singled out for some reason or other. The threat of black magic was much feared by the common people. Even the princes were wary of it, for the priests had been able, perhaps by bribery, to introduce poison into the food of some nobles.

The use of black magic was not limited to major matters such as the coal-mining episode. Gonzell said it was also used as a common means of extorting money and gaining other ends desired by the lamas. "Recently a patient I was treating was threatened with black magic if he continued to accept treatment from me. Most lamas are very anti-foreign."

Also recently, three priests had worked themselves up into such a paroxysm through their incantations that they became extremely threatening. On the order of a prince, the soldiers seized the three and threw them into prison. Two of them were executed. "Too bad we didn't think of this before Manfred went back to Guihua with Georg," Gonzell said. "He could have shown you a photograph he took of the third lama in

prison, bound hand and foot, with
a wooden bit clamped securely in
his mouth to prevent him from
pronouncing his black magic
imprecations."

Georg and Gonzell both said
that time was running out for
Prince De. Change was proceeding at a snail's pace.
Gonzell tended to fault the
prince for not proceeding fast
enough. Georg placed most
of the blame on the Chinese.
Typical of the slow pace, they
said, was the way things were
going with the plans to establish
a new capital at the Temple of
the Larks where Prince De
would preside as the head of an
Inner Mongolia autonomous
region. There was obviously
a considerable difference of
opinion between Mongols and
Chinese as to the meaning of

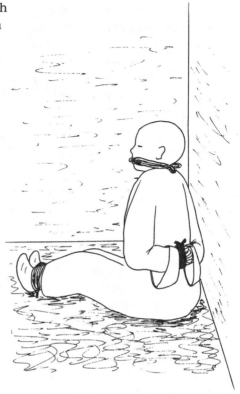

"autonomous." And the Chinese did not share the Mongols' sense of
urgency about establishing the capital on a firmer basis. At present the
capital consisted simply of a small village of tents set up close to the monastery. These were supposed to be temporary quarters, while more permanent buildings were constructed in a valley some five or six miles to
the northwest.

Martin and I decided to fill in our impatient wait for our camels by hiking to where the capital was going up. We set out along the dried riverbed. Although there was no water in the river, it was apparent that the
course was toward the north, away from China, showing that we were in
the real Mongolia, territory whose water does not drain into the sea. After
following the riverbed for a short distance, we plunged into the hills
toward a pile of white stones on the top of the largest hill in the vicinity.

Such cairns, called *obos* by the Mongols, are not only landmarks but
shrines as well, where each traveler adds a stone to the pile and leaves
some small offering to thank the local spirits for allowing him safe passage

through the area. Some of the obos attain a considerable height. Their function as landmarks is increased by implanting poles beside the stones from which flutter white strips of cloth inscribed with Tibetan prayers. The Mongols call these flags that carry the prayers to the gods "galloping wind horses." In some areas of sandy desert the Mongols also add a bell tower to an obo atop a high dune. The tolling bell, in constant motion from the wind, is to desert caravans what the bell buoy is to mariners.

Our white obo, which Gonzell said was called the Obo of the Sun, was a landmark for us as we wandered in and out of some pretty but quite isolated valleys which, in contrast to the treeless plain, boasted an occasional tree or two growing in the dried bed of the river. The trees were mainly elms. All were gnarled and twisted, and very old. There were no saplings, a fact which lent weight to the theory that the present climatic cycle is too dry for young trees to obtain a foothold. In a wry commentary on this situation, the Mongols, Gonzell told us, have a saying that if you want to hang yourself you have to ride a hundred miles to find a tree. As we drew closer to the obo we encountered a series of hills and valleys in which black slate predominated, giving the landscape a particularly dark, almost sinister, appearance.

On reaching the obo we were struck by its enormous size, much larger than either of us had seen so far, and by its whiteness. This turned out to be due to whitewash that had been splashed over the stones. A pole with prayer flags surmounted the obo. Others were placed all around the cairn. Apparently all this was designed to propitiate some particularly potent spirits that resided in the vicinity.

We stopped to chat with the Chinese workers at the nearby site of the capital. This was located between the river and the hills, on an incline that sloped gently toward the river. There were about a dozen workers, all Chinese, who were chiefly engaged in cutting some tall grass that was to be used to reinforce the mud walls of the buildings. The plans called for the construction of a number of buildings containing, in all, about one hundred rooms.

Work was progressing very slowly. It was being held up by the failure to receive poles that were to be used as ceiling beams. These had to be carried here from some distance, as no timber was available anywhere in the vicinity. Completion of the construction work was not expected for at least two years. The Chinese seemed to be quite unconcerned about the slow pace of construction.

Not so the Mongols.

"They're annoyed about it," said Gonzell. "And worried about the deteriorating situation. The Chinese aren't giving them any significant help. Yet it's obvious that the Japanese are pushing deeper and deeper into Mongol territory. Georg thinks they've already infiltrated agents into this area. Prince De is madly running around trying to keep the Mongols from being overwhelmed —by the Japanese, by the Chinese, and by their own backward elements."

"Sounds like a hopeless mess," said Martin.

"It sure is. Georg says the atmosphere is especially tense farther east. For now, at any rate, things aren't too bad around here, especially for foreigners."

"That's a relief." I said.

A few weeks later, in July, Garrett Jones, a correspondent for the British *Manchester Guardian,* was captured and killed by "bandits" in the neighboring province to the east. The foreign community in Peking was convinced that he was murdered at the instigation of the Japanese because he had learned too much in the course of his snooping around in the areas they were infiltrating.

8 / A Day in the Life of a Desert Traveler

‡‡‡‡‡‡‡‡

Some years after my return from China, New Haven, Connecticut, which used to be called "The City of Elms," was hit by a blight that killed off most of those stately trees. Seeing a dying elm reminded me of a place called Elm Tree in Mongolia. Desiccation there, blight here in the United States; death in both places.

What a fragile planet we inhabit!

It's not all nature's fault, of course. We, Americans and Chinese alike, help create dust bowls by plowing up the thin layer of top soil that is just enough to grow grass for animals but not enough to grow food for humans. And it's awfully hard to reverse the process.

After they came to power, the Chinese Communists launched a grandiose project to keep the desert at bay by creating a new Great Wall, a massive belt of trees that would cover the Gansu Corridor and the great bend of the Yellow River from the area north of Lanzhou all the way into Inner Mongolia.

It would be worth a trip to the area, if one is permitted to go there, to find out just how much of this tree-planting plan, and related desert-control projects, has been carried out, and with what success.

‡‡‡‡‡‡‡‡

We never did catch up with Prince De, because our camels arrived (finally!) before his return and we took off the very next day. They arrived late in the evening, so it was not until the next morning that we could get a good look at them and attend to final details before starting out.

Manager Guo had sent us four camels and a camel driver called Zhou.

In addition he had sent another camel driver, the paragon named Xiao that he had tried to foist on us, who was to accompany us, with his own camel and food, as far as the Black River. He was not to be paid, which was one up for us, but the fact that he was to accompany us at all was something that neither Martin nor I were pleased about. Xiao had been presented to us by Guo as one of the chief camel drivers in the firm, so he naturally would be Zhou's superior. We could foresee conflict between his wishes and ours.

"You really don't have any choice in the matter," Gonzell told us. "The custom of the road requires that a caravan accept a lone traveler who wants to attach himself to it."

Our annoyance at Guo's maneuver was almost dissipated by our hilarity at the thought that our scruffy little group of animals was considered a caravan comparable to the long trains of hundreds of camels that stretched out over a distance of more than a mile. Well, if there was nothing to be done about it, we could at least enjoy our elevated status as a caravan. "Welcome aboard," we said to Xiao, with as much grace as we could muster.

All five of the camels were females.

"There isn't a really good one in the lot," Gonzell's teacher said. "They're in poor condition. You'll be lucky if they survive as far as the Black River."

That really shook us. We didn't mind taking risks, but we had no desire to have our camels die on us and find ourselves in the position of those cartoon figures crawling on hands and knees across the desert toward the enticing mirage of a palm-shaded oasis. So we queried anxiously as to what we might do to spare the camels as much as possible. George had mentioned not riding them all the time. Was there anything else?

Well, for one thing, we could reduce the weight that our camels would have to carry by eliminating some items that could be dispensed with in a pinch—and a pinch there certainly was, we were forced to acknowledge. Martin undertook the painful task of going through his two big boxes of books, a veritable traveling library, and eliminating as many as possible, mainly a lot of general reading matter and other items not related to our travels. He insisted on retaining an annotated edition of Marco Polo's *Travels,* half a dozen books by Hedin and other desert explorers, a multivolume history of the Mongols, and quite a few other works that he insisted we would need to consult or should have as reading matter. I reluctantly sacrificed my big dictionary, keeping only a small one along with a couple of light-weight Chinese books and a goodly supply of note paper and character-cards, indispensable aids for the never-ending study of Chinese.

Altogether, between the books and other discards, we figured on sparing our camels about 200 pounds. We estimated that now each camel would have to carry no more than about 325–350 pounds. This was in contrast to the 375–400 pounds that comprises an ordinary load and the 500 and more pounds that first-class camels can manage. If camels, as the cliché has it, are ships of the desert, then ours appeared to be in danger of foundering even before being launched. Here we were jettisoning part of our cargo so as to stay afloat on a voyage that had not even begun.

And that was not all. We were also advised to adopt a routine that would spare our camels as much as possible. We should avoid travel during the hottest part of the day. It was best to start each day's march about three in the afternoon, so that the camels would have only one or two hours of the worst heat. Second, we should not push them too fast or too far on these treks. It would be best to keep to the normal caravan pace of two and a half miles per hour, and to go for no more than about six hours a day, so that our daily march should average only about fifteen miles. In contrast, camels in good condition can easily cover twenty to twenty-five miles a day. And finally, we should not work our camels for more than a week or so at a time without a full day's rest. This meant that it would take us more than a month, perhaps five or six weeks, to cover the six hundred miles to the Black River.

I passed on the advice from Gonzell's teacher to our camel driver in Xiao's hearing. Both took it all as a matter of course, as if it was self-evident and they had already thought of it.

Apart from the fact that our take-off point was the cluster of yurts belonging to Georg and Gonzell rather than our own tent, our first day on the road turned out to be fairly typical of the routine we followed in more than two months of travel by camel. After breakfast Zhou took the five camels out to pasture. The rest of us busied ourselves with various chores for the rest of the morning. At noon Zhou brought the camels back from pasture. We had dinner (this was always our biggest meal of the day) and then got everything ready for loading the camels. We had previously decided what we wanted to have access to on the march, such as windbreakers in case the weather turned cold, what would be needed when we made camp, and what would not be needed for several days or even weeks. When we ended our march for the day it would be nighttime, too late to search for fuel for our camp fire, so we would have to carry some with us. Martin and I took a small basket reserved for this purpose and went scouting for the only sure fuel in camel country.

The Mongols call it *argol*. It consists of camel droppings about the size of the briquets popular in American outdoor barbecuing. One needs only a squishy mistake or two to learn to distinguish between fresh droppings and sun-baked ones. Well-seasoned "camel briquets" burn a little more slowly, and with a little less heat, than charcoal briquets, but they serve quite well in the absence of better fuel. After filling the basket with enough argol, we hung it on one of the camels along with a few other things that needed to be readily available.

The men brought each of the loaded camels to its feet by giving a tug on the cord attached to the peg thrust through the cartilage of its nose—gently at first, not so gently if the beast tried to ignore the summons to rise. Then they tied the cord of one camel to the load of a preceding camel so that all five of them were joined together in a string.

In larger caravans a string consists of ten or a dozen camels led by a man known as the camel puller. The last camel in his string has a bell attached to its neck so that, if no longer hearing the clanging sound behind him, the camel puller would be alerted to the fact that one or more of the camels had broken loose.

Zhou went to the head of the string and took hold of the cord of the lead camel, since he had been designated to have the first stint as camel puller. We were to take turns at the task of leading the camels.

We exchanged final handshakes with Gonzell and thanked him for his hospitality. Then we were off. Martin and I walked alongside the camels. Xiao brought up the rear.

We climbed the low hills west of the Temple of the Larks and at the top turned for a last look at the hill-girt plain in which it was situated. We lin-

Xiao checking our start from the Temple of the Larks

gered for a moment, almost reluctant to make a final, irrevocable break with the lifeline that had sustained us so far. Then we turned and set our eyes toward the distant oasis six hundred miles across the desert, in the very heart of the Gobi, a vast expanse three times the size of Texas.

Our route took us over terrain that in patches was still fairly good pastureland, for this area stood at the western edge of what the Chinese called the Great Grassland. Throughout the grassland, especially farther east, where the growth was taller and of better quality, the grass was a sweet variety particularly favored by horses, cattle, and sheep. Camels ate it also, but reluctantly, for they preferred a salt grass that grew in more alkaline soil, such as abounded in the area we were traversing and was to become dominant farther west, especially in the area of the Great Gobi.

The term "Gobi" requires a bit of explanation. It is a Mongolian word with the literal meaning "gravel desert." The term "Gobi Desert" is therefore redundant, but it is now firmly established in general usage, where it is applied to an area extending seven hundred miles from north to south and twelve hundred miles from east to west. This is centered along the border running east and west between Inner and Outer Mongolia.

But this huge expanse, the central portion of which is often designated "the Great Gobi," actually consists of stretches comprising different kinds of terrain—sandy belts, barren rocky hills, patches of grassland, and gravel-covered soil. It is only the last of these, the gravel-covered stretches, that Mongols refer to as "gobi." Foreign travelers in the area soon learn to use the term in both the restricted sense of the Mongols and the looser sense established by popular usage.

The distinction, which is sometimes expressed in writing by capitalization versus small letters, is important if we are to make sense out of a statement like "After crossing this sandy stretch we'll have a belt of gobi before running into more sand." When hoofing it through the desert one can hardly fail to be impressed by the differences in terrain and by the utility of the restricted Mongol usage of the term. And after slogging through a stretch of sandy soil it is a relief for one's legs to come to a belt of good firm gobi.

We developed a refined feeling—literally a feeling—for the differences in the ground under our feet. Sight was not a completely reliable guide. Except for differences in color, one stretch of gobi often looked much like another. But our feet felt a difference.

Some stretches of gobi consisted of a thick layer of hard-packed gravel that held up well under our weight and made walking a pleasure. Others consisted of a thin covering of gravel on a friable crust that gave way to softer earth underneath. Walking over such terrain was almost as tiring as walking on sand.

There were differences between sandy areas too. Wind-blown sand that covered the ground with drifts and dunes was so tiring to walk on that we often made long detours to avoid such areas. Sand in dry riverbeds was occasionally somewhat compacted and so provided better footing.

Zhou said that there were actually five kinds of gobi—white, black, yellow, red, and blue. These colors refer to the kinds of gravel that covered the ground. The sand, soil, and rocks in their various hues added still more color to terrain that not only varied from place to place but changed shape before our eyes, sometimes because we saw the wind literally remaking the face of the land, always because in our progression we saw things from constantly changing perspectives. We found no little pleasure, or at least fascination, in the desert kaleidoscope.

Walking at the camels' snail's pace of two and a half miles per hour turned out to be more tiring than a brisker pace. So we soon took to walking off from the caravan—sometimes together, sometimes separately —whenever we saw a curious outcropping of rock or something else that seemed to warrant a closer look. Our zigzag excursions away from and back to the caravan added considerably to the distance we walked. Later we were fond of saying that of the total distance of a thousand miles covered by the camels in the course of our trip, we walked at least twelve hundred.

After we had been walking for a couple of hours we decided to ride a bit. Not that we were tired. It was just that we were curious to know what it was like to ride a camel, in particular whether it was really the case, as Georg had assured us, that there was nothing to riding a loaded camel, in contrast to an unloaded one, something that required at least as much skill as riding astride a horse.

There were, we knew, two ways to mount a loaded camel: one when it is standing, the other when it is squatting. If it is standing and you want to make it squat, you accompany a downward tug on the nose-cord with the command "Sook, sook," which is camel talk for "Lie down" or "Squat down on your knees." The squatting position brings the low point of the arched neck low above the ground. You step onto the neck with the left foot and simply scramble up to the top of the load, where you sit with your legs stretched out in front. This is very easy and requires only that you be alert when the camel rises from its squatting position.

It does so by first thrusting up suddenly with the hind legs, so that you are snapped violently forward and are in danger of being pitched over the head of the beast. Without giving you time to recover from that jolt, the camel lurches up with its front legs, so that you are whipped backward toward its rump. During all this you have to remember to keep your legs stretched out in front with the weight of the body evenly distributed on the top of the load, which you have to grasp with a firm hold to keep from being unbalanced and thrown off.

Later in the trip I came a cropper once when I absent-mindedly mounted a camel in this way and forgot to hold on when it stood up. As I

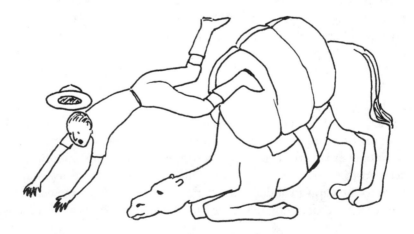

was about to be thrown off, I clutched wildly at one side of the load, thereby unbalancing it. As I fell off, Zhou quickly seized the nose-cord and kept the panicked animal from bucking and running off. I shame-facedly helped readjust the load.

On our first try at riding a loaded camel we mounted it by an alternative method that does not require it to squat down and so is often used in the course of a march. This is a bit more difficult to execute because it demands careful coordination.

You begin by taking the nose-cord of the standing camel in your left hand and pulling down on it to force the arch of the camel's neck as low as possible. Next, still pulling down on the cord, you place your left foot on the low point of the neck and your right hand on the load to steady yourself. Then, relaxing your grip on the cord and letting it slip slowly through your hand so that the camel is free to raise its head, you balance the weight of your body on the left leg and follow through with the upward momentum of the camel's neck and body to scramble onto the top of the load. It's a bit like riding up a jerky old elevator standing on one leg.

This technique can be used even when the camel you are mounting is attached by the nose-cord to the load of the preceding camel. You simply bring your camel as far forward as possible so that there is enough slack on the nose-cord. Then in mounting, instead of letting the cord slip through your hand, you release it completely, leaving both hands free to help in scrambling to the top of the load. If the camel is not attached, however, you have to be ready at all times to tighten your grip on the nose-cord so as to be able to control the animal.

When we mounted our camels for the first time they were standing attached as part of the string. Zhou helped us by pulling down on the nose-cord of the camel each of us had selected to mount so that we had both hands free to help pull ourselves up. Later we grew adept at mounting by ourselves.

After we had mounted our camels, we sat with our legs stretched out in front, feet slightly apart, and our weight evenly distributed along the center of the platform formed by the loads on each side of the camel. As the camels plodded along on their cushioned feet, the pads of which expand with the pressure each time the foot is placed on the ground, we felt a gentle swaying motion, as in a rocking chair, with just a bit of side motion too, for camels proceed at an amble, that is by moving both legs on one side together. It was almost like sitting in a forward-moving rocking chair five or six feet above the ground. Gentle rocking motion, warm after-

noon sun, rhythmic thudding of camel pads, and sound of creaking ropes
—it all made for a somnolent ride.

"What do yo think?" Martin called over to me. "Not bad, huh?"

"Georg is absolutely right. I'm relieved. Riding this way is very pleasant. Nothing to it."

It was a pleasure in which we could not indulge ourselves for long,
however. In order to spare the camels we dismounted after less than an
hour. Dismounting is easier than mounting. You simply slide forward
toward the front of the load so that both legs are dangling down one side
of the camel's neck. Then, without causing a break in the camel's stride,
you jump clear of both the beast and its burden. The main thing is to pro-
pel yourself sufficiently far so as not to be knocked over by the protruding load.

For a while I walked alongside Zhou in order to talk with him, partly
just to practice handling the language, one of my major objectives on the
trip, and partly to ask about the route we were taking and related matters.
It turned out that he actually didn't know much about our route, as he
had never been over it before and was merely following the directions
given by Xiao. The latter would point to some distant landmark toward
which we should work our way, as it seemed best given the terrain we
encountered.

It was generally a simple enough matter to do this. At least that was
true in the early stages, over terrain that was traveled over enough so that
although there was, strictly speaking, no real road, there was occasional
evidence of what might be called a desert highway. Sometimes this was a
path made by thousands of camels over the years; sometimes it consisted
of tracks made by carts and even motor vehicles.

In some areas where the ground was harder under foot I lost sight of
the telltale marks of travel over our route. Zhou's eyes were sharper than
mine. From time to time he pointed to evidence that I had missed. The
Mongols, he said, were even more skilled at reading the signs left on the
ground. I matched his tales of Mongol tracking with similar stories involving American Indians.

Zhou said that a few years before a number of people had joined
together to form the Xin-Sui Motor Company in the hope of developing
truck transport between Xinjiang and Suiyuan via the Black River route
across the desert. I had heard of the venture also, from Georg. Zhou
agreed with my doubts that the Xin-Sui Company would be able to
replace camels in the face of the appalling difficulties that I had heard
about. Already several trucks had been wrecked in the rough terrain.

I had heard that there were, nevertheless, sporadic crossings of the desert by motor vehicles. Some of these were made by opium runners, apparently operating with the connivance of the authorities at both ends and in between. They carried the drug from the growing areas in western Gansu to the market areas of the northern and eastern provinces. Special cargoes such as this paid off handsomely despite the risks and the cost involved in motor transportation. It appeared that opium, although ostensibly illegal, was readily available to anyone who wanted it. Many people were addicted to it, Zhou said. Even some of the camel drivers.

"But not those of our firm," he said virtuously. "The company would not hire anyone who had the habit."

That led us into more personal conversation. I asked Zhou about his family. There were only a wife and mother at home, he said.

"No children?"

He hesitated for a moment before answering, "No children."

It was months before I learned the reason for that hesitation.

Zhou asked about my own situation, particularly my family background, and seemed politely skeptical when informed that I did not come from a rich family. How else to account for my being able to come to China as a student and to undertake this trip just out of curiosity? He was, however, moderately impressed by my attempts to learn Chinese, especially its written form. Illiterate himself, he was particularly impressed by the fistful of character-cards that I carried with me at all times. I invited him to look at the bulging left pocket of my jodhpurs. That was for cards still to be learned. The pocket on the right was for those already mastered. There were always more cards in the left pocket than in the one on the right, I said dolefully, and all too often some right-pocket cards kept returning to the left. Zhou laughed.

"Yes," he said, "learning characters is truly not easy."

But he complimented me on my speaking ability. I took that with a shakerful of salt, for Chinese etiquette requires that foreigners, however fractured their Chinese, must be praised for their wonderful mastery of the language.

Zhou, and Xiao also, patiently answered my questions about the specific meaning and usage of the new terms that constantly cropped up in our conversation. Xiao, who like Zhou could speak Mongolian, generally gave me the Mongol name of places we encountered and followed this with the Chinese meaning of the term. I had the impression that he was sometimes unsure of the Mongol name, and even less sure of its meaning, but that he was trying to humor me by coming up with something I could note down. It was also apparent that there was a great deal of repetition in the names, as many were based on local features that were by no means unique. Often the name of a place on our route was the same as one I recalled in the accounts of other desert travelers, but the locations were quite different, separated at times by hundred of miles.

From the spoken rendition of the Chinese terms given to me I tried to find the characters to represent them. This was difficult, sometimes impossible. I occasionally had trouble converting their dialect pronunciations into the standard forms on which my dictionary was based. And this was too small to have many of the everyday terms, especially the colloquial and technical ones, that peppered our necessarily nonacademic exchanges. Moreover, dictionaries of Chinese are among the worst in the world, generally reflecting a literary and archaic bias. Nevertheless, as we plodded along, I kept plying the men with questions and getting answers that I would check on as soon as possible. In one of my hip pockets I carried a small notebook in which I jotted brief penciled notes along the way. Later, as soon as the opportunity arose, I wrote up the notes in greater detail.

About twelve miles into our march we passed a place whose Mongol name Xiao rendered into Chinese as Yu Shu, an expression that can be translated either as Elm Tree or Elm Trees, since there is no distinction of singular and plural in Chinese nouns. Here it was apparently meant in the singular, for there was only one tree in evidence, a huge, oddly twisted, decrepit veteran that was holding out stubbornly in its desiccated surroundings against its tragic destiny of extinction without progeny. It was sad to reflect that the lone tree was sufficiently remarkable to serve as a landmark in this ill-favored land.

The speck on the landscape that, if mapped, would be marked down as Elm Tree appeared to be uninhabited. It was, said Xiao, the winter headquarters of a few Mongols, as it lay south of some hills that gave shelter to the pastures lying in their lee. The Mongols were doubtless north of the hills, in their summer pastures, and would return only when the cold northerly winds drove them to seek shelter for their herds.

About two miles farther along we came to a Mongol encampment known as New Well where we decided to camp for the night. Here, as throughout our desert marches, where we stopped was determined by the availability of water. In the first week or so this presented no particular problem, as wells, real wells with buckets ready for use, occurred at fairly frequent intervals and were well marked. But as we progressed into drier areas, and as habitations decreased and then petered out completely, finding water became increasingly difficult and worrisome.

In this matter we were completely dependent on Xiao's previous experience and on his ability to recall landmarks that would pinpoint the location of water. In the worst areas we had many anxious moments as we waited while Xiao scanned what seemed to us to be a featureless landscape before deciding, with varying degrees of assurance, that we should aim for this or that spot which seemed familiar to him.

At New Well we made camp not far from a Mongol family whose womenfolk were busy milking the cows while the head of the house, a lama, lounged about.

Our camels were made to lie down in a row preparatory to unloading. This was much easier than loading. It was done with dispatch, in a clearly prescribed order, so that at the end everything was neatly arranged on the ground and readily accessible when needed.

After being unloaded the camels were tied to several of the heavier crates to prevent them from wandering off or feeding during the night, as Zhou said the nighttime dew on the grass is likely to give them colic. Camels normally graze during the day, especially in the morning, and chew their cud during the night.

Martin and I watched the unloading carefully so that we would be able to help out in the future. We were of more immediate help in the easier tasks, such as setting up the tent.

After that operation we brought in our bedding rolls and arranged them so that Martin and I had one side of the tent and Zhou and Xiao the other side. Then we made a fire in the tent with the argol we had gathered earlier. By now, after sunset, the temperature had dropped enough so that we were glad to have the warmth of the fire inside the tent. We knocked off a piece of brick tea, threw it into boiling water, and when the tea was brewed, poured ourselves bowlfuls to which we added a few handfuls of roasted millet. This was our evening meal.

We had barely finished this spartan supper when a few drops of rain sent us scurrying to cover the camels by tying the padding over them. This was to keep them from catching cold. Camels normally cool down slowly after a march. It is dangerous for them to suffer a sudden chill. Our camels had shed so much of their wool that without this protective covering they were unusually sensitive to the rain and changes in temperature.

In the course of settling down after supper we discovered that we had left our thermometer behind in Georg's yurt. This, along with a compass, made up the sum total of our scientific equipment. It wasn't absolutely essential, but we felt it important enough for me to go over to the Mongol yurt with Xiao to see if we could work out some way of getting it. The lama there offered to rent us a horse for the approximately thirty-mile round trip for M$2 or to go himself for M$1. We arranged for him to go fetch it the next day before we broke camp around three o'clock.

"Interesting," said Martin. "He charges twice as much to rent us a horse as to make the trip himself."

"Maybe he figured in the additional wear and tear if I rode it," I said.

"Or if anyone rode it. The Mongols are pretty fanatical when it comes to their horses."

Since we had no good nighttime illumination, and there was nothing much to do anyway, we soon decided to turn in. The fifteen or so miles that I had walked had made me pleasantly tired, not really worn out, which meant that my legs were beginning to get into shape. Sleep came quickly to all of us.

9 / A Desert Diner's Guide

‡ ‡ ‡ ‡ ‡ ‡ ‡ ‡

One of the nice things about being a China specialist is getting to eat a lot of Chinese food. That's not an inevitable bit of serendipity, of course, but it's one I've been happy to enjoy to the full, for to my mind—and taste— Chinese cooking is the best cuisine in the world. Among my favorite dishes is noodles with fried bean sauce. It not only tastes good but evokes a lot of memories.

Those memories are pretty idiosyncratic. I doubt if it would come to anyone else's mind to make an association between noodles with fried bean sauce and the noodles with cameleer's sauce that we had in Mongolia.

Incidentally, that matter of evoking idiosyncratic connections, a process psychologists like to use in their association tests, is an important factor in my recollecting a lot of details about that journey of long ago.

‡ ‡ ‡ ‡ ‡ ‡ ‡ ‡

Our breakfast the next morning, like our supper the evening before, consisted of a few handfuls of dried cereal mixed into our tea. These simple meals, which were typical of all the other morning and evening meals during our desert travels, reflected our decision to live on the same food as the camel drivers and to conform in other respects as well to their caravan life. For us the details had been fixed in the course of long conversations with Georg and Torgny.

In our negotiations with Manager Guo about our camels, we also discussed the equipment and supplies, including food, that we would need for the trip. Torgny was a big help in seeing to it that we were properly supplied. He arranged one day to have some sample items—food, tents, and other equipment—sent over to his home for our inspection. He also had his cook prepare a sample meal that would introduce us to typical caravan food.

We started by drinking a bowl of "brick tea." This was tea made by hammering off a chunk from a brick measuring about 6″ × 10″ × 1″ that weighed about two and a half pounds and was formed by compressing tea leaves into the least possible space in order to reduce the cost of transportation. Such bricks were widely used as a medium of exchange in the barter trade between Chinese and Mongols.

There is wide variation in the quality of brick tea. At best it is a far cry from the fine jasmines that we had become accustomed to. We opted for a medium grade in the hope of minimizing the non-tea-leaf ingredients—twigs, tea dust, and warehouse debris—that are often compacted with the leaves.

The chunk broken off from the brick is pounded, usually in a mortar, to loosen the compacted elements. Most teas are steeped in hot water according to the taste of the drinker. Brick tea is made by boiling. Mongols and Tibetans drink tea *au lait,* with added milk, butter, and salt. Chinese prefer it straight.

We had ours Chinese style. At first sip the tea tasted a bit like water in which a strip of rubber has been boiled. It improved only slightly with more sips.

Next we had a bowl of roasted or parched millet. Although millet is generally considered to be poor people's fare, especially in contrast to high-status rice and wheat, it seemed to me not a whit inferior in taste to many of our cereals that are well known to be the breakfasts of champions. The manner in which it is eaten, however, is another matter, for the Chinese, as the eminent scholar Berthold Laufer has pointed out, belong to the category of people characterized by the curious coincidence that they neither drink milk nor produce epic poetry. Camel drivers generally eat the millet dry, washing it down with copious bowls of brick tea. Others prefer the somewhat more efficient technique of pouring handfuls of the cereal into their tea and then slurping down the combination. This was my preference, too, perhaps owing to some sort of Pavlovian conditioning by an auditory stimulus to the otherwise banal act of eating.

We also had a small taste of two other cereals. One was a kind of oatmeal, not the flaky sort such as graces American breakfasts, but rather a finely ground flour, also roasted or parched. We ate it in a bowl of hot tea, making a sort of porridge, with the optional addition of a bit of sugar. I found it quite tasty. The other cereal, also a parched flour, tasted like bran. We sampled a few spoonfuls in our tea, again with a bit of sugar. It too seemed to me quite palatable.

As our main course our maitre d' presented us with a dish of noodles boiled in water and served with a salty sauce. The noodles were made of white flour mixed with water and kneaded into a big lump that was then rolled flat and cut into strips. The use of flour in this main dish reflected its importance in the diet of northern Chinese. Rice hardly entered into their diet, being eaten only on special occasions, and so it was not part of our caravan fare either.

The sauce served with our noodles was a caravan staple that came in many varieties depending on which of the possible ingredients were actually included, and in what proportions. All versions had as their base a kind of fermented bread and bean paste. To this was added a small amount of chopped meat of indeterminant origin. Other ingredients might include bean curd, garlic, ginger, and chili pepper. An indispensable addition was a considerable quantity of salt, both for flavoring and as a preservative, for the sauce had to keep indefinitely without refrigeration even throughout the hottest summer months.

A helping of noodles was served to us in a wooden bowl like those favored by Mongols and caravan Chinese as being less fragile than ceramic ware. This was actually the same bowl that we had used for tea, since in caravan travel there is nothing so luxurious as a change in service. We added sauce to suit our individual preferences and optionally enlivened the dish with a splash or two of vinegar for further flavor.

This "noodles with cameleer sauce" reminded me somewhat of *zhajiang mian,* or "noodles with fried bean sauce." Brita tartly remarked that I must have a pretty underdeveloped set of taste buds to compare the low-grade "cameleer sauce" with the much more delicate flavor of "fried bean sauce." Moreover, the *zhajiang mian* dish wasn't just noodles but was always served with fresh vegetables such as beansprouts, slivered cucumber, and diced radishes. Vegetables of any kind were unknown in Mongolia. Still, I found the noodle dish quite acceptable and asked for a second helping. Brita shook her head in disbelief. Martin had a small helping and made the rather disconcerting admission that he didn't much like noodles or pasta of any kind and cared even less for the "cameleer sauce." He stoutly maintained, however, that he could handle this dish and the other food served to us.

On the same day when we were introduced to this food, Torgny also arranged a demonstration of other equipment and supplies we would need for the trip. One of our major purchases was a tent. Two of them, one blue, the other white, were pitched in a courtyard for our inspection. We decided in favor of the larger white one, at a price of US$11, since in addition to its having more room, its white color would throw off the heat of the sun better than the blue one. Apart from a small first-aid kit, the limited size of which accorded perfectly with our limited knowledge of such matters, the rest of our equipment comprised fairly standard caravan items.

However, in the matter of food we unexpectedly found ourselves taken to task by the redoubtable Brita Oberg. Fine cook that she was, she was aghast at the thought of our limiting our coddled stomachs exclusively to fare that she was sure the camel drivers could endure only because of the evolutionary selection of the fittest digestive tracts. Torgny scoffed at this theory. I objected to her line of thought on different grounds, the cost of acquiring all the Western luxuries that she insisted were essential to our well-being, indeed to our very survival. Martin took the high ground of principle.

"Our way of travel," he said, "should conform as much as possible to conditions of earlier years, especially the time of Genghis Khan."

At this, Brita leaped in with a thought that had not occurred to our slower wits.

"You frauds!" she exclaimed. "Then leave behind your first-aid kit. And change your boots for the felt-soled slippers that the Chinese wear."

It was my turn to be aghast. I had to admit it was a matter of historical record that Genghis Khan had conquered China without the benefit of Band-Aids. But give up my beloved boots! They had been painstakingly shaped to fit a pair of feet the likes of which had doubtless not even been dreamed of in all the centuries of travel across the desert wastes. And I shrank at the spectacle of myself attempting to hold an audience enthralled with tales of crossing the desert in bedroom slippers.

I could see that Martin was wavering. That's the trouble with persons of principle. You can't count on these fanatics not to push good principles to bad lengths.

"How about compromising by taking just a few Western items?" I asked. "For example, a dozen or so cans of vegetables. We could have one can every few days. That should make it possible for us to ease ourselves gradually into caravan fare. And it wouldn't really compromise our determination to live like ordinary people."

Brita protested that that was just weaseling, but Torgny backed me up vigorously. After a struggle, Martin gave way to his baser nature, and he too agreed to the compromise.

In the course of subsisting on typical caravan fare for the thirty-eight days it took us to get to the Black River, where we were able to add a few things to our diet, I came to regret my close-fisted resistance to Brita's advice. Not Martin, though. In his infatuation with authentic hair shirts he felt guilt at any departure from ordinary caravan life.

There were actually few such departures. Day after day we had pasta for our main meal and a cereal in tea for breakfast and supper. As soon as we got up in the morning we started an argol fire—outside the tent if possible, inside if it was too cold—and heated water to make tea in our tall teapot. We did the same thing in the evening at the end of our day's march, usually after nightfall. At both times all we had to do was pour out a bowlful of hot tea and add one of our three cereals to it.

Cameleer Zhou

My own preference was the parched millet. I had this at least once a day, always in the same fashion, that is, added by the handful to my hot tea. I liked the oat flour and bran well enough but had them only occasionally. The gruel that they made when added to the tea stuck a bit to the bowl. The millet didn't, so all I had to do at the end of the meal was to give the bowl a light rinsing instead of the washing needed after eating the other cereals.

At noon, when Zhou brought the camels back from their grazing area, we all pitched in to prepare our big meal of the day. We built a fire of argol that had been collected around our camp and prepared to boil water in the big iron pot that was our only cooking vessel. While that was in process we mixed water and flour, kneaded it into dough on a board balanced on our two water kegs, and then proceeded to get it ready for cooking.

First we rolled the dough flat. Then we sometimes cut it into noodle strips called *miantiao,* or "flour strips." In one variation we cut the

dough into little squares, called *mianpiar,* "flour squares," about one and a half inches on each side. Sometimes, especially if we were in a hurry, all four of us joined in simply tearing off little chunks of dough from the big pile and pinching them flat between our fingers before flinging them into the pot. On a few occasions, in still another variation, we rolled the dough into ropelike lengths about half an inch in diameter that we proceeded to cut up into little cylinders about an inch long and then pressed with the side of the thumb to form what the Chinese aptly call *mao'er,* "cat's ears." These are the same shape as what Italians call *gnocchi.*

To the cooked pasta, whatever the shape, that we ladled into our bowls we added some of the salty sauce according to our individual preferences. Usually all of us except Martin fell to with gusto.

I always had three or four bowlfuls, as did the camel drivers. Martin had only one or two.

At first that worried me. Our diet was going to be pretty monotonous, with our main meal having variety chiefly in the three shapes of the pasta. I was confident of my own ability to handle our restricted fare, having had plenty of experience along that line, along with a capacity that never seemed to be impaired by monotony. I told Martin that my invariable lunch for three months when working in the steel mill had included four thick sandwiches, more than any of the other hard hats, who marveled at my capacity. It was a matter of concern now if Martin, who probably had more fastidious eating habits, could not handle a diet that the rest of us found acceptable enough, even if monotonous. He assured me, however, that he could manage.

"Don't worry about me," he said. "I'm not a big eater. Even at home."

Eventually I did stop worrying about Martin's limited appetite. We both seemed to be doing all right despite our disparate eating habits.

As a matter of fact, it was I, rather than Martin, who first began to chafe at the monotony of our diet, after only three successive noonday pasta meals that exhausted the three ways of preparing the dough. At first I tried to adopt the psychological technique of restaurateurs by telling myself that dough slices with cameleer's sauce would taste better if Frenchified to "médaillons, sauce chamelier," but that didn't work. Then I thought of going beyond just boiling our pasta to cooking it over an open fire.

I started by rolling fair-sized chunks of dough into extra thin pancakes. Next I washed clean the only flat-surfaced utensil we had, a shovel that we carried to heap earth against the bottom edge of our tent in case of heavy winds. Then I cooked each pancake on the shovel by holding it over the flame of the argol campfire. Everyone agreed that the result tasted fine, reminding us variously of tortillas or chapatis or the wrappings used with Peking duck. The thought of that ambrosial filling led me to wild dreams of other improvements. I expressed surprise that there

was not more variety in the caravan style of cooking. It should not be too difficult to add a skillet or wok for toasting or frying and some sort of device for steaming.

I was considerably deflated, however, on being told that camel drivers do in fact make something like my tortillas. Called *laobing,* they are made by rolling dough flat and cooking it in a dry pot such as the one we have. They can then be eaten as a sort of sandwich with the same sauce that we add to our boiled pasta. At times Chinese eat them with a scallion or two. This led me to hunt for the wild onions that Martin said he had read about in accounts of desert travelers. I never did succeed in finding any.

The men pointed out, and I had to admit they were right in this, that my little experiment, and *laobing* too, involved rather more work and took considerably more time. The same was true of steaming. As to frying, cooking oil cost money, and anyway what was there to cook in this way? Certainly not vegetables. Whoever heard of vegetables in Mongolia? Meat, yes; but it was expensive, to be eaten only on special occasions. And what was the point of frying it without accompanying vegetables? As to steaming, yes, it might be possible, but that too took a lot of time, and it just wasn't done in caravan travel.

A further point that occurred to Martin and me was that the difference between caravan fare and our usual Western diet was infinitely greater than in the case of our two Chinese, who even at home subsisted on what, for us, would be a very restricted and monotonous diet. There just wasn't the same incentive for them to go to the additional bother, not to mention expense, that my bright schemes entailed. It was enough to get a bellyful of food.

The incentive that existed for Martin and me led us to indulge ourselves by breaking out one of the cans of tomatoes that we had brought along. It was so delicious that we regretted having brought only ten cans with us. The tomatoes were delightfully cool and soothing at midday when the temperature reached 100°.

About a week into our march we passed a Chinese farmstead that operated a small family-run trading post where we were delighted to add to our larder by buying up what Xiao said was the family's personal store of two dozen eggs, a peck of potatoes, and a pint of oil. All this cost less than half a dollar in Chinese currency. Cheap, yes, for us. But not for the Chinese. For them half a dollar represented more than a day's wages. Only rich foreigners like ourselves could indulge in such extravagance.

Xiao had arranged, however, for some of our flour to be made into steamed buns. That pleased us mightily, until we learned that the process would take so much time that our departure would be delayed several hours.

For breakfast the morning after our shopping spree I grandly offered to serve everyone a feast of fried potatoes and eggs. I heated some oil in our iron pot, fried nine or ten potatoes, and added a dozen of our precious eggs. I served everyone a big helping of the potato omelet. We all dug in at the same time. And we all gagged simultaneously.

We spat out our mouthfuls of food and tried to wash out the taste of oil that had gone sickeningly bad. In vain. We only succeeded in burning the insides of our mouths as we swished hot water around and spat it out in repeated rinsings. The vile taste lasted for hours.

As I threw out my failed feast, I nearly wept at the loss of all that hard-bought food. And after going back to our usual breakfast of roasted cereal and tea it was a further letdown at dinnertime to be able to manage nothing better than boiled potatoes and hard-boiled eggs.

That was our one and only non-pasta dinner. After that, we had thirty-one straight days of either noodles or dough squares or cat's ears or, on one red-letter day, fried dough.

That happy day occurred about two weeks into our march when a Mongol family near whose yurt we had pitched camp sold us some butter and two kinds of cheese. One kind was the delicious cheese we had encountered in our visit to Arash's family. Called *naipi,* literally "milk skin," by the Chinese, it is a very soft creamy cheese made by simmering large quantities of milk in a cauldron until a thin crust forms that can be lifted out of the pot. We had some of this delicious cheese in our tea and saved some to have with our parched cereal.

The other kind of cheese was in the form of a small brick, dry and very hard. It did not have much taste, and was dirty and full of hair to boot. We ate it anyway, as it represented a change from our monotonous diet.

The butter was our real find. It gave me an idea to make up for the earlier failure with our spoiled cooking oil. I attempted to duplicate the fried dough that my sister used to make for me on my visits to her home. I melted a lot of butter in our iron pot, tore off fair-sized chunks from our usual mound of dough, and instead of rolling them flat tried stretching them out into thin sheets. It seemed easy when my sister did this, but when I attempted it the dough stuck to my fingers and came out in blobs rather than sheets. When fried, the dough ended up like irregular puffy fritters, heavier than my sister's, but tasty enough so that we all made our whole midday meal out of them. Even Zhou and Xiao, who I thought might now shy away from any culinary experiments of mine, especially if cooking in butter was involved, appeared more or less content with my creation.

That they were not simply being polite became apparent when they rejected my invitation to share the only fresh vegetable we were to have in the whole of the journey to the Black River. This came about when I spied some dandelions growing wild near the edge of a marshy depression that we encountered about halfway there. Martin was dubious about them, but I told him how my mother used to add this free food to our diet every spring. (Actually, I hated dandelions, even in early spring, when they were still relatively tender and not so bitter as they became later in the season.)

I also discoursed about the problems that camel drivers were reputed to have with their gums because of the lack of fresh fruits and vegetables. Scurvy was not limited to sailors. Martin was skeptical, both as to the incidence of scurvy in the desert and to the efficacy of dandelions in preventing it. Wasn't it citrus fruits, not vegetables, that were needed?

I wasn't sure about this, but argued that we also needed fresh vegetables to keep our innards in good working order, though again I wasn't sure about the details. I hoped the dandelions would do us more good than the limited diuretic effect suggested by the popular French name *pissenlits,* or "piss-in-beds." Martin pointed out that we had some dried prunes that were supposed to keep us regular. He finally agreed, however, that dandelions were unlikely to do us any harm and might possibly do us some good, so we might as well give them a try.

I cooked a big batch, which Zhou and Xiao, after a brief taste, flatly refused to share. We almost joined them. The dandelions were of a bitterness that even my thrifty mother would not have dared to foist on us. Nevertheless, by repeatedly admonishing ourselves that all this was for our own good, we finally managed to down the lot. It nearly took away our appetite for anything else. And we never did resolve the question of whether this worst of all meals really did us any good.

Whenever we passed a Chinese settlement or a Mongol yurt we often attempted, largely at my prompting, to buy some food that would add a bit of variety to our diet. We did not have much success. The Chinese usually had only the same grain foods that we did, except for some occasional fresh things which they were able to raise only in such small quantities that they simply had no surplus to sell. The family that had sold us the eggs and potatoes must have been an unusually prosperous one. The Mongols, too, rarely had any surplus they could sell. They, as well as the

Chinese, seemed to be eking out a bare subsistence that teetered precariously on the thin edge of inadequacy.

What Martin and I had to eat was thus perforce largely the same as what the camel drivers normally lived on. And their diet probably had not changed much in the millennia of caravan travel across the desert.

10 / From Grassland to Gobi

The Chinese tourist industry is missing a bet in not publicizing places like the Grand Canyonette, Sheepguts River, Tiger Pass, and Wolf's Head Mountains. Of course it would be a tremendous undertaking to prepare those places for tourism. But I suspect that most Chinese don't even know about the existence of those natural spectacles in an area that may still be as inaccessible and little known as when we visited there years ago.

After Nixon ended the estrangement between China and the United States (having helped to create it in the first place), I repeatedly asked the Chinese for permission to redo as much as possible of my earlier trip in the hope of writing a "Then and Now" book. I gave up my attempts to revisit those out-of-the-way places when the Chinese, in their maddeningly polite way, said "No" in a dozen different ways without ever resorting to such a crude and forthright brush-off.

In the first two and a half weeks after leaving the Temple of tne Larks we made the transition from grassland to gobi (with a small *g*), that is, from good pastureland to terrain dominated by gravel-covered soil.

From the start our route took us across a succession of north-flowing streams that started in the mountains to the north of Guihua and Baotou and ended in salt lakes farther north. Most of the time the riverbeds were dry, or nearly so, with water rushing down only at the time of the recurrent rainstorms.

The stretches in between these ephemeral rivers consisted of plains and low hills. Most of the latter were bare and rocky. The more or less level areas included some patches of good grassland, but these increasingly gave way to some areas of salty grass and still others of gobi and occasionally sand. We encountered even more sand in the riverbeds, which were often quite wide, for the flash floods tended to cut away a high bank on one side and deposit the soil in an ever-widening bed.

Our route was fairly well marked in the beginning and even had a fair amount of traffic—two or three passing groups of travelers per day in the first week. On our second day out we passed two Chinese with unloaded camels who said they had come from the Black River. They shook their heads and clucked sympathetically on hearing that we were just beginning, in the opposite direction, the trip that they were about to conclude.

Not long afterward we encountered a number of gazelles, or Asiatic antelope, exquisitely graceful creatures, with long slender horns, which called to each other in queer, quacking bleats. We were impressed by what seemed to us to be a large herd of over a hundred, but Zhou said that was nothing, that herds of more than a thousand were common. The antelope ran swiftly, like a smooth-flowing stream, except that through-

out the herd scattered individuals, while still keeping their place in the compact mass, popped up randomly from the rest in bounding leaps of fifteen feet like exuberant show-offs in a four-footed corps de ballet. In their spectacular progression across the plain they had a curious tendency to run parallel to our line of march for a while and then, instead of continuing straight ahead, to wheel in formation and cross only a hundred yards or so in front of us before disappearing from view.

These antelope can maintain, indefinitely and seemingly without effort, a speed of twenty-five to thirty miles per hour. They have been clocked by pursuers in automobiles as achieving short bursts of fifty to sixty miles per hour. The antelope also reminded me of the huge herds of animals that once roamed the great open ranges of the American West. I stuck out my elbows, reveling in the immense empty space that surrounded us, and regaled an unappreciative audience with

> Home, home on the range,
> Where the deer and the antelope play.
> Where seldom is heard a discouraging word,
> And the sky is not cloudy all day.

On our second day out we made camp after dark at a spot that Xiao said marked the border between two Mongol princedoms. We were still preparing to settle ourselves in when a violent storm broke that prompted us to see first to covering the frightened camels. Rain pelted down, thunder crashed in rapid succession, and almost continuous lightning flashes lit up the landscape so that we were even able to see a distant obo or cairn that Xiao said we would be aiming toward the next day. We felt small and beleaguered as we waited out the storm in our frail shelter.

We got an earlier start the next day but went on so long that a considerable distance was covered in the dark. Xiao and I walked well ahead of our little caravan in order to find a likely spot for our camp. On locating one near a dried-up salt lake with the half-Chinese half-Mongolian name Da Nor, or Great Lake, we built a little grass fire as a beacon to guide Zhou and Martin to us.

This was our longest march so far, a distance of twenty miles. Having walked all of it, and more, I was pretty well tired out, so after we had pitched the tent and finished our supper of roasted flour in tea, I slipped into my sleeping bag and immediately dropped off to sleep.

The following day the temperature went up to 100° by noon. Though it had gone down slightly by the time we broke camp, it was still so hot that I continued the practice I had started as soon as it warmed up enough of doing without my shirt so as to soak up as much sun as possible. In the weeks that followed I became a veritable sun-worshipper. At times I even stripped down to my undershorts, sun helmet, and boots. Martin, on the other hand, insisted on always being sartorially correct, in boots, jodhpurs, shirt, and creased fedora.

Martin thought I was overdoing it to continue my regimen of solar therapy after my skin turned from its original color of a belly-up dead fish to a nice golden tan and then to deepening shades of black. I told him that the rays of the sun penetrated beyond the skin. They mercilessly zapped those mean cold germs that fled from one cell to another, cowered in the

Getting a tan

innermost recesses of my lungs, and finally were found out and zapped to extinction. After that, I thought of myself as a recharged battery storing up the means to deal with future intruders.

I had always thought that "O sole mio" was only sung by gondoliers for tourists. After becoming a worshipper of the sun, however, I sang it myself with the fervor of a new convert. Xiao and Zhou looked amused, and Martin looked pained, when I belted out

Che bella cosa	What a beautiful thing
'na iurnata'e sole,	a day of sun,
N'aria serena	Calm air
doppo 'na tempesta!	after a storm!

When doing without my shirt I hung it on a camel so that it would be readily available when needed. Perhaps that camel was to blame for my discovery one day of a louse. Only one, to be sure, but an inevitable harbinger of more to come. This one was minuscule in size, with a coating of yellow fuzz, and, unlike us, had apparently dined well, for when I popped it between my thumbnails in the approved way of dealing with these creatures, out splattered some nice rich blood that was certainly not its own.

I anxiously wondered whether my deceased companion came from a family of particularly minuscule lice or whether it was merely an infant member of a somewhat more impressive species. The issue was of some importance. Doctors at Catholic University in Peking had shown me some good-sized specimens which they said were the carriers of typhus, that dreaded scourge endemic to the border area and neighboring provinces. The question became academic later when both Martin and I found several large lice that were unquestionably of the type we had been warned against.

The doctors had also injected us with an antityphus serum which they frankly acknowledged was still in the experimental stage. During the preceding years, especially during the terrible Great Northwest Famine of 1929–1933, the disease had hastened the death of many hunger-weakened Chinese among the millions who died of starvation, especially in Suiyuan and the neighboring province of Shaanxi, where almost half the population was wiped out. The doctors were pleased to report, however, that the death rate among foreigners had been greatly reduced. Among those who had been inoculated with their serum only a few missionaries succumbed.

Not all lice, of course, actually carried the disease. We could only hope that ours did not, or that we were effectively inoculated against it.

Although there was no point in dwelling on the matter, I had occasional twinges of fear upon realizing that medical attention, if we should need it, was too far away to be reachable in time.

We had occasion to do a bit of amateur doctoring on our own when Xiao complained about his eyes hurting. They were badly inflamed and looked very ugly. We hoped it was nothing more than the common complaint in desert travel of eyes constantly irritated by the glare of the sun and by dirt blown into them, but we also knew that this common ailment could lead to blindness. We had him apply an eyewash consisting of a mild solution of boric acid. He was hardly more relieved than we were when our treatment proved completely effective.

Our success in clearing up Xiao's inflamed eyes led Zhou to ask us to check his eyes too. I was upset at what my amateurish examination revealed. Zhou had sight in only one eye. The sightless one could distinguish only light and dark.

The "good" eye did not look very good. It seemed to have some dirt under a film, but whatever was there could not be washed out because of the filmy cover. The pupil itself also seemed to be damaged. Zhou said he had had many bouts of eye inflammation in the course of desert travel but had no recollection of an injury to his eyes. He had never had them examined by an eye-doctor. I felt a kind of rage at his having to seek help from an ignoramus with no better treatment than useless washings with boric acid.

There was no avoiding having sand blown into our faces. The problem increased as we left grassland for gobi, was worse in the sandy riverbeds, and was worst of all in areas of high dunes.

One of the more important streams we encountered was called the Sheepguts River. It was aptly named, for in the first thirteen miles of our march on the day we first encountered its mostly sandy bed we crossed its tortuous course no less than eight times. We snaked in and out of a succession of grim valleys, some of them really just narrow gorges, that were made by the river as it cut its way through the surrounding hills.

After nightfall we climbed out of the river valley onto a plain. Here we pitched camp within the dimly discernible sight of a dark mass called Abuder, meaning "box" or "boxes," a common place-name the significance of which we were able to appreciate only in the light of day.

In the morning, as I lazed abed in the early dawn, I was entertained by the antics of a couple of jerboa—jumping mice, as they are known to the Chinese, or kangaroo mice, as Westerners know them. These little rodents have a body about four inches long, a powerful tail of equal length, and a coat light tan in color. When they cock an ear to listen they assume a sitting position with their stunted forelegs dangling in the air. They run only on their hind legs, with body erect. Their Chinese name comes from the fact that they are said to be able to jump as high as eighteen inches.

My two visitors darted about sniffing out the prospects for something to eat. One of them found something. It sat erect, tail outstretched, and nibbled away daintily at the morsel held in its front paws. Both scampered off at the slightest movement on my part. But when I lay very still they came to within a few inches of my head before taking alarm and darting off again.

The plain where we had pitched our camp was almost completely surrounded by hills and was even dotted by a number of lower ones, some rounded, some flattened on top. Among the latter was Abuder. From a distance this actually looked like two enormous boxes lying close together on the ground, but when we approached it later in the day it turned out to be a ridgelike rise thrusting sharply up from the plain, with its center half eroded so that it was divided into two boxlike parts. From our limited understanding of geological matters, we took Box to be a so-called volcanic neck, or vertical pillar of lava from which the earth surrounding it at the time of eruption, eons ago, had eroded away.

Martin's traveling library included a small paperback on geology. He and I read in it from time to time and discussed it together in the hope of at least partially overcoming our ignorance about this subject. The attempt only made us feel all the sorrier not to have taken a course or two in geology so that we could look at terrain with a more understanding eye. There was so much that needed explanation!

In our march through here we passed a place the Mongol name of which, Shirit Obo, it seemed appropriate to translate as Obo on the Mesa. Martin and I climbed to the top of a nearby high point for a better view of the whole area. From that vantage point we were able to survey a vast panorama in which adjacent hills had, stratum by stratum, the same pattern of multicolored striation. It also carried down below the level of the plain into the canyons formed by rivers that now had little, if any, water.

As far as we could see the area was uninhabited except for a distant horseshoe-shaped valley to the north, where we made out a yurt near a small flock of white sheep, or more likely goats, that dotted the predominantly black slopes. The scene was incongruously reminiscent of a stadium in which scattered spectators were watching a poorly attended football game.

On the whole, the terrain with its flat-topped hills reminded me of the mesa country of Arizona and New Mexico. One area we traversed closely resembled a smaller version of the Grand Canyon. Although this was not on the same grand scale as the original, I was, in a way, even more awed by it. I had seen the Grand Canyon in the company of several classmates when we drove across country. Impressed as we then were by that magnificent spectacle, our relationship to it was merely that of fleeting and detached visitors, and pampered ones at that, who approached and left it, with little effort, in a modern conveyance over roads prepared by others for our convenience. In a personally nontrivial sense, we came and went as masters over the almost inconceivable power of nature that had formed that awesome landscape.

Now, as we plodded along step by dogged step in our Grand Canyonette, we were more acutely aware of our own insignificance and vulnerability. Here we were not merely fascinated, not merely awed, but even somewhat intimidated, to an extent we had not yet experienced. The faint aura of menace that we felt here, and indeed throughout much of our travels, was heightened by the fact that we were aliens in a land not our own. In contrast, during the whole course of my automobile drive from New England to California, from sea to shining sea, I had had a sense of belonging, of attachment, of deepened appreciation for that favored land under spacious skies.

Our feelings of alienation here were heightened by the realization that we were probably the first foreigners to traverse this region. Martin, who knew the literature on Mongolia much better than I did, said that no previous traveler in this general area had described terrain that matched what we were seeing. This puzzled us somewhat, for the Sheepguts River had clearly been encountered by others and referred to in their accounts. Martin speculated that they had crossed the river in some other area, for the route west was more a direction than a specific road, and as a result they had missed our discovery.

Our reactions were further affected by our encounters with sand and wind. These were hardly new to us, of course, but here we encountered them both together in a combination that was particularly fearsome.

Previously we had trudged through belts of sand in river bottoms or in ordinary terrain of mixed grassland and gobi. In such areas walking was, for us, slower and more tiring than over firmer ground. The camels, thanks to their cushioned pads that spread on contact with the ground, had less difficulty in negotiating these stretches, though even they preferred gobi to sand. Wind was hard on them as well as on us. It caught against the camels' burdens and forced them to push against the wind.

The trying combination of wind and sand that we had to contend with here was further aggravated the next day when we experienced one of those sudden changes in temperature that characterize desert weather. Although the day started out with its usual scorching sun, which I took advantage of by shedding my shirt, at midmorning the wind suddenly rose and began to whip sand about so strongly that we were almost literally sand-blasted. First I put on a shirt, and then, as the temperature dropped from over 100° to the mid-seventies in a little over an hour, I joined the others in hastening to cover the camels and to get out some additional clothing.

After a vain wait for the wind to die down, we broke camp in the hope of making at least a short march. However, as we progressed, the wind increased in intensity and the temperature continued to fall, dropping into the forties. We fished out sweaters to wear under our windbreakers but were still chilled through by the biting wind. As protection against the windblown sand we walked holding our sun-helmets in front of our faces with one hand while the other clutched our clothing close to our bodies. We plodded along, twisted edgewise and hunched over to shoulder our way against the wind, and sought shelter in the lee of the camels, as they helped somewhat to break the force of the wind for us. Sand pattered against our helmets and stung our hands. I regretted not having had the foresight, summer notwithstanding, to bring along my lined gloves and fur hat with the nice warm earflaps.

After a march of only a dozen miles, which was slowed down by the combination of soft sand and cold wind, we hastened to make camp at the base of a small hill. Only with all four of us working together were we able to get the tent up. We hammered the stakes as deep into the ground as possible and shoveled sand and stones along the bottom edge of the canvas in order to keep the wind from sneaking under it and blowing everything away. It took quantities of hot tea made over our argol fire in the tent to thaw us out a bit. Not until we crept into our sheepskin sleeping bags were we able to get thoroughly warm. Our exhausted sleep was troubled by the howling wind and flapping canvas of the tent.

On Day 12 Xiao complained of a headache and pain in his leg, saying that they were so bad he thought we should rest for a day. That reminded us that we should have had a day's rest before this. Caught up as we were in the rhythm of caravan life, we had forgotten all about the advice of Gonzell's teacher to give the camels one day's rest every week or so.

Xiao wasn't very specific about his ailments. All we could think to do was to dose him with aspirin, feed him a can of tomatoes so he would not have to digest only the heavy dough that the rest of us had, and advise complete rest, all of which he seemed happy to go along with. He surprised me by doing a lot of groaning and sighing. I had though that Chinese, at least those without access to good medical attention, were quite stoical when confronted by pain or discomfort. We suspected that maybe Xiao was putting on an act to remind us of the need for rest.

The next day Xiao said he felt well enough to go on despite the fact that the temperature at noon rose to 108°, the hottest so far. En route we saw in the distance what looked like a long file of troops headed toward us. It turned out to be a caravan about half a mile in length, consisting of three hundred camels split into two sections, each of which had on the lead camel a fluttering red, white, and green triangular banner with the name of the trading firm written on it in big black characters. Accompanying the caravan were a number of dogs, some chained to camels, others chained to each other, and still others free to keep up an incessant patrol by running in an out among the camels and some distance from them along both flanks of the column. At night the chained dogs in such caravans were freed to join in a virtually impenetrable defense against marauders.

This long column of animals belonged to a Mohammedan firm with headquarters in Guihua. It was one of the most important firms in that city, possessing a thousand camels. The caravan was on its way to Baotou from Xinjiang with a cargo consisting chiefly of sheep wool, camel wool,

Martin photographing the Xinjiang caravan

dried grapes, cedar wood for incense, deer antlers for making Chinese medicine, and untanned skins of sheep, fox, and wolf. At Baotou the cargo would be taken off the camels and shipped by rail to Guihua, while the unloaded camels would proceed there to rest up somewhere in the vicinity for the rest of the summer.

In the fall the camels would set out again for Xinjiang. After arriving there they would be let out to graze and rest before the return trip in the spring. Thus the camels normally make one round trip a year.

This trip from Xinjiang to Baotou was taking a good three months, somewhat longer than usual, and was now running late. The caravan was following a particularly tortuous route in order to avoid as many as possible of the insatiable tax vultures who would be only too eager to pounce on such a juicy prize. Indeed, the fact that the caravan was going to Baotou rather than to company headquarters in Guihua was precisely in order to avoid taking our route back and having to pay a tax at the Temple of the Larks.

One of the unusual things about this caravan was the fact that it included some women. There was even a child, who was being carried in a large box swinging on one side of a camel. Something else that I thought unusual, but was actually quite commonplace, as I discovered later, was the sight of caravan men perched atop camels placidly engaged in making yarn and even knitting. One strapping young fellow who exchanged friendly smiles and greetings with us was making yarn from the hair of the camel he was riding. He would reach down and pluck a handful of wool from his molting camel, work it between his palms into a thread, and then roll the yarn onto a spool. There was no lack of wool, for a camel sheds about six pounds of first-grade hair, plus some of lower quality.

Most of the men were knitting, a task we usually think of as women's work, but a man's job here, as in much of Asia. Socks and sweaters were their main products. One of the men proudly showed us the fancy patterns, some done in cable stitch, of the sweater he was working on. Xiao and Zhou, both of whom said they also knitted, joined us in complimenting him on his fine eye for design. I refrained from pointing out that it did not extend to color. Patches of the sweater were of varying hues, from a very light tan, almost an off-white, to a dark brown. This reflected the variety of shades to be seen on different camels and even on different parts of the same camel. Of course, one could hardly expect yarn found on the hoof to match the uniformity of yarn found in dry-goods stores.

Cameleer of the Xinjiang caravan making yarn

The Gobi was the only place in the world that produced camel wool fine enough for clothing purposes. Much of what was produced there was brought to the major collecting center at the Temple of the Larks. From there the best camel wool was exported abroad.

After parting company with the big caravan we continued through terrain that was even more rugged than what we had encountered so far. For a week we climbed up and down a succession of jumbled hills, through valleys that narrowed into gorges, along riverbeds some of which actually contained water, past patches of marshy land with vegetation that supported a few small herds of horses and cattle. It took two days to thread through the narrowest part of Tiger Pass, another day to cross Wolf's Head Mountain.

I gave silent thanks to the nameless camel drivers who had thought up these names. They seemed to fit perfectly the mood evoked by vistas of savage beauty. From high vantage points on our route it seemed as if powerful forces of nature had clawed deep gashes in the terrain, leaving scarred hillsides where huge boulders and fractured slabs of rock, brilliantly variegated in their diverse patterns of oxidation, teetered menacingly, ready at any moment to crash down and join the debris already scattered throughout the lower reaches of the valleys. For a whole day we passed an area where streams had scoured ugly gashes, bleeding red against the dark hillsides, like the slashes on the face of a disfigured duelist.

The changing moods of the weather fitted right in with the menace lurking in these rugged hills. While crossing Wolf's Head Mountain we were overtaken by a storm that seemed to materialize from nowhere. Before we could prepare to take cover, a cold wind blew down upon us, the sky blackened, lightning streaked across the heavens, and claps of thunder rolled through the hills. Driving rain soon turned to hail. Most of the hailstones were the size of little peas, but some were as big as marbles. They stung our bodies and rattled against our hats, which we tilted at a rakish angle to protect our eyes.

The camels became badly frightened. They screamed, attempted to run off, jostled each other in panic. At shouted commands from Xiao and Zhou, we all grabbed nose-cords and brought the milling animals to a halt, forcing them to their knees, holding their noses close to the ground so they could not scramble erect. We crouched in the lee of the camels for whatever slight shelter we might obtain against the gusting wind. Without even the frail protection of a tent, we felt like insignificant animalcules cowering in the open country against the unleashed wrath of heaven.

Just as suddenly as it had come up, the storm died down. Out came the sun, as hot as ever, and soon dried out our clothing, which was clinging clammily to our bodies.

The next day we decided to attend to some long overdue household chores. We started by darning some socks. While Martin and I plied needle and thread, Zhou joined us with his knitting needles and a half-completed sweater. We made a fetching domestic scene, caravan style, as we accompanied ourselves with lively chatter, interrupted by the occasional search of an itching spot for a louse, which we delicately popped between our thumbnails.

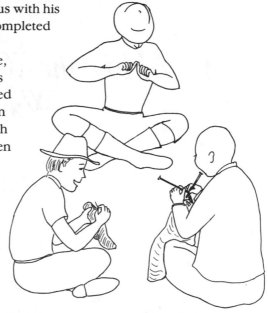

In a further attack against these creatures, we took advantage of a good supply of water to indulge ourselves in the first baths since our start more than two weeks before, and we also did a big laundry. I washed three pairs of socks, four handkerchiefs, a towel, four pairs of shorts, and my jodhpurs. There were still a couple of shirts to go, but at this point, my knuckles rubbed raw and my temper frayed to the limit, I called it quits.

The shirts presented a problem for which I found what seemed to me to be a perfect solution. This was based on what I came to call my relativity theory of cleanliness. My two shirts, which I seldom wore in order to get as much sun as possible, were not equally dirty. I decided to wear the cleaner, or at least the less dirty, shirt until the erstwhile dirtier one became the cleaner one. By alternating them, I was thus always able to wear a shirt that was relatively clean.

It was well that we had done our big washings when we did, for after emerging from our week-long trek through mountainous country we entered upon a drier area marked by smaller hills in an extensive plain of gobi and sand. At this point we were a bit short of halfway to our destination. So far we had traversed what was described as the easier part of our journey over comparatively good country. From now on water would be harder to find. We would have to make longer marches.

11 / How the West Was Lost

‡‡‡‡‡‡‡

Whether you consider land as won or lost depends on your point of view. In America, whites exult at how the West was won, Indians mourn at how it was lost. In our travels through the western part of Inner Mongolia we saw how the Mongols were literally losing ground before the influx of land-hungry Chinese.

In the years since then, there have been some changes in Chinese policy owing to the establishment of the new regime in 1949. For one thing, the Mongols, along with other minority peoples, have been exempted from the one-child policy that has been applied to the the major part of the population, those called "Han Chinese," so named from the great Han dynasty of 206 B.C. to A.D. 220. For another, the Mongols' demand that their tribal lands be merged into a single unit has been at least partially met by the de-gerrymandering of the old provinces and the establishment of the Inner Mongolia Autonomous Region. However, the boundaries are still drawn so that Chinese far outnumber Mongols there. While the population of Inner Mongolia has increased fivefold, the Mongols themselves have increased by only 50 percent. Today they comprise only 2.5 million out of a total population of 20 million.

The more things change. . . .

‡‡‡‡‡‡‡

While trekking west of the Temple of the Larks, we noted a pattern of Chinese penetration that differed somewhat from what we had encountered in the region directly north of Guihua. There the Chinese had taken over large tracts of land and settled close together in villages similar to

118

those that dotted the farmland of North China. From these villages the peasants went out in all directions to till their plots of land.

In the area where grassland merged into gobi, however, Chinese families lived separate from each other, a pattern more closely approximating that of the United States in the frontier days. We encountered these isolated farmsteads only at long intervals in the course of our daily marches.

Another point of difference was that some of these farmsteads doubled as trading posts. Many of the families settled in this region did some supplementary buying and selling. They either acted on their own or served as agents of the trading houses based in Guihua and Baotou. It also happened that some Chinese who started out primarily as traders took to farming and sheep-raising as sidelines. The goods sold at these trading posts were supplied by caravans belonging to the parent companies with which they were affiliated. Supplies were dropped off by caravans on their outward journey to the Black River. On the return trip the caravans picked up the items that had been acquired by barter with the Mongols.

For all these little trading posts it seemed to be a pretty miserable existence. Only the Mongol princes who permitted the alienation of tribal lands, and the Chinese authorities who promoted the whole business, made any real profit out of it all. The worst losers were ordinary Mongols, who bought and sold at prices largely set by the Chinese and saw their best-watered land being taken over by these immigrants.

Xiao referred to the trading establishments as *maimai,* literally "buy-sell," a term usually applied to small stores or trading enterprises of various kinds. Here it seemed to refer to farmstead establishments that were a cross between the trading posts of the American West and the ma-and-pa grocery stores of the days before supermarkets. They catered to both Chinese and Mongols who lived in the area or passed through it.

We passed the first sign of Chinese settlement three days out of Temple of the Larks. This consisted of several abandoned mud huts and was called by a Chinese name that Xiao explained as meaning Great Profits Company. It was the former site of a Chinese establishment of some ten people who were driven out of there by bandits a few years before and had not returned. Only the dilapidated buildings remained, and the name, which even before the bandit attack must have reflected more hope than reality.

"Who were the bandits?" Martin wanted to know. "Chinese or Mongols?"

"Chinese," Xiao informed us.

Martin said he expected as much. "Mongols don't often go in for ban-

ditry. And there's a different pattern here from your American experience. The Indians resisted the encroachment of the settlers. They went down fighting. The Mongols just retire farther out into the Gobi where conditions are unsuitable for settlement."

"They didn't have much alternative. After all, their own princes sold the land out from under them."

"Yes, that's generally true, but some Mongols fought their princes over this. Those in the Ordos did. Not here, though."

A little beyond the abandoned settlement we dipped into a valley that had been taken over by several Chinese families. Xiao said that at this point we were about a hundred miles north of Baotou. The Chinese had penetrated into this area from there in order to eke out an existence by farming and sheep-raising.

They were amply protected, or at least forewarned, against any prospective marauders. As we were passing in the dark, half a dozen huge dogs dashed out in a baying chorus to surround us in a snarling, snapping circle. One particularly big brute rushed up as if he was going to come right at us and was only brought to a halt in a cloud of dust within a few feet by Zhou's stout cudgel striking right at his face. He followed us for about ten minutes, always so closely that we had to keep driving him off with sticks and stones. It was not until we were some distance away from the settlement that he left us in peace to camp for the night at a place with a Mongol name meaning Well in the Valley.

Although the name suggested that this was a watering place for Mongols, there was no evidence of any of them there. Xiao said that they had probably gone into the hills to graze their animals in the summer pastures. When winter set in they would be coming down into valleys like this. But now they would have to share the limited supply of water with the Chinese, who were monopolizing it for irrigation purposes.

The next morning we found that our camp was not far from some Chinese settled along the dry course of a river who, in addition to growing a few crops, did a bit of trading on the side. In most places, Xiao said, these trading establishments had little food to offer beside such standard long-keeping items as wheat flour and parched cereals of various kinds. They rarely had any surplus of fresh food, since what they raised was usually barely enough to meet their own needs.

Not far from there we encountered a place called Great Stone where a fairly good-sized piece of land was under cultivation, probably by dry-farming, though a little garden gave obvious evidence of being irrigated by water from a big well. This was some fifteen feet in diameter and had a water level only about ten feet below the ground. When we peered down into the well we were startled to see a dozen or so larks and other birds fly out.

Farther along we passed a trading house called Four Big Shares that Xiao said was started by four partners, each of whom had a share in the business. The shares must have been profitable, unlikely though it seemed to us (and I suspected Xiao of pulling my leg), for only a mile or so farther on we passed another place of the same name that Xiao said was a branch of the first. They certainly weren't open for business. When we passed them in the dark we saw silhouetted against the skyline an enormous dog, even bigger than the one we had encountered farther back, with eyes burning like red-hot coals. As he dashed at us Martin shouted: "Watch out! Here comes the hound of the Baskervilles!" We had our cudgels ready against him and several other brutes that came rushing at us.

After running that gauntlet and passing some distance from still another establishment, this one with the grandiose name Six Big Shares, we made camp at a spot near the Sheepguts River. Xiao said that the land here was largely given over to the growing of opium.

Although in most places the river disappeared completely, in the areas under cultivation water either appeared on the surface or was readily available underground. A distinctive method was used here for drawing water from wells of shallow depth: the bucket for drawing up water was counterbalanced at the other end of a long pole by a heavy stone firmly tied in place.

As we continued our progress it became clear that on leaving the valley of the Sheepguts River we had left behind the main area of Chinese settlement. Only rarely now did we encounter Chinese settlers, and even more rarely a Chinese trading post. While threading our way through the low-lying hills, we continued to cross occasional north-flowing streams, but

Cameleer Xiao
drawing water

these were smaller now, almost always completely dry, with greater stretches of intervening sand and gobi. Most of these stretches were dotted with small mounds of sand, a few feet around, covered with a coarse shrub that Martin said reminded him of gorse in the Scottish highlands.

The land here was distinctly poorer than farther east. Herds of animals were noticeably fewer—predominantly goats, with only occasional small flocks of sheep and even smaller herds of horses and cattle. In walking through this sort of country we tried to keep as much as possible to gobi areas, as the sand was so much more tiring to negotiate. Sand was a particularly serious problem for cars, as we noted in our repeated encounters with a convoy of several trucks.

On our first day out of the Temple of the Larks, when I was walking some distance from our caravan, I was surprised to see a truck and a car pass me going in the same direction. The truck was loaded down with furniture and other household goods. Several women and children clung uncomfortably to the top of the pile, constantly thrown this way and that as the truck bumped and swayed along. Apart from the driver, the accompanying car was occupied by a couple of Mongol passengers who looked like officials, They grinned good-naturedly at the spectacle of a lone foreigner walking about in the open countryside. Perhaps they were as puzzled about me as I was about them.

A few days later we saw a convoy of trucks drive up to a dry stream less than a half-mile from our camp. They were still there when we struck camp, passed us a bit later, but then in turn were overtaken by us seven or eight miles farther on, where some of the trucks were stuck hard in the sandy bed of another river. All of the passengers had dismounted and were standing around waiting for the trucks to be extricated from the sand. As we came abreast of the group we exchanged greetings. From some among the passengers came the mellifluous sounds of the Peking dialect, to my ears almost like the sounds of home in a foreign land, so I decided to let our little caravan go on ahead while I stopped to jaw a while with a friendly fellow with the common surname Zhang.

The convoy consisted of six trucks belonging to the Xin-Sui Company that were bound for Xinjiang via the Black River route. To make the transit, Zhang said, they were dependent on gasoline carried by camels and deposited in company depots strewn along the route. The logistics involved in this aspect of the Xin-Sui venture made one wonder.

Each camel carried ten five-gallon tins of gas, five on each side, wired together. The trucks were getting between four and five miles to a gallon. For the twelve hundred-mile trip to Xinjiang, that meant 240–300 gallons, or five to six camel-loads per truck, thirty to thirty-six camel-loads for the whole convoy. In addition to carrying forty-four passengers, the trucks were heaped high with household furnishings and personal belongings, like the one we had encountered early on with its Mongol escort. In fact, said Zhang, they hoped to rendezvous with that truck somewhere along the way.

The convoy represented a sort of postscript to the Japanese seizure of Manchuria that had taken place four years earlier in 1931. It seems that when the invaders overran the armies of Zhang Xueliang, known as the Young Marshal, who was the independent warlord of that region, apart from the troops which had fled south with him to the Peking area, a remnant took refuge in Soviet territory to the north. From there they were transported via the trans-Siberian railway to Xinjiang, where they joined a local warlord who had thrown in his lot with the Soviet Union, at least for however long as it might suit his own purposes. The passengers in the convoy included wives and children of the transplanted soldiers, together with various officials and their wives.

Zhang said they hoped to reach their destination in ten more days. That seemed unlikely to me, since it generally took two to three weeks to make the trip by car, compared to two or three months by camel. Zhang admitted that to meet their hoped-for schedule they would have to improve considerably on their dismal progress so far, which averaged less than fifty miles a day. Small wonder, I thought, they had made such slow progress, considering how badly the trucks were being driven. These drivers had none of the finesse that Georg had shown in maneuvering The Bedbug through terrain not much better than this.

The Chinese drivers were a lordly group whose driving technique suggested a need for some elementary lessons in their trade. Here, where the trucks were stuck in the sand, they insisted on gunning the engines dozens of times in succession while the wheels spun uselessly and the overheated motors strained noisily before dying out. Finally, even the drivers conceded that it would be necessary to resort to the special equipment carried along for just such contingencies.

The equipment included picks, shovels, special jacks, wire hawsers, wooden planks, and rope mats about thirty feet long made of half-inch knotted cord. One of the mats was placed under the front wheels of a truck and planks were forced under the rear wheels. This generally enabled the truck to advance to the end of the mat, whereupon the process was repeated as many times as needed to carry the truck over the stretch of sand to firmer ground. Some of the trucks were so deeply sunk in the

sand that planks had to be placed under the axles to hold jacks so that the vehicles could be lifted up enough to fill in with stones the deep ruts they had dug with the incessant spinning of their wheels. In some cases it was necessary to pull a badly stuck truck by attaching it with a hawser to a vehicle that had succeeded in making the crossing. Zhang said that if camels or horses had been available they too would have been pressed into service.

Since there were only three rope mats for six cars, it took quite a while to get all the trucks out of the sand trap. By that time our camels were a long distance off. I hitched a ride on Zhang's truck, the last in the convoy, finding a perch along with half a dozen other passengers on the top of the swaying and bone-rattling load. After having become accustomed to travel at camel-pace, it was almost frightening to be bounced along in a cloud of dust at the breakneck speed of twenty or thirty miles per hour. When we overtook our camels the driver slowed down enough so that I could jump off, to the accompaniment of much hand-waving and the conventional farewell, "Peace on the whole journey!"

It was apparent from what I had seen and heard about motor transport across the Gobi that, although it went almost entirely through Mongol territory, it did not involve them at all in the enterprise and brought them no benefit whatsoever, except perhaps for some princes who might be paid off a bit as the price for passing through their territory.

We encountered another case of Chinese gaining at the expense of the Mongols not long after the truck caravan episode.

As we continued our march, we found ourselves in an area where the low hills both to the north and to the south of us appeared gradually to draw closer together. Up ahead, said Xiao, the hills would almost converge at a place called Hoshot, a name referring to a sort of saddle-shaped depression between two hills. On our way there we passed two good-sized open watering-holes where several hundred camels from a Baotou caravan were grazing and resting.

This area was important as a point where two main caravan routes intersected and then went their separate ways. Here our route from Guihua west to the Black River was met by another route taken by cara-vans from Baotou that circled the mountains northwest of the city and then turned southwest to run parallel and west of the Yellow River and the Alashan range, ending up finally in the central Gansu city of Liang-zhou.

Befitting the importance of this caravan juncture, Hoshot was the site of a small mixed Chinese-Mongol garrison, and also a tax station, all housed in a motley collection of mud huts and yurts. The Chinese sol-diers had been sent here from Baotou by the warlord who had his center of power in that city. The Mongols belonged to a local noble known as the Eastern Great Duke.

The tax station was run by the Chinese, ostensibly for the Mongols, since this was, again ostensibly, territory under Mongol jurisdiction. At this point, as in many others located on caravan routes, whatever regular or irregular authority could get away with it would exact payment from passing caravans on the pretense of providing protection. Here a tax of sixty cents Mex, more if deemed expedient, was levied on every camel passing through.

On our approach to Hoshot I happened to be lagging a bit behind the others and arrived at the head of our halted caravan just in time to over-hear Xiao saying to a Chinese officer, "They're German missionaries and they don't speak Chinese." I was furious but immobilized, fearful of say-ing or doing anything that would reveal Xiao to be lying, as could have been ascertained by a mere glance at our passports. This could be a repeat of Xiao's earlier caper in trying to avoid payment of a tax at the Temple of the Larks by sneaking our camels around the tax station there, a failed maneuver that had caused a considerable delay in our plans. The last thing we wanted here was to run afoul of the law, to give the local preda-tors a polite name.

I was further upset when a bright-faced youngster of eight or nine years ran up at the sight of us and, with a big cheerful grin, shrilled, *Ni shang nar?*—"Where are you going?" I would have loved to bandy a few words with him, but I had to play dumb and shake my head in the pre-tense of not understanding him.

This time Xiao's tactic worked. He got us, and of course himself too, out of paying the tax, for he claimed to be one of our retainers.

Xiao laughed away my protests at the risk he had taken in trying to pass us off as German missionaries. Perhaps the idea of calling us Germans came to him from the similarity between my Chinese surname and the first syllable of the Chinese name for Germany, derived from Deutschland. He did not deign to explain why that identification entitled us to exemption from taxation. To all my questions and remonstrances he replied simply, "It doesn't matter." And he ended with the clincher that we had, after all, managed to avoid paying the tax.

That certainly did a lot to soothe my feelings. There was enormous satisfaction in the thought that we had in effect stolen from thieves. Clever fellow, that Xiao.

It was a couple of days beyond Hoshot that we met up with the big Mohammedan caravan of three hundred camels. We warned the caravan leader about the tax station, but he said he already knew about it and was going to try to dodge that one too, as he had others along the way. From the caravan grapevine he knew that the soldiers were sent out on forays to catch would-be tax-dodgers, but they prudently operated only during the day, so he was going to make a forced all-night march past there in the hope of keeping out of their clutches. We wished him luck.

This part of our trip was marked by a slightly different pattern of Chinese penetration. We had left behind farming settlements such as those in the valley of the Sheepguts River. There we had encountered peasants living in dwellings of dried mud who tilled fair-sized plots of land and carried on family trading enterprises as a sideline.

Here families were few, single men more common, all living in yurts and occupied mainly as traders with the Mongols and passing caravans. They secondarily engaged in raising goats and other animals and only occasionally cultivated a small garden for a few vegetables to supplement a diet otherwise hardly more varied than that of the caravan men. These trading posts were also more scattered, initially about one every ten miles, with the distances between them increasing as we progressed westward. Finally they completely petered out as we got into the worst part of the Gobi.

12 / Tales of Cameleer Zhou

‡ ‡ ‡ ‡ ‡ ‡ ‡

The camel bell that Zhou helped me buy at the end of our trip hangs in the pass-through between my kitchen and dining room. It makes a nice conversation piece. Whenever the bell is rung to summon guests to the table, newcomers comment on its mellow tone and ask about its origin. If they seem really interested, I tell them some of the stories that Zhou told us as we sat around a campfire after the day's march.

‡ ‡ ‡ ‡ ‡ ‡ ‡

We were only partly right in our early impression of Zhou as a rather mousy person who deferred to Xiao and was even more deferential toward Martin and me. Not that he was really obsequious. It was more a case of a sort of passivity that led him to await the lead of others.

Xiao, on the other hand, was clearly a person with initiative. There was nothing overtly aggressive in this, but rather a calm and matter-of-fact making of decisions that largely determined our daily routine.

Chief among those decisions were the all-important ones involving the specific road we should take on each day's march. Only he had knowledge of these matters, as he was the only one to have traveled to the Black River before. It was therefore natural that we should wait for him to look over the terrain and dredge up from his memory the landmarks that would help him to direct us on our way and to call a halt near a likely source of water.

We were startled one day when there was something of a reversal of roles. It happened on an evening shortly after the sky was set aflame in a variety of reds in one of the most dazzling sunsets we had yet seen. In the darkness that soon engulfed us the enormous banks of clouds that had given us that brilliant spectacle suddenly released a heavy downpour.

As we hastened to make camp, Zhou was galvanized into a frenzy of activity. He dashed about among the frightened camels, forced them down on their knees with brutal tugs on their nose-cords, loosened the ropes to release the loads, all the while shouting peremptory orders for everyone to hurry and join in tying the nose-cords to heavy loads and covering the animals lest they catch cold. By the time we had gotten the tent up and a big fire going in it to make tea and dry out our things, Zhou had reverted to his usual self-effacing role.

One morning when we were still in the grassland area, Zhou and I happened to be alone in the tent when a lone Mongol from a nearby yurt dropped in for a visit. I could only manage a hesitant "Sain baino!" but Zhou rose to the occasion by giving him a fuller greeting and engaging in the usual exchange that is the equivalent of our handshake.

Ordinarily, when two people meet in Mongolia, they greet each other by exchanging snuff bottles. Both men and women have these little vials and carry them around at all times. After the exchange they raise the bottles to their noses; sometimes they also take out the stopper and inhale a bit of the snuff. Often they simply lower the vials and admire them a while. Then, holding their hands close together, they return the bottles with a bow.

I was not prepared for this social exchange and so rather doltishly did nothing. Zhou was likewise unprepared but displayed greater presence of mind.

The Mongol took out a flat snuff-bottle about three inches long made out of tawny onyx. It was delicately incised on one side with a seated Buddha and on the other with a sprig of bamboo. He extended the bottle to Zhou. Not having a vial of his own, Zhou instead offered his pipe in return. Our visitor took a puff or two from the pipe and handed it back. In the meantime Zhou had been turning the bottle over in his hands,

making a great show of admiring it. He received his pipe and returned the bottle with a polite bow. The Mongol carefully extracted the green-topped stopper with its attached stick and held it to his nostrils to inhale a little of the snuff. After he and Zhou had chatted for a while our guest took his leave.

Another side of Zhou came out in the course of our evening periods of rest before turning in for the night. When we were not too tired and the weather permitted, we relaxed around the campfire outside the tent and engaged in desultory talk. All except Xiao. He sat for only a while and then, apparently bored with our idle chitchat, went in to sleep. It was then that Zhou blossomed. He told stories, talked on all sorts of topics, and did not hesitate to express views in contradiction to ours.

One of our disagreements was on the relative size of the sun and the moon. That came about on one of the best nights of the trip when the moon rose bright yellow and perfectly round, as big as a wagon-wheel, according to the Chinese cliché. We sat around a glowing campfire that provided companionable warmth against the slight chill. The air was so still that we could hear the faint rhythmic clanging of camel bells from a caravan passing in the distance. I made some offhand comment about how much larger the moon seemed than the sun.

"Of course," said Zhou. "What do you expect? That's because the moon *is* bigger."

I explained that the moon only looks bigger because it is closer. The sun is far away, much farther away than the moon. Zhou would have none of this. He overwhelmed me with precise statistics.

"The moon is six hundred of your Western miles across, the sun only four hundred miles. How do I know this? Why, everyone knows it. All you have to do is look at the sun and moon to see which is bigger."

Zhou's commonsense approach applied also to sunrises and sunsets. These come about, of course, because the sun revolves around the earth. He brushed aside my assertion that it was the other way around.

"No. just look at our Chinese words. We say that the sun comes out, and that the sun falls."

"Well, in English we also say that the sun rises and the sun sets, but that's because that way of speaking comes from a time before people dis-covered the motions of the moon around the earth and of the earth around the sun."

Zhou shook his head at all this bookish theorizing. "Trust your senses," he said.

Another time our conversation turned to automobiles. I made a passing reference to our cars' carrying license plates to identify each vehicle. That reminded Zhou of a story dealing with the equivalent of this for the rickshaws in Guihua. It seems that one night an official engaged a rickshaw to take him from the New City to the Old City. The rickshaw-puller took him down a dark alley, pulled out a knife, and demanded his passenger's money. The official reached inside his gown, ostensibly for his purse, but instead drew out a gun that he leveled at the would-be thief. The upshot was that the rickshaw-puller had his head chopped off and exhibited on a stake as a warning to would-be thieves. And all Guihua pullers were required to go about with a prominently displayed number on their jackets.

One evening, after a day of trudging through gobi country, our campfire talk included discussion of a strange phenomenon that we observed not far away. We saw to the south what seemed like a huge campfire that alternately grew very bright and then disappeared entirely. I wondered if it might be something called Saint Elmo's fire. Actually, I had only heard the term and had little idea of what it really referred to, except that it was said to be an electrical discharge that accompanies thunderstorms.

"But we haven't had any rain for days," said Zhou.

Martin said it was probably an ignis fatuus, or will-o'-the-wisp, a term applied to the mysterious fires that are especially common in England. They are caused, he said, by combustion of gases from decomposed matter in swamps.

Zhou rejected that explanation too. "How could there be a swamp in this desert area?"

No, Zhou said, it was what the Chinese call ghost fire, for the very simple reason that it is actually caused by ghosts. There are all sorts of spirits in the desert, good ones, evil ones, passive ones, others waiting to pounce on travelers who go against desert rules of propriety.

The matter of propriety came up another day when we passed a temple that Xiao called by a Mongol name meaning Yellow Rock Temple. The name was apparently derived from the color of the hills near which the temple was built, for the gray rocks were covered with a yellow and light-brown oxidation.

On the way to visit it we saw a mirage. It was a long expanse that betrayed itself by the heat waves dancing above it. Had it not been for that, I would have sworn that there was a nice big lake ahead of us.

The temple was built snug up against the base of a rocky hill. It was almost wholly in the Tibetan style of architecture. Only the central gabled building with its upturned eves showed Chinese influence. From a distance the temple presented an attractive appearance, but close up it proved to be in a condition of semidilapidation. Only the main central building was in moderately good repair. Sand blown up against the western wall of the enclosure and partly covering it added to the impression of a structure sinking into oblivion.

A service was being held as we approached. From a distance we heard only a sort of hum, which increased in intensity as we approached and finally was differentiated into the monotonous, loud chanting of the lamas that accompanied the equally monotonous beating of drums and clashing of cymbals. On the way back, the humming sound that we had first heard on approaching the temple seemed to accompany us for some time.

Our mention of the service, especially our impression of a humming noise heard for a long distance, led Zhou to tell us some tales of what he called singing dunes and buried temples. In fact, he himself, on his various journeys by camel, had heard some dunes emit humming sounds just like the chanting of priests at their prayers and other sounds just like those made by drums and cymbals. Some people believe, he said, and he was not one to gainsay them, that these sounds come from buildings that have been overwhelmed by sand. What one hears is the lamas still carrying on their prayers in their sand-buried temple.

There are also demons in some of these sand dunes. They call out to passing caravans in the voice of lost travelers seeking help. But if one should go to give assistance, the voice recedes, sounding always just a bit farther off, so that the would-be rescuer is lured farther and farther off the beaten path, until he in turn becomes lost and adds his voice to those calling for help from anyone within hearing of the sound-emitting dunes.

I mentioned to Zhou that when we were staying with Torgny in Guihua he had told us of encountering singing sands in the Ordos desert when attending the services commemorating the birthday of Genghis Khan. He said the dune emitted a low hum, which changed to a roar when you attempted to climb it. Zhou almost shuddered. He would not think of climbing such a dune. However, yes, he would draw our attention to a singing dune if we should encounter one in our travels.

Zhou especially delighted in telling us stories in the evening. We were amazed at his knowledge of historical and legendary figures. His tales were often garbled, however, an intermingling of historical figures from different epochs, a mixture of fact and legend that was derived chiefly from listening to professional storytellers. Zhou himself narrated these tales with relish, punctuating his remarks with histrionic gestures with his pipe, his one good eye gleaming in the light of the campfire. He could hardly restrain his impatience as he waited for me to translate for Martin.

One little story involved Li Shimin, a heroic figure in Chinese history who lived from 600 to 649 and was instrumental in founding the great Tang dynasty that raised China to the heights at a time when Europe had sunk to one of its lowest points. He was a man of action, whose widespread travels were not limited to this mundane world. With only one companion he once made a trip to the Nether Regions. There he was delighted to find an insect of great beauty that he called the Fragrant Bug. He brought it back to earth, but was angered one day when it committed lese majesty by taking a nip out of the royal body. The emperor thereupon renamed it the Stinking Bug, and that is what the Chinese have called it ever since, that pestiferous beastie that westerners call the bedbug.

Among Zhou's favorite stories were some drawn from a book of historical fiction dealing with a period of disunity, known as the Three Kingdoms period, that followed the collapse of the Han Dynasty in A.D. 220. That book is a cornucopia of romantic and swashbuckling tales that storytellers have narrated for almost two thousand years.

One of the most popular figures of that period was a prime minister famed for his clever stratagems in opposing his emperor's two main rivals. Popularly known as Kong Ming, this great strategist, said Zhou, had among his many accomplishments the invention of the lamp and pipe used in smoking opium.

"But wait!" I exclaimed. "Kong Ming lived long before opium was known in China. The Arabs are said to have brought it to China in the ninth century. But for a long time it wasn't used much, except as a remedy for dysentery. After the westerners appeared in the sixteenth century, they brought in large quantities and later forced the Chinese to buy it."

Zhou corrected my version of what had happened. Foreigners actually brought in opium during the Three Kingdoms period. The Chinese did not know how to use it until Kong Ming showed his sovereign and high officials how to enjoy it by using the lamp and pipe he had invented. He recognized the danger of the drug, however, and at his insistence the smoking of opium was prohibited. Kong Ming could see into the future. He foretold the reintroduction of opium many years later and the hold it would acquire over the Chinese. For all his prescience he was unable to change the course of history.

"Kong Ming had a daughter," Zhou said, "who in some ways was even more clever than he was. She was given in marriage to a foreigner and went to live abroad. While there she invented the steam engine."

"The steam engine?"

"Yes, and the steamboat too."

"But. . . ."

"She also invented the airplane."

I attempted to lay claim for a more recent Western role in these inventions.

"Westerners are always claiming credit for things that we Chinese have done," said Zhou.

I had to admit that was true as far as printing was concerned, and a lot of other things too. That didn't satisfy Zhou. I couldn't shake his belief, which I suppose was generally held, in the Chinese origin of much that westerners claim as their own. There was no doubt in his mind of China's cultural superiority over the rest of the world.

More solidly grounded on fact, or at least on historical records, was a story Zhou told us about the attempted assassination of the king of Qin. The episode was familiar to me, for it so happened that I had read about it shortly before leaving Peking. It was narrated in a biography of the assassin written by China's first historian in the second century B.C.

The story had to do with the great unifier of China, who destroyed the numerous kingdoms into which the country was divided and went on to become the first emperor of China in 221 B.C. He was also a megalomaniac who burned books that expounded a diversity of views, buried alive scholars who protested his actions, and arranged for many things of this world to be buried in his mausoleum in Xi'an to accompany him to the other world. The small kingdoms, Zhou said, were in terror, as one after another fell before the armies of the king of Qin. One of the last to hold out was the small kingdom of Yan near present-day Peking. The prince begged his highest minister, called Jing Ke, to think of a way to save the kingdom.

After much thought Jing Ke devised a desperate plan. He would gain an audience with the king of Qin and assassinate him with a dagger concealed in a rolled-up map of a strategic area leading to the heart of the Yan kingdom. But offering the map would not be enough to gain him an audience. How could that be accomplished?

There was in the court of the prince of Yan a former general of the king of Qin who had fled and now had a huge price on his head, a fantastic sum of thousands of pounds of gold. Jin Ke went to see the general.

"General," he said, "you have suffered much from Qin. Your family has been wiped out. I have a plan to avenge your suffering and to save the kingdom of Yan."

"What is the plan?" asked the general.

"Let me have your head so I can present it to the king of Qin under the pretense of claiming the reward. That will surely gain me an audience. When I approach the king I'll take out a dagger concealed in a map and assassinate him."

The general cut his own throat.

Jing Ke put the head in a box and prepared to make his departure. He had with him a dagger made of specially tempered steel. Its blade was coated with poison that had been tried out on several men who died on the spot although they had suffered no more than a little scratch.

The prince of Yan and his retainers accompanied the solitary figure of Jing Ke beyond the city gate. All wore the color of mourning and sang a dirge as they bade him a tearful farewell.

Jing Ke carried the head to Qin. There he was immediately admitted to an audience. He approached the king and began to unroll the map to display it. When the dagger appeared he seized it and lunged at the king.

"Like this," said Zhou, whipping his long pipe toward me in a lunge that caused me to recoil in surprise.

"The king ran from the throne. Jing Ke chased after him, thrusting away like this with his dagger, his eyes glaring. They circled around a pillar."

"Yes," I said, "I've seen pictures of that. It's a famous scene."

"The king's retainers were taken by surprise, and since they weren't permitted to have arms in the throne room, everyone milled about in confusion as the king fled from pillar to post, with Jing Ke in pursuit. Finally the king managed to draw his sword and slash Jing Ke's left thigh. As Jing Ke fell he threw the poisoned dagger at the king. It missed and hit a pillar. Jing Ke slid down to the foot of the post, his back against it, his legs sprawled out before him, and cursed the king: 'You turtle's egg! You dog-reared swine!' Finally the courtiers rushed in to finish him off."

This story of the attempted assassination of the military genius who first united China was Martin's favorite tale. Mine was the one I thought of as the camel drivers' idea of paradise.

To the northwest of China, said Zhou, far to the west, beyond the farthest reaches of caravan travel, is a land called The Country Ruled by Women. They are like other women in every respect, except that they are

far more beautiful. There are no
men in this land. The women
conceive by gazing at their
reflection in a still pool of
water. They bear
only girl-children.

These women receive very
hospitably any men who
might happen to wander
into their country. Those
who do, love it so much
that they never want to
return, for they are
entertained with the
best of food and drink.

"What about. . . ?"
I began.

"Here their pleasures
end," said Zhou, fore-
stalling me.

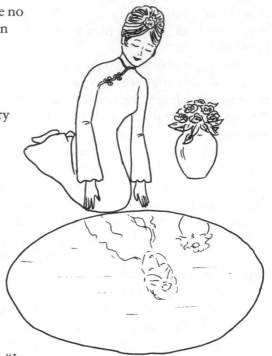

Martin and I felt let down. "Is
that really all?" we asked. "That is all,"
said Zhou firmly. "Should the men desire to return, the women would
not permit it. However, it has never happened that a man had to be kept
against his will. They are all quite content to remain. Upon their death
their bodies are cremated and the ashes are divided among the women."

"Why is that?" we asked.

"The women carry a small amount of the ashes in little pouches
attached at their waists. In that way they are able to conceive. This is a
second method of conception and is the preferred one of the two, but if
ashes are not available, the women can fall back on the usual method of
gazing at their reflections in water."

We sighed. We could think of a better way.

13 / Camelot Peachy and Other Bactrians

‡ ‡ ‡ ‡ ‡ ‡ ‡ ‡

Used-*X* dealers are all the same. It doesn't matter how you fill in the *X*.

What evoked that global insight was a cartoon I saw recently that led me to link my two worst used-*X* experiences. The cartoon showed an isolated desert shack festooned with banners like those in a used-car lot. Several rows of camels stood nearby. A cigar-smoking man lounged on a chair near a sign "New and Used" placed below an illuminated signboard that read CAMELOT.

The cartoon reminded me of a used-car dealer I encountered in Seattle on my way back from China. On a scale of one to ten, with ten indicating highest approval, that dealer rates zero. Manager Guo was a far more ethical sharpie.

To this day I still seethe at the thought of the American despoiler of innocents—myself and two brothers I met on shipboard who were also going to the East Coast and joined me in pooling our limited resources to buy a second-hand car.

Like the One-Hoss Shay, the car gave out completely less than a hundred miles from Seattle. We had to steal rides on freight cars to get back East.

Even my blackest thoughts of Manager Guo while serving as camel puller to Peachy are honeyed panegyrics in comparison with the maledictions I heap on the Seattle Swindler.

‡ ‡ ‡ ‡ ‡ ‡ ‡ ‡

If absence makes the heart grow fonder, presence certainly had the opposite effect in our constant association with the camels. Our unfondness for them grew with every step across the desert.

The very first sight of them filled us with distaste. When they arrived at the Temple of the Larks their burdens had made them seem bigger than they actually were. After they were unloaded Martin said they seemed tiny compared to the strapping geldings he had seen at Georg's ranch. They were made to appear even smaller by the fact that they had shed half or more of their wool, exposing big pinkish blotches of skin. Although such shedding was perfectly normal, the mangy appearance gave them an air of utter decrepitude.

This impression was heightened by the forlorn way in which their two humps lay all flopped over, like the limp watches in a Dali painting. These stand firmly erect on camels in good condition. Contrary to popular belief, the single hump of Arabian dromedaries and the two humps of our Bactrians are reservoirs of fat, not water. The limp humps of our camels showed their complete lack of any reserve of fat that they might draw on.

We might have felt pity for the beasts if they had not had about them an air of hauteur that did not at all accord with their actual appearance— ungainly bodies with spindly legs, serpentine necks with reptilian heads, misshapen faces with doubly cleft harelips and unblinking eyes, protruding mouth and jaws that chewed the cud with a silly sideways motion. They made me think of scrofulous aristocrats with frayed cuffs and dirty collars, monocle in eye and ivory-handled cane aswing. At first I felt almost guilty to have such a visceral dislike for these supercilious creatures, but then I remembered reading that camels never evoke in humans the sort of relationship that dogs and horses often do.

A camel never looks you in the eye, the way an adoring dog does. They hold their arrogant heads up high and look right past you, as if you were not there, and indeed they appear to be totally indifferent to anything in their environment. It is not that they are lost in their own thoughts, for thinking, to redirect the male conceit of Henry Higgins, is something that camels never do. It takes them several years to learn to kneel, and even then they constantly need to be reminded by a sharp downward tug at their nose-cord.

Even the basic intelligence needed for survival is lacking. Other animals learn to avoid poisonous plants, but they have given their name to a plant called "camel poison" because only they are so stupid as to eat it, with dire results that they never foresee. From time to time disaster strikes whole caravans whose camels have all succumbed to the plant.

The poor condition of our camels made it necessary to handle them with special care when it came to the burdens they carried. These had been reduced as much as possible at the very beginning of our trip. The men always took great care in loading the camels. I had been impressed with that process the first time that I witnessed it, and I continued to be impressed at the way the men handled both the loading and unloading.

In preparing to leave the Temple of the Larks, when we packed some of the things into wooden boxes, we had taken care not to have any box exceed what we guessed to be two hundred pounds, the maximum weight of a half-load. The tent and our sheepskin sleeping bags were rolled up into big bundles which again were carefully kept within the required weight limit. Everything was divided up into ten half-loads of approximately equal weight in preparation for arranging them in two parallel rows of five half-loads each. The men made slings for each half-load. They did this by lashing it with a series of ropes knotted in a fashion that would have done a sailor credit. The end result was a securely tied box or bundle that near each end had a rope terminating in a loop.

The camels were made to squat down on all four knees between the half-loads. First the two men, working as a team, placed a strip of reinforced felt around each of the humps of the first camel as a sort of under-padding. On each side of the camel, high up against the upper bulge of the rib-cage and just below the humps, they held in place with one hand a thick flat pad made of hair or hemp that was filled with straw stuffing and had sewn into it a birchwood stave that extended several inches beyond the humps forward and backward. The two staves were then lashed together front and rear so that the felt strips and the stuffed pads were held securely in place.

This done, the men proceeded to put the loads in place. Each of them swung one of the half-loads up onto one knee, balanced it there between himself and the camel, and then settled it into position against the stuffed pad. One of the men threw over the looped end of a rope on his side. The other caught the rope, matched it up with the corresponding loop on his side, and inserted a stout wooden peg through the two loops to hold them together. The looped ropes on the other end of the half-loads were joined in the same way. Now the men were able to stand back from a load that was hanging securely on both sides of the camel. The men swiftly proceeded to load the other camels in the same way.

What impressed me most about all this was the apparent ease with which the men handled the heavy loads, especially the clumsy big boxes. Martin made some offhand remark about the men being stronger than they looked. I was intensely annoyed at his casual acceptance of the way these stevedores of the desert, neither of them weighing more than about

140 pounds, lifted, balanced, and delicately maneuvered the unwieldy half-loads of 175–200 pounds onto impatient and unpredictable beasts that might at any moment scramble erect and throw off the loads precariously balanced between them and the men. It had taken a combined effort by Martin and me to move the big boxes when we repacked them earlier. No, it was also skill, not just brawn, that accounted for the routinely remarkable performance on the part of these camel drivers.

I tried to impress this on Martin by telling him of another remarkable performance I had witnessed while working in the steel mill. One of the hard hats, a worker only about the size of our camel drivers, had the job of stacking iron ingots. I couldn't even budge them. Equipped only with a small steel hook, he would snake a number of ingots to one spot and stack them crisscross to a height of about three feet. Then I attached chains around the stack and to an overhead crane that whisked the pile away. When this worker was about to finish a pile, those of us hard hats who happened to be nearby would pause to watch. We gathered around, as at a theatrical performance, with the crane operator looking on overhead in his dress-circle crane cabin.

The stacker would snake the last ingot over to the foot of the pile, study it for a moment, and then, placing the hook under the ingot at just the right spot, with a swift jerk of his arm, twist of his body, and nudge of one knee would flick the ingot to exactly where it was supposed to go at the top of the pile. We all felt like applauding at the end of the performance.

I felt like doing the same when the camel drivers finished loading the camels.

I also felt considerably abashed on thinking back to our negotiations with Manager Guo. We had blithely insisted that it would not be necessary to take on a second camel puller, as we expected to share fully in all the tasks connected with our trip. Well, I was now uncomfortably aware that that expectation was presumptuous on our part, a product of our crass ignorance, since there were some tasks that required professional skill beyond our competence. I suppose we could have managed somehow, perhaps with the two of us clumsily taking over Xiao's share of the loading. But at best that would have been inefficient, and at worst might even have endangered the trip.

I recalled accounts of how camels, with their well-deserved reputation for general skittishness and unpredictability, are particularly sensitive regarding the loads they carry. If a load is unbalanced to begin with, or moves slightly on the march, as when a camel stumbles a bit and causes a slight shift in the load, the beast may suddenly panic. Then it tends to buck wildly in an attempt to throw off the pesky encumberment. If it succeeds in breaking away, it may even run off and disappear. Sometimes a camel resists being loaded just out of sheer cussedness.

Clearly, loading camels was not a job for amateurs.

The infrequent occasions when we rode the camels were the only time we felt any pleasure in associating with these beasts. At other times we merely walked along with them, helped with the various chores attendant on handling them, and endured their general surliness and outbursts of ill humor. Never in the best of temper, they often became especially restive, spitting, snorting, grunting, snarling, and occasionally screaming, a piercing sound that set us on edge too. One, in particular, usually the fourth in our string, stood out in her display of ill temper.

On the march I had gotten into the habit of hanging my things—packets of flashcards, clothes, and other odds and ends—on the third camel. Right behind came a camel that early on distinguished herself as a particularly nasty beast. The Chinese described her as *piqi da,* "having a bad temper." From how the first part of this expression sounded to his ears, Martin nicknamed her "Peachy," a name that was appropriate only if you like the kind of humor that refers to a seven-footer as "Tiny."

From time to time on the march I had occasion to go to my camel to fetch something or other. Several times, as I was preoccupied with my task, Peachy would sneak up close to me and let out a piercing scream within a foot or two of my head that would cause me to jump half out of my skin. The men laughed at my slowness in catching on to this camel's nastiness. It was humiliating to be constantly outwitted by this stupidest of creatures.

About a week into our travels it was Xiao's turn to run afoul of her. On that occasion Peachy scrambled erect twice in the course of being loaded before Xiao and Zhou had succeeded in tying together the two half-loads they were holding precariously against the sides of the animal. The second time she rose up and threw off her load, a water cask gave Xiao a glancing blow on one foot. He let out a stream of curses as he hopped around on the other foot.

Xiao seized Peachy's nose-cord and handed it to me with a request to hold her in place for a few moments. I faced her warily, recalling stories of attacks by enraged camels, and I pulled this way and that on the nose-cord to keep her snarling face and gaping mouth as far from me as possible.

Herodotus was probably passing on a tall tale when he wrote of a

camel biting off a man's head. At least I
hoped it was a tall tale as I imagined
my moderate-sized head fitting into
that drooling maw. There were, in
any case, plenty of authenticated
stories of camels biting off arms
and inflicting serious wounds.
And the sight of those powerful
jaws evoked a bizarre statistic:
in an average day of chewing
the cud a camel makes 28,000
grinding movements.

It struck me, too, that we
would be in deep trouble if that
cask had fallen full force on
Xiao's foot and fractured it. I tried
to keep my mind from dwelling
on the even worse calamities
that might befall us, like being
stranded in the worst part of the
desert without the help of the only
person who could guide us to water.

While Zhou busied himself with again rearranging the fallen burdens
for a third try at completing the loading, Xiao limped over to the camel
that was carrying our tent, returned with one of the stakes, and drove it
deep into the ground near where I was standing. Then he took Peachy's
nose-cord from me and with a vicious pull downward brought her
screaming to her knees. He tied the cord to the stake in such a way that
Peachy's nose was almost touching the ground. Now it was impossible for
her to scramble erect or even to move her head more than an inch or two
in any direction. With Peachy thus immobilized, the men proceeded to
complete her loading and that of the other camels.

Insofar as one can speak of camels having any thoughts, we encountered one that could be characterized as having a one-track mind. This
incident happened on the day when we met the trucks bound for Xinjiang and I stayed behind for a chat.

On rejoining our caravan I found that a stray camel had joined our caravan as an unwelcome hanger-on.

"He attached himself to us a few miles back," Martin said. "I think he's come a-wooing. He insists on walking behind our camels. We can't shoo him off."

As we were wondering what else we might do to get rid of the beast, a Mongol leading a couple of horses rode up and attempted to detach the camel by riding between it and our animals. The persistent suitor kept working his way back, however, so after several fruitless tries the Mongol gave up and rode off.

Shortly afterward a Mongol girl appeared, a superb rider sitting far forward on her horse, in the Mongol style, who galloped up and reigned to a stop in a cloud of dust. She made a striking figure in her long-skirted, high-collared, plum-colored robe buttoned on the right side and slit on both sides so as not to interfere with riding in the saddle. A wide silk belt wound several times around the waist proclaimed her to be unmarried.

Her hat, tilted at a rakish angle, was adorned with beaded strings of jewels that dangled about her head and flashed this way and that as she deftly maneuvered her steed around the camel. Not at all shy, she gave us a big smile, white teeth flashing against her dark face with its high cheekbones and almond eyes, and laughed with us at her attempts to chase off the persistent suitor. After a while she managed to put a halter on the camel and led him away. As our captivating visitor rode slowly off with her recovered animal in tow, we felt a sort of sympathy for the camel's thwarted ardor.

Zhou leading our camels and an amorous hanger-on

I had a run-in with Peachy several days later when Zhou tried to rest a while by riding her separate from the other camels that were being led by Xiao. He mounted her when she was squatting down, but despite his comical kicking at her with his short legs was unable to get her to rise. I yanked her erect for him, but she still refused to move, so I had to take on the role of camel puller for a while. The skin on my bare back prickled with fear as the enraged beast followed behind me, snorting, belching, screaming, mouth wide open, drooling green slime.

With a particularly piercing scream, Peachy suddenly regurgitated a bellyful of slimy cud and spat it out all over my back. I reached behind me to wipe off the reeking mess.

"Don't do that!" Zhou called down to me. "Wait until the sun dries it out. Then you can just flake it off. That's the only way to get rid of it."

Having gotten Peachy to start moving, I handed the nose-cord to Zhou so he could control her himself while I tried to hasten the drying process by turning my back to the direct rays of the sun. Even when I finally succeeded in brushing the stuff off, the stench continued to surround me. I noticed that Martin was careful to walk upwind from me.

It was obvious that Peachy and the other camels were becoming increasingly bad-tempered because we were continuing to work them instead of letting them have their usual summer rest. We were still not halfway to the Black River. The worst was yet to come.

Martin was the only one who seemed uncon-cerned about what lay ahead.

14 / Death Row in
the Desert

‡‡‡‡‡‡‡‡

Picasso's *Guernica,* which he painted in 1937 to protest the Fascist bombing of that Spanish town, evokes in my mind the memory of death in the desert. The screaming horse, mouth agape, and the anguished human figures, especially the one with upraised arms, face pointing straight up to the sky and wide-open mouth crying out to heaven, capture the essence of brutal death as we encountered it in the Gobi.

Time and again in the years since then something or other has brought vividly to mind a long-forgotten episode from that distant past. That is especially the case now, as I deliberately seek to dredge the dim recesses of my memory in order to make that past live again.

‡‡‡‡‡‡‡‡

Unlike humans, camels die in a uniform fashion, even though, like humans, they die for various reasons. Most perish from simple exhaustion, from being literally worked to death. Our introduction to their manner of dying came about when we encountered a camel that had been attacked by wolves.

That episode occurred on Day 19, shortly after we emerged from the Wolf's Head Mountains onto a vast sand-and-gobi plain dotted with low-lying hills that Xiao said would largely characterize the terrain from here on. As we were plodding along I spied a grove of trees far ahead on our line of march. At first I dismissed it as just another mirage. Then, as it persisted, I quickened my pace with the idea of getting there a bit ahead of the others and enjoying the shade of the trees until our caravan caught up with me.

145

The grove consisted of several large elm trees in the dried bed of a stream. Their limbs were bent and twisted and came so close to the ground that I was able to sit on one of the lower branches after shooing away a dozen or more hawks. These reluctantly gave way, but flew only as far as the other trees, which were likewise covered with dozens of these birds of prey.

Hidden by the trees was a yurt that I hadn't noticed before. It looked shabby and run down. I was surprised to have been able to come so close to it without being challenged by the usual protective pack of dogs. After I had been sitting a while, a man and woman, a very old and dried-up Mongol couple, came out of the yurt. On noticing me they took a few steps in my direction and bowed. I got down from my seat and returned the greeting. They made gestures to invite me into their yurt.

For a moment I was tempted. A few days back, when Xiao and I had visited a Mongol yurt, we were entertained with the usual Mongol-style tea and in addition with a thin buckwheat pancake topped with whipped butter, all so wonderfully delicious that I made rather a pig of myself by accepting the offer of a second helping. But the old couple here seemed so poor that I gestured a polite refusal.

As we were standing there our caravan came up. Zhou and Xiao paused for a few moments to engage the couple in conversation. Then we went on.

Just beyond the grove of trees we passed a squatting camel that Xiao said belonged to the old Mongols. It had been attacked by wolves the previous night before the owners were able to drive them off. There were great open wounds on its legs, flanks, and, most seriously, throat, where the hair was matted with blood. Its head was drawn so far back that it was touching the front hump. Its mouth was wide open, pointing straight up to the sky, as if crying out to heaven.

Xiao said that is the way camels die. Invariably, as death draws near, a camel falls to its knees. While in that sitting position, the animal gradually throws its head farther and farther back until it touches the front hump. The mouth is wide open, but silent, except perhaps for some rasping sounds, as in the present case. At the moment of actual death

the camel topples over to one side and all four of its legs convulsively straighten out.

Since this camel was obviously in its death throes, I asked why the owners did not end the animal's suffering. Both men reacted sharply against the idea of killing a camel, even a dying one. They carefully avoided using such terms as "killing" and "dying." Instead they spoke of "throwing away" camels, of animals "thrown away" in the desert. The forbidden terms suggest something irrevocable, whereas there is always the possibility of a miracle happening to save a camel that has been "thrown away." Taking a camel's life also risks having its troubled soul seek out other camels and bring them bad luck. Fearful things have happened to whole caravans because someone meddled with a camel that had been thrown away. Xiao reminded us that we had already passed several skeletons of camels in the familiar posture of death—body lying on its side, head pulled far back, jaws agape, all four legs stiffly extended full-length.

"We'll be seeing many more from here on," he said. "In places our route will be marked by a row of such skeletons."

And so it was. There were stretches where we were rarely out of sight of the bleached bones of camels—single ones at irregular intervals, occasional groups of two or three clustered close together, more than a dozen in particularly deadly areas of mixed gobi and sand where the difficulty of the terrain was compounded by the increased severity of the windstorms.

A death row camel

Here, in some gobi areas, little backwashes of sand found sanctuary in the lee of small bushes behind which the sand stretched out, in a long narrow band, like the tail of a comet, lashed this way and that by the wind. There were also great expanses of sand that resembled a tempest-tossed sea where the crests of waves were broken off and driven forward in a continuous streaming spray.

At times the wind was so strong that we had to fight our way against it. Some sandstorms made breathing difficult. We tied handkerchiefs over our noses and mouths and tilted our hats over our eyes. Martin said he had read of sandstorms so strong that people actually died of suffocation.

Occasionally we encountered little whirlwinds, miniature tornadoes that appeared sometimes singly, often in pairs, occasionally in disorderly swarms. These funnel-shaped sand spouts, or dust devils as some people call them, came dancing across the gobi, darting this way and that, stopping for a moment in one spot, pirouetting before scurrying off in another direction, like a broken-field runner in a football game.

I played a game myself with a dust spout that seemed small enough not to be dangerous. To see what it was like, I tried to jump into the middle of the whirlwind. It sidestepped me, but I succeeded in outwitting it. For a brief moment I felt myself in a semivacuum being whipped about and pummeled by sand and small stones. Then the dust spout darted away from me. I recalled that in Guihua we had seen a little boy bawling in terror when he was momentarily engulfed in such a miniature tornado.

Zhou was horrified at my playing games with the wind. "Don't you know that desert demons hide themselves in these whirlwinds? Those pairs of sand spouts are male and female demons. You can tell the difference by the way they wrap the sand around themselves. They whirl about looking for victims to suffocate and strip bare of flesh inside their shrouds of sand."

The wind that brought these dust devils also imaginatively sculpted the landscape into a variety of intriguing shapes and blew the sand about in shifting patterns that almost seemed to bring life to inert terrain. In one place light-colored sand blown into the crevices of a slate-covered hill gave the appearance of snow lingering in valleys not yet reached by the warming sun. In another, several orange-red mounds stood out prominently in the distance, one like a conical peasant hat, another like a square tower, still another like a Chinese stone tortoise, all losing these distinctive shapes as we passed and viewed them from another angle.

In a stretch consisting chiefly of reddish earth, the soil was eroded to form a low, flat mound with a top layer of deeper red than that underneath, giving the appearance of hardened frosting spread over the top of a cake and flowing down the side in irregular patches. On another low plateau of dirty white color a strip of orange-red soil ran across the top and down one side like a waterfall of pale blood.

We passed through an extensive depression that was remarkably colored, with red, brown, and gray soils predominating, interspersed here and there with big patches of blue and white. It reminded me of the Painted Desert in the American Southwest. Martin mourned that his camera would leave us only black and white mementos of these immense swatches of color.

In contrast to these varied and variegated expanses there were monotonous stretches of gobi only occasionally relieved by low hills and sandy dunes, some topped by and partially engulfing dried-out trees and shrubs grotesquely twisted as if in the agony of death. The bleakest areas of all were those that the Mongols called *khara gobi,* or black gobi. Our mood matched the somber landscape as we trekked over seemingly endless miles of such terrain.

On one of our marches here, Martin walked off from our caravan in one direction while I climbed a low hill for a panoramic view of a particularly desolate area. Seeing Martin trudging alone in that wasteland of black gobi, tawny dunes, and skeletal trees evoked Dante's wanderings beyond the Gate of Hell, with its inscription "Abandon hope all ye who enter here."

Our caravan in the *khara gobi*

The worsening of the terrain was matched by the worsening of the weather. Previously the highest temperatures had rarely exceeded a hundred degrees, cooling off at night into the comfortable seventies and even sixties. Now it was a rarity for the high to fall below the century mark. In the first week or so of trekking after Day 18, when we left the Wolf's Head Mountains, the average high was 106°. Mercifully, it cooled off during the night. There was a memorable day when the temperature got no higher than 75°. More nearly typical in this area was the day when the thermometer read 105° in the tent and 117° in the sun. Later, as we approached the Black River and then camped on it, we encountered even greater blasts of heat.

Among the most uncomfortable days were those when the heat was accompanied by no wind or by wind from the southeast. From that direction came monsoon weather. By the time the monsoon reached the Gobi, however, it was no more than a blanket of damp air capable only of stirring up a bit of dust and depositing it on our sweating bodies. At night the temperature dropped no lower than the dank eighties. Fortunately, we experienced this rainless monsoon weather for only a few days.

Of greater concern to us than terrain and weather was the problem of water. The length of our marches and just when we made them were largely determined by the need to find water in an area of increasing aridity. Our previous marches had averaged fifteen miles. Now they lengthened to nineteen.

Shortly after entering the gobi plain beyond the Wolf's Head Mountains, we encountered the kind of water that was to be all too typical during our travels in this area. We came upon a shallow well that contained a dead bird and innumerable scavenger bugs floating on the surface. There was also a peculiar smell that I thought came from these dead creatures. But it turned out later, after we had boiled the water to make tea, that the odor came from the water itself. It was slightly alkaline and contained sulfur as well. We drank large quantities of tea, but it quenched our thirst for only a short while and coated our mouths with a sticky film.

Finding water of any kind became harder and required longer stages. Nor could we count on success by the end of a day's march. On Day 28, for example, after a march of seventeen miles, we had still not found any in the spot where Xiao thought some might be available. So the next day we had to make a forced march, starting out at dawn with the sun to our backs for the first time since leaving the Temple of the Larks. It was another ten miles before we reached a well, a shallow one with just a little water in it.

A few days later we had to make not one but two forced marches. A severe storm the previous evening had forced us to camp short of the place where we expected to find water. So at dawn we resumed our march, again with the sun to our backs, to a well seven miles farther on. We were dismayed to find that the well had caved in. On we continued, for another thirteen miles, right through the scorching noon hour. Our tiring trek of twenty miles finally brought us to a well where there was also a patch of good pasturage with salt grass for the camels.

From time to time we had to make other forced marches to reach water. The worst occasion was on Day 31, another day of heat well above a hundred. Having made a waterless stop the evening before after going a tiring seventeen miles through sandy country, we now had to go an additional ten miles in the morning before we came to a well. Then, as usual, in the afternoon we started out toward the next well, a dozen or so miles away. Again no water.

Xiao said water was so uncertain here that it was best to continue until we came to a likely source rather than wait until the next day to continue our search. So on we plodded, long after dark, straining toward shadowy landmarks in the distance, our minds dulled by the effort to put one foot before the other. The stage lengthened to twenty-three miles, the longest single trek on the whole trip. Added to the morning's march, that made a total of thirty-three miles for the day, much of it over the worst kind of terrain.

After making camp we fell exhausted onto our sleeping bags without taking the time to make a fire or have anything to eat.

The scarcity of water that forced us to such extraordinary marches of course severely limited the number of people who could live in this area. Two days after our encounter with the old Mongol couple and their dying camel, we passed several yurts in a tiny oasis where some Mongols were raising goats and camels. They were the last Mongols that we saw in the remaining distance of over 250 miles to the Black River.

The only other people we encountered were two small groups of Chinese, who were mainly involved in illegal trade with Mongols from across the border. Xiao said that the long range of mountains immediately to the north of us, which we had been skirting for some time, was actually located in Outer Mongolia. It was a simple enough matter for Mongols to slip across the border in order to barter with these Chinese.

One of the groups consisted of three Chinese in charge of seventy or eighty camels that were fattening up on the good salt grass in the oasis. They belonged to a nearby trading post with headquarters in Baotou. The

Mongols from the north who came across the border to trade here brought mostly camel wool of high quality, which suggested that while conditions on both sides of the border were similar, the north probably had more extensive pasturage and was better supplied with wells.

Our second encounter occurred close to the first when we stopped at a tiny oasis with a Mongol name meaning White Grass. It wasn't the excellent salt grass that was white, but the surrounding gobi. This was almost a desert metropolis, for it boasted both a trading post and a gasoline dump. In addition to excellent pasturage it had a good supply of water that we took advantage of to indulge in long overdue baths. In honor of the occasion I got out my Sunday-best white duck trousers. It was odd how they boosted my morale for a few hours before having to change back into my grimy jodhpurs.

There were two men at the post engaged in the usual barter trade with the Mongols, though here these were from across the border. Another man ran the gas dump. He was a pleasant young Muslim named Ma who refused my offer of a cigarette because it was against his religion. That rather startled me considering what I had seen and heard of addiction to the greater vice of opium-smoking by Chinese, regardless of religion. In general, Muslims in northwest China did not have a high reputation for

strict adherence to the tenets of Islam. They were, to be sure, fierce defenders of their faith as a mark of their separateness from other Chinese. But strict religious practice was another matter. On several occasions we heard variations of a story that non-Muslims in the Northwest were fond of telling to illustrate the point.

It seems that a hungry Muslim encountered a Chinese peddlar hawking a tray of deep-fried pork-balls. He pointed to one of the meatballs and said, 'What's this?"

"Pork-ball."

He pointed to another. "And this one?"

"Pork-ball."

He tried again. "How about this one?"

"Oh, *that* one," said the peddlar, catching on at last. "*That* one's a mutton-ball."

We had a nice long talk with Ma about his work and his life here. On indefinite assignment to this remote spot, he was well informed about the truck transport system as well as the politics of the region so uncertainly served by it. The politics were of the warlord variety—the tragicomic brawling of rapacious bullies.

There was some uncertainty as to whether the oasis was located in Gansu or Ningxia. It didn't really matter, since this was merely an out-of-the-way stop for caravans and motor transport that could be intercepted at more readily accessible points. The oasis was too distant and insignificant to attract the interest of the warlords who controlled those two provinces. So we were fairly safe from this scourge.

But Ma warned us of the physical difficulties facing us between here and the Black River.

"You'll find hardly any grass for the camels," he said, "and very little water either for them or for yourselves. There's nothing but sand, gobi, and barren hills. It's the worst part of the desert."

We debated whether to push right on or to stay a bit longer at this oasis in the hope of getting into a little better shape for the final push, as all of us, men as well as beasts, were feeling somewhat the worse for wear. What finally decided the matter in favor of forcing ourselves to continue was the realization that we needed much more than just a few days of rest.

In our eagerness to push on we decided to forego the normal rest stop that was actually long overdue at this point. Our initial resolve for a periodic rest had somehow gone by the board. The only times we interrupted our advance was when someone became sick.

The first had been Xiao, on Day 12. Then, on Day 23, Martin was felled by a bout of diarrhea that had started the previous day. There was good grass at that stop, an additional reason for calling a halt and giving the camels an overdue rest. The next day, with Martin feeling worse and raising the specter that he might have dysentery rather than just the lesser runs, we stayed encamped while he dosed himself with medicines, which fortunately proved effective.

A week later Zhou complained of not feeling well. Since we were dangerously low on water just then, he insisted we go on, asking only that we help him mount a camel.

Martin and I replaced him in working with Xiao to load the camels, a task that we found most demanding on the arm and shoulder muscles, and also hard on the hands, as the ropes were stiff and abrasive. It took the combined efforts of the two of us to perform, clumsily and with wasted energy, Zhou's share of the task that was now easier than it would have been a few weeks earlier, since by now we had lightened the burden of the camels by using up a considerable amount of our supplies.

Zhou had no sooner recovered than Xiao had a recurrence of whatever had ailed him earlier. It was not as bad this time, however, and he was able to continue without a halt by riding one of the camels.

Apart from physical ailments, we were also beginning to suffer from a surfeit of each other's company. When Xiao was sick, he groaned and sighed so much during the night that I dragged my sleeping bag out of the tent. The wind blew sand in my face. I countered by wrapping a shirt around my head. It was a bad night. During the day's march I plodded aloof from the others to avoid their grating presence.

Martin particularly aggravated me with his incessant chatter, especially about military matters, which he somehow managed to bring into the conversation on just about any topic. And nothing seemed to ruffle him. That imperturbability was itself a matter of annoyance, as it accentuated my own shortness of temper.

Shortly after leaving the gasoline dump, during a march when Zhou and I happened to lag behind the others, he launched into a litany of complaints against Xiao. I was surprised that he would confide in me to such an extent. I had already noted with irritation that Xiao was curt and domineering toward Zhou. And I was becoming increasingly exasperated at the way he doled out information and preempted decisions regarding our marches. He seemed to be rubbing in our dependence on him.

"We're not really that dependent on Xiao's knowledge of the route," Zhou said. "At this point we're less than a week from the river. All we need to do is head west with the sun and we'll be sure to reach it."

It didn't seem quite that simple to me. What about water? We had already experienced many anxious moments when Xiao had difficulty remembering where water might be found. It seemed positively suicidal for us to attempt a crossing of this last worst stretch of the desert on our own. Apart from the problem of water, if we made an error that extended the distance we had to cover, even by a little, would the camels be able to hold out? Only two of them were in relatively good shape. The other three ranged from bad to very bad. It would be nothing less than a catastrophe if these three gave out completely and left us stranded in a waterless expanse of desert.

The one in worst shape was Peachy. Some time back the men had stopped riding her, long before we completely gave up riding any of the camels in order to spare them for the more urgent task of carrying our equipment and supplies. Then part of her burden was shifted to the other camels. A few days before she had simply refused to get up until the men took off the rest of her load and distributed it among the other camels, which, despite their own weakening condition, now had to carry an even heavier burden. Even then the men only succeeded in getting Peachy to her feet by savagely beating her legs and pulling so hard at the nose-cord that her nostrils bled. Now all that kept her going was the excruciating pain of that cord constantly pulling at the sensitive cartilage of her nose.

Peachy was so far gone that she no longer screamed and spat. Nor did the others have much spirit left in them, especially on the march, when they seemed resigned to simply going on and on, without end. Whenever my turn came around to be camel puller, we all trudged along in silence, and my back no longer prickled in fear at being spat upon or bitten. Now placed last in the caravan, Peachy plodded dully behind the others. Whenever we stopped I wondered if we could get her going again. It seemed increasingly likely that she would join the bleached bones of other camels that marked our way.

In the course of his complaints about Xiao, Zhou presented a startling bit of news about Peachy. She was Xiao's camel, not one of ours! Because she was usually placed fourth in the string, we had assumed that she was the last of our group. My relief at learning she was not ours was followed by anger at Manager Guo for having provided poor camels in the first place.

The day following Zhou's outpouring of grievances against Xiao, we had to make another forced march, a long one, in the morning. In order to make plans for the rest of the day, I asked Xiao whether it seemed advisable to make another march in the afternoon, and if so when we should leave and how long he estimated that stage would be. He refused to commit himself or to provide any helpful information. I decided that it was time to make it clear he was traveling with us, not the other way round, so I said we would make another march starting late in the afternoon because of the heat. He had no choice but to go along with us, for it was now apparent, in view of Peachy's condition, that if we needed his knowledge, he also needed our help.

The next few days were an ordeal of sand-and-gobi terrain, heat that soared above 130°, desperate noonday marches to reach brackish water, and grassless stops where we drooped with the camels in silent exhaustion. Getting Peachy to her feet and on the move involved such frightful beating on the legs and tugging at the bloody nose-cord that even Xiao was almost ready to concede that she had to be "thrown away."

Somehow, though, she made it. And so did we. On Day 37, Xiao pointed to what I thought was just another mirage and said it was our destination. After a final stretch of sinister black gobi dotted with the white skeletons of camels, we came to the tree-lined river.

Anticlimax. The river was bone dry.

"The river is always dry here at this time of year," Xiao said. "The peasants upstream are still using the water. It will be a few weeks yet before they release the water so it can flow north to this area."

And we weren't quite yet at our destination. We camped overnight before making a final march of fifteen miles north along the bed of the river to what turned out to be a veritable community of trading posts. Several firms were represented, including Manager Guo's, which had a contingent of four or five men housed in a couple of yurts and a log cabin chinked with mud.

When we arrived, well before sunset, the men from all the posts warmly welcomed us, Chinese style, with broad grins and a chorus of the simple greeting Hao, "Hi." I would have preferred a good handshake and a bit of backslapping.

The men did do us the kindness of unloading the camels and putting up our tent. They also entertained us with a stomach-distending feast of meat and cabbage and steamed bread washed down with many convivial jiggers of "white dry."

And when Martin, Zhou, and I turned in for the night, a full moon shining through the trees provided a theatrically satisfying ending for our journey across the desert.

15 / The Mongols That
Time Passed By

‡ ‡ ‡ ‡ ‡ ‡ ‡ ‡

In August 1945, in the closing days of World War II, a small but powerful Mongol army, riding tanks and planes as well as horses, erupted across the frontier of the Mongolian People's Republic. This army formed the right wing of a combined Mongol-Soviet force that, in a week of sharp fighting, crushed the Japanese and their Mongol allies in Manchuria and Inner Mongolia.

This event, little noticed and less remembered, revealed the striking difference that had developed between Outer Mongolia under its new regime and Inner Mongolia under the antiquated rule of its princes and priests.

Ten years before this, during a period of forced rest on the Black River after our desert crossing, a book by a Chinese political agent that I started to translate there alerted me to the emerging disparity by revealing that the Outer Mongols were at the beginning stage of a profound social revolution. In contrast, what we saw of the Mongols in the Black River area showed a people stuck even farther back in time than the Mongols we had encountered in the east.

‡ ‡ ‡ ‡ ‡ ‡ ‡ ‡

Imagine visiting an isolated corner of Appalachia, where Shakespearean English is said to be preserved to this day, and running across people wearing eighteenth-century knee-breeches and cocked hats and pining for the good old days of King George III.

We experienced something like the equivalent of that among the Mongols we encountered during our stay on the Black River. So did a

Chinese political agent, Ma Hetian, in a book he wrote recounting a trip through there a few years before us. His account confirmed our view that the Black River Mongols, a tiny offshoot of what had once been a major tribe called Torguts, seemed suspended in a time long past.

Some of these Torguts still wore pigtails. This style of hairdo had been imposed by the Manchus on their subject peoples when they conquered China in 1644. For the Chinese, the queue was a hated symbol of subjection. They made it a political point to cut off the pigtail when they overthrew the Manchu regime in 1911.

Many Torguts, especially officials, also continued to wear apparel dating from the Manchu period. One day, not long after reaching our Black River rest stop, we encountered a couple of Mongols on horseback whose Manchu-style round caps topped by a button proclaimed them to be officials attached to the office of the prince who ruled over this area. Earlier, when Ma Hetian was received in what he referred to as the prince's "palace," which consisted of a number of mud buildings and a half-dozen yurts, he had noticed a rack holding a brilliant summer hat of the Manchu period with a white button, a feather, and a red fringe. He also noted that subordinate officials addressed their superiors in the Manchu style by dropping on one knee

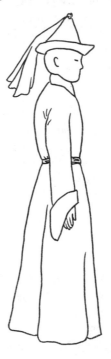

and touching a hand to the ground. People knelt in the presence of the prince; only by his leave did they dare to rise.

Ma Hetian reported a conversation with some Mongols in which he asked what kind of government they hoped to see in China. They expressed a preference for the restoration of the Manchu dynasty and the installation of the Panchen Lama, next in the Lama hierarchy after the Dalai Lama, as their spiritual leader. "Ridiculous!" he fumed. "Pitiful!"

He blamed the Chinese government for not "educating and civilizing the Mongol people."

The Black River Torguts had particular reason to be so attached to the Manchus. Most Mongols acquired territory by fighting for it, but this group of Torguts had been placed on the Black River in the eighteenth century through the kindness of the Manchu emperor. How that came about is part of the epic story of the Torgut diaspora that I'll tell about in the next chapter.

When we were there, the Black River Torguts numbered only about five hundred people. They constituted an independent "banner" not subordinate, as were most Mongols, to a larger tribal grouping. Their territory nominally covered some 25,000 square miles—250 miles from north to south and 100 miles from east to west. The habitable area was less than one-fifth of that, though, for the actual width was only a few dozen miles in the delta area of the two lakes and a mere few hundred yards farther south, where the desert had a tight fist-hold on the river before it branched out, so that overall the river complex was rather like a spindly bouquet of flowers in the desiccating embrace of the Gobi. That made for a population density of one Torgut to ten square miles.

The population was increased somewhat by the presence of some Outer Mongols, perhaps one to two hundred of them, whose dissatisfaction with the changes taking place in their homeland had led them to decamp with their herds. In addition, there were several dozen Chinese attached to various trading posts, gas depots, and other facilities. And of course two visitors—one Canadian and one American.

I stretched out my arms. Nope, not too crowded. It would be, though, if Ma Hetian had his way.

Our first contacts with the Torguts were on our food-hunting expeditions. We turned to them shortly after our arrival on finding that the trading posts had only the staple grains for sale and, saddest of all, no fresh vegetables. The men grew barely enough for themselves in their carefully irrigated little gardens. But the Mongols, too, had little beyond their own needs.

One of the men from our firm offered to take us around to some nearby yurts to see what we might find. We all took care to arm ourselves with stout cudgels. It was well that we did. I was the last one to enter the first yurt, and while I was still halfway in the door, a big brute came charging up at me, his lips drawn back in an ugly snarl. I had to stop and beat him off with my stick.

There was no one at home in this tent, but we found a taciturn old

Mongol in a nearby yurt who was willing to provide us with a daily supply of milk and to sell us some freshly made sour-milk cheese. In both its
fresh and dried forms, this cheese was one of the main items in the diet of
the Mongols in this area. To my disappointment, it seems that not many
Mongols here made the delicious "milk-skin" cheese that we had been
introduced to in our visit to Arash's yurt.

In payment for the cheese we gave the old Mongol a silver dollar. With
a fine gesture of disdain he tossed the coin into a little basket without taking the usual precaution of biting it to check whether it was genuine. Pah.
Money.

We smiled. He loosened up, offered us a drink made from fermented
goat's milk. I found the taste barely tolerable, but Martin was quite taken
by it. He arranged to acquire several bottles, some of which he planned to
send to friends in Canada.

On returning to our camp I mixed some of the sour-milk cheese into a
batch of dough, rolled this into little patties, and dry-cooked them in our
iron pot. The result was a sort of cheese cracker that went well with little
sips of our Mongolian liquor.

Our cocktail hour was further enlivened by the spectacle of a Mongol
couple doctoring a horse and a camel near our tent. They forced the
horse to lie down on its side and immobilized it by tying up its feet. The
strong-armed young amazon held the horse's head firmly on the ground
while her husband forced a quantity of soap shavings into an ugly open
wound in the corner of the animal's mouth.

After finishing with the horse they tied up a camel in the same fashion.
This time the wife sat on the animal's head to keep it from moving. Her
husband cleaned out an enormous wound in the camel's belly, emptying
it of a mass of maggots, and then filled the wound with soap shavings.

The Mongols were a cheerful young couple who repaid our interest in
their doctoring by coming over to the tent for a visit. They turned out to
be the prince's niece and her husband. The two inquisitively looked over
our possessions, chatted a while with Zhou, and then left.

That visit was typical of many that we had from the Mongols in the
neighborhood. They would greet us with "Sain baino! and then, on realizing that we did not speak their language, would turn their attention to
Zhou.

One day, though, I was surprised when a young Mongol first turned
toward me and offered me his snuff bottle by way of greeting. For a
moment I was at a loss what to do. I accepted his bottle and had just
enough presence of mind to present him with my unlit pipe that was

lying close at hand. He pretended to puff, and I, to smell. I returned his snuff bottle with both hands, hoping I had not committed any breach of etiquette.

We had somewhat more extended contacts with the Mongols thanks to taking on one of them as our guide for a projected trip to the lakes. Old Wang, one of the senior members of our firm, found him for us.

Wang took us to a yurt not far from our camp that he said belonged to one of the more important families in the area. There were four people there—two young men, one young woman, and a somewhat older woman. One of the men was a lama who had visited our camp several times, just out of curiosity, as he had never seen foreigners before. The other man was introduced to us as Dorji. In the course of our negotiations with him, through Wang, Dorji seemed to defer to the older woman and to discuss everything with her. We were not introduced to the women and never did find out just what the family relationships were.

Both women had a peculiar style of headdress that we had not seen before. They had buttered their hair so that on each side of the head the hair stuck hard together to form a flat projection that pressed the ears from behind in such a way as to cause them to stick out almost at right angles. We thought the ears must surely become deformed if the hair was done up in that style for a long period of time.

The two women set out quite a repast for us. Especially delicious were some pancakes topped with large dollops of a heavy white cream the consistency of whipped butter. I ate more than good manners dictated.

After we left, Wang did his best to satisfy our curiosity about the women.

"I'm not entirely clear about the relationship of the people in the yurt. But I know who the older woman is. Her name is Hanta. She's the prince's first wife. He has a second wife. I've never met her. They say she's a strong-willed younger woman who has the prince pretty well in hand."

Wang regaled us with further gossip about the prince. It seems that he was so riddled with syphilis as to be incapable of fathering a child. Fearful that the princely line would not be continued, he had his brother, who was a monk, renounce his calling and become a "black man," a lay person who could marry and have children. (The term comes from the fact that in contrast to priests, whose heads were shaven, under Manchu rule other men had long black queues.) Then a search was made for a likely mate for the ex-monk.

The local Khutukhtu, or Living Buddha, was asked to invoke his powers of magic to find a wife capable of bearing children. He discovered, doubtless by means not requiring magical powers, that the unmarried daughter of a certain rich man was pregnant. The Living Buddha informed the prince that the mother-to-be would make a suitable wife for the ex-monk. Thereupon the two brothers opened negotiations to secure her.

Here they ran into a snag. The girl's father was overjoyed at the prospect of obtaining a grandson to inherit his wealth. He was quite unconcerned, Wang added, about the uncertain paternity of the child. But he was furious at the thought of losing a prospective heir.

Finally a solution was reached that satisfied all parties concerned. The prince's brother would marry the girl. The first male child was to be handed over to the prince. The second would be given to the girl's father.

Things turned out even more auspiciously than they might have hoped. The girl proved so prolific that the ex-monk, who was now quite happy to remain a "black man," also came to be supplied with a male heir.

The day after we had arranged with Dorji to guide us to the lakes, he came to our camp accompanied by the young lama we had seen in the yurt with him and the two women. Bowing politely, the lama draped a pale blue silk scarf, called a *khatagh,* on the outstretched palms of his hands and presented it to me. I received it in the same way, on my outstretched palms, bowing politely in return, very flattered to think he was paying Martin and me a special honor, as this was the formal way of expressing friendship, presenting gifts, and inaugurating various ceremonial acts.

The lama accompanied his presentation with a little speech that Zhou, interpreting for us, said had to do with building a temple somewhere in the Alashan area, far to the east. In case we failed to get the point, Zhou added that this was the Mongol way of asking for a contribution. If our gift was large, we would be entitled to keep the scarf. If small, the scarf was to be returned with our contribution on it.

Feeling a bit like the dinner guest who drained the finger bowl, I placed two silver dollars on the khatagh and presented it to the lama with an apology for the smallness of our gift.

Dorji repeated our names several times before coming to a decision as to their proper rendering in Mongolian. Then he noted them down on a large sheet of paper partially filled with the names of donors.

We asked the lama about temples here in Torgut country. He said there were two of them, not counting a temple just south of there that had been destroyed many years ago. We knew about that temple. We had passed the ruins just a few miles short of our final destination. All that remained were the partially collapsed walls of a dozen or so small buildings, most of them probably the living quarters of the monks, and somewhat more substantial enclosing walls about ten feet high made of mud and baked bricks reinforced with wooden beams. The longest side was only about two hundred yards. That made for a rather small temple, at least compared to those we had seen farther east, but it still seemed fairly impressive for a population of only a few hundred people. Xiao had called the ruins the Old Temple. He said it had been destroyed more than a hundred years before in an attack by Muslims.

Our lama visitor said that of the two currently existing temples one, called East Temple, was located not far from here at the seat of the prince's administration. The other, called West Temple, was located farther south, just beyond the westernmost channel of the river. East Temple was the larger of the two.

Besides these temples there was a little encampment consisting only of three yurts in an area of fine pasture and leafy poplars where the Living Buddha of the Torguts preferred to live. Accompanied only by a few disciples and some shepherds to tend his flocks, he kept himself apart from the two temple populations of lamas and monks. He was, however, readily accessible to anyone who sought his counsel, as many people did, for he was full of wisdom and magic powers.

I wondered if this Living Buddha was the same one that Ma Hetian had met a few years earlier. The Chinese writer remarked, rather sourly, that when Torguts came into the presence of the Khutukhtu they all kneeled down on one leg to accord him a greeting worthy of an august Manchu monarch.

The nearby temple mentioned by our young lama was some seven or eight miles away at a place the men in the trading posts referred to as Beile. Martin said that this term, which they applied as a place-name to the official quarters of the prince, was actually a Manchu title referring to a prince of the third rank, the lowest of the princely ranks. The possessor of this rank was distinguished by insignia dating from imperial times, which included an official hat topped by a sapphire button and a peacock feather hanging backward from it.

Shortly after we had settled into our camp, the men informed us that etiquette required us to make a courtesy call at Beile. They delegated Xiao to guide us there and provided us with splendid mounts that Martin said were sure to impress the Mongols.

Martin was mounted on a spirited white horse. I was provided with a gentler brown one. Xiao rode a donkey and had put on his best clothes for the occasion. The horses had Mongol saddles made of birchwood on a pattern that has not changed since the days of Genghis Khan. Martin said they were narrower than those he was accustomed to. We found them rather tight-fitting but on the whole not too uncomfortable when a blanket was placed over them. Our saddles were just ordinary workaday ones, a far cry from the saddles padded with colorful leather or cloth and studded with silver and gold that are the pride and joy of the Mongols who can afford such ostentatious displays of wealth.

Our route was well traveled. For the most part it consisted of a single well-defined path, but in places there were two or three paths running side by side. Throughout most of the trip our route was bordered by heavy vegetation with occasional groves of Euphrates poplars, a curious tree with willow leaves below and ordinary poplar leaves above. Our horses ate the bark.

Beile, like Gaul, was divided into three parts. The most impressive, which we saw only at a distance, comprised the personal quarters of the prince. These consisted of several flat-roofed buildings made of sun-dried mud bricks that had been whitewashed to present a dazzling appearance as they lay somnolent and silent under the blazing sun.

A small nearby temple that housed sixty to seventy monks presented a similar appearance except for some tiled roofs and a number of yurts in the courtyard. From the temple came the low murmur of the monks chanting their scriptures.

We thought of visiting the temple but decided against it, as a service seemed to be in progress. Xiao also seemed very reluctant to approach the place. He spoke of the priests there with unusual harshness.

"They're an ignorant lot. I'm told that at most they have a smattering of Tibetan so they can intone the scriptures. Not a single one is able to read Mongolian. And as for those who know Chinese, they're as rare as phoenix feathers and unicorn horns."

This diatribe on the ignorance of the priests surprised us in view of Xiao's own illiteracy. We wondered if there was bad blood between him and the priests, perhaps a history of conflict between them and the men at the trading posts. Xiao muttered something about black magic but seemed reluctant to discuss the matter further.

The administrative quarters of the prince consisted of half a dozen yurts and a single mud building with several rooms. There was no sign of life. Not even the usual protective pack of dogs sallied out to contest our approach. Only the susurration from the temple disturbed the eerie quiet.

Puzzled, we entered several yurts, only to find them empty. Finally we came across a Mongol who described himself as a caretaker. From him we learned that the prince, with a large part of his entourage, had just left for Tibet on a visit to the Panchen Lama. Xiao remarked that such mass pilgrimages were quite common. In the old days, before the border was officially closed, large groups of Outer Mongolia and Buriat Mongols, located in Siberia in the Lake Baikal area, also used to pass along the Black River on their way to Lhasa.

We had brought along a gift consisting of a satin scarf and a bottle of wine, but the caretaker said he did not have the authority to receive our gift. Finally he routed out someone in another yurt, who turned out to be not a Mongol but a Chinese from the upriver town of Maomu. He had been taken over by the Mongols as a child and spoke only a little Chinese. We presented our gift to him, chatted a while, and then left for the pleasant ride back to camp.

We thought that after our courtesy call at Beile we would have no further involvement with Torgut officialdom. To our surprise, a few days later we received a visit from a representative of the prince. He rode down from Beile with a live sheep, which he presented to us together with a khatagh as a return gift. That was the Mongol custom, we were told.

The men at the trading post offered to take on the task of killing, skinning, and cutting up the animal. Two of them came over to our camp. One of the men held the sheep while the other slit its throat. He drained the blood into our washbasin for later use in making blood sausages. Then they skinned the sheep, cut it into two parts, and separated the meat from the skeleton.

The Torgut official who presented us with a sheep

We presented the men with one half of the sheep, together with the skin, blood, and inner organs. Zhou was very happy to be called upon for advice about reserving a few cuts to be cooked immediately. The rest we hung to dry in the sun on a cord tied between two hitching posts.

Several black vultures circled watchfully overhead. Their shadows crossed and recrossed the space around us as we sat outside the tent to keep them from swooping down on the unexpected addition to our larder. Actually, I would not have been too unhappy had they succeeded in making off with the meat, for mutton jerky was not my idea of a gourmet addition to our diet.

Zhou was particularly happy at the prospect of having some meat dishes. He had been pestering us for days to try to acquire a sheep from our Mongol neighbors, but neither Martin nor I had much enthusiasm for the idea. As jaded Western carnivores, we had failed to realize how much it meant to Zhou. Some people may be vegetarians by preference, but Zhou had no choice in a lifetime diet where meat was a luxury.

We had one meal of lamb chops grilled on a fire made from dried tamarisk wood instead of our usual argol. The root of this tree imparts a slightly bitter taste to water touched by the growth, but the dried branches provide excellent fuel, as they burn steadily with a blue flame. They added a distinctive woodsy flavor to our nicely grilled lamb chops.

The next day Zhou persuaded his friends in the trading post to make him a present of some cabbage. He combined this with slivered pieces of lamb, added seasoning begged from his friends, and cooked everything with loving care in our big iron pot. We ate his creation with lavish but sincere praise for his culinary skill.

Zhou said that in a Mongol feast, where it is customary to boil or roast whole animals, the part of the sheep offered to guests depends on their status. The meat along the back is considered the most delectable and is therefore given to the person of greatest importance. Next in order is the meat near the upper spine, then the armpit, the thigh, and finally the calf. The breast, with charming appropriateness, is given to women.

In our contacts with the Mongols on the Black River there was no occasion when we might participate in the elaborate feasts that Zhou described. I didn't mind. Our Torgut neighbors near the camp, and those we visited thanks to Dorji, provided samples of ordinary items in the Mongol diet that were more to my taste. Martin was especially happy to encounter such staples as dried sour-milk cheese because, he said, that was doubtless a standard item that Genghis Khan's hard-riding troops could easily carry with them over long distances. I liked the taste of that cheese.

So we were both happy, though for different reasons.

16 / The Torgut Diaspora

The tide of the Torgut diaspora washed up even on the shores of the United States. This human flotsam comprised a group of Mongols called Kalmyks who were kin to the Torguts I met on the Black River. In the 1950s and 1960s almost a thousand of them settled in this country in little enclaves, chiefly in New Jersey and Pennsylvania, after migrating from Germany, where they had assembled from all over Europe at the end of the war. Some of them had left the Soviet Union at the time of the revolution. Others were wartime emigrés from the Kalmyk Autonomous Soviet Socialist Republic, located in the lower reaches of the Volga River, which Stalin dissolved in 1944 on the ground of collaboration with the Nazis. The Kalmyks were exiled en masse to Soviet Central Asia, but were permitted to return in 1957 and to reestablish themselves as the Kalmyk ASSR, where 83 percent of the Soviet Union's Kalmyks, estimated at 147,000 in 1979, are located.

These twentieth-century shifts of population were the latest in an odyssey that began in the seventeenth century in the heart of Central Asia.

We tried to find out from Dorji how much he knew of the amazing odyssey of the Torgut Mongols. It wasn't much. Although he could read and write, no mean accomplishment given the conditions that prevailed on the Black River, he had little access to historical records relating to his people. He had some bits of knowledge that had been passed down by word of mouth, but they were mostly in the garbled form of legends. To get the full story we had to rely chiefly on the materials that Martin had brought along.

The story begins with the infighting that followed the collapse in the fourteenth and fifteenth centuries of the vast empire brought into being by the conquests of Genghis Khan and his successors. At the time of the collapse, the Torguts, along with several other Mongol tribes, shared control of territory in northern Xinjiang that was known as Dzungaria, after the name of the Dzungar Mongols, the most powerful of the four tribes in the area.

It is a characteristic of nomad societies that they are seldom satisfied with their own land but constantly seek to expand into someone else's territory. This was especially the case now that the Mongols could no longer count on a share in the spoils squeezed out of the Chinese and other subject peoples.

As an aftermath of the jostling for land and power that took place among the Mongol tribes in northern Xinjiang, in 1618 a group of Torguts under a chief named Boro Orolok decided to seek greener pastures to the west. By an unrelated coincidence, that was just two years before a group of pilgrims started a westward trek that others completed across the American continent.

With twenty-five thousand of his followers, Boro Orolok moved north and then west along a line that was later followed in the building of the Trans-Siberian Railway. It was slow going. The land was already occupied by Kazakh and Kirghiz nomads, Turkish tribes whose attachment to the Muslim faith gave them an additional reason to resent the incursion of Buddhist infidels. When they could, the Torguts set up their yurts and stayed a while, combining their usual peaceful pursuits with their equally usual forays against assorted enemies. When fighting against these rivals proved too much for them, they pulled up stakes and pushed farther west.

By 1630 they had reached the Ural mountains. On they pushed, into the middle reaches of the Volga River, contesting that area with the Tatars, another nomadic people adhering to Islam, and with the Russians, who occupied towns and villages along the river. Boro Orolok was killed in 1643 while laying siege to Astrakhan, in the delta area of the Volga, but by that time his people were fairly well entrenched along both banks of the river. It had taken these Torguts twenty-five years to cover the three thousand miles from northern Xinjiang to the Volga, a distance greater than that between the eastern and western coasts of the United States.

Other segments of the Torguts followed the example of the first contingent in the exodus from their Xinjiang homeland to the new land along the Volga. Eventually, just about all the Torguts were transplanted to the

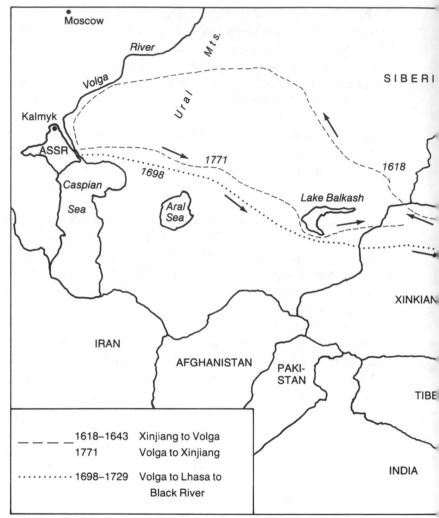

area north of the Caspian Sea, leaving the Dzungars as the dominant tribe among the Mongols who remained.

You would think that after all they had been through in getting to their new location the Torguts would have been content to settle down to a peaceful life of raising their herds of animals in steppe country ideally suited to this pursuit. No doubt most of the ordinary people did just that. You'd never know it, though, from the chronicles that concentrate attention on the internal rivalry for power and the external struggles with the Russians and a variety of nomad tribes.

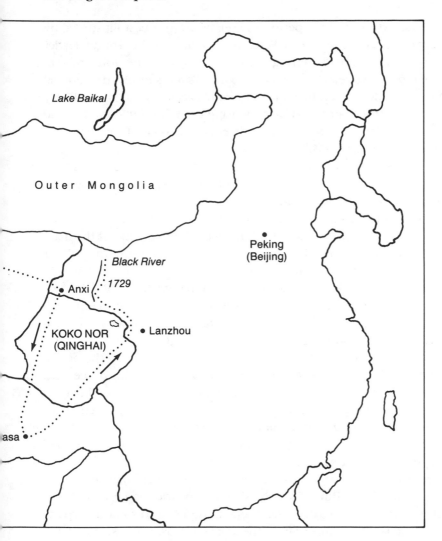

Most Torgut princes had more than one wife and produced a big brood of sons, who constantly brawled with each other for a bigger share in the spoils of leadership. Martin enjoyed trying to work out family trees for the bewildering multitude of names that peppered the historical records. He also liked to work out what came to resemble a child's aimless doodling as he mapped the frenetic forays and campaigns that preoccupied both the Torguts and their chroniclers.

In their relations with the Russians the Torguts appeared sometimes as vassals, sometimes as equals, depending on the shifting balance of power between the two. For a long period the relationship is best illustrated by an agreement reached between Peter the Great and the Torgut leader Ayuki Khan that was made during a visit of the tsar to the Volga region. According to that agreement, the leader of the Torguts received an annual stipend of two thousand rubles, two thousand sacks of flour, and military supplies for his troops in return for promising to be faithful to the tsar and to act, as one chronicler put it, "as policeman to some of the turbulent tribes north of the Caucasus."

The Torguts served in other areas as well. In 1707, at the time of the Swedish invasion of Russia, the mounted Mongol warriors harassed the marching columns of Charles XII.

Over time, the Russians gradually increased their ascendancy over the Torguts, leading to increasing friction between the two. One of the main bones of contention was who had the authority to bestow the title of khan on the supreme leader of the Torguts. The tsar contended that only he had this authority. The Torguts maintained that it was the Dalai Lama. One of the princes tried to establish this position by sending an envoy to Lhasa to seek its help in the matter. Then he had himself proclaimed khan in an elaborate investiture ceremony in which his Grand Lama read out for all to hear the Holy Missive of the Dalai Lama proclaiming the prince to be khan of all the Torguts. A rival prince who had made his peace with the Russians countered this move by having himself proclaimed khan by the tsar. Then he sought to reinforce his position by sending an envoy to ask for investiture by the Dalai Lama. The issue was finally decided, as were most such quarrels, on the field of battle. There the tsar's man showed that might made right.

The appeals of the Torguts to the Dalai Lama reflected their profound attachment to Tibetan Buddhism. Russian missionaries had no more success in winning converts than did their modern Swedish counterparts like Reverend Gonzell. Rivalry with the adjacent Muslim Turks was made all the sharper by intransigent religious attitudes on both sides.

The greatest desire of devout Torguts was to make a pilgrimage to the holy city of Lhasa. So it came about that in 1698 a prince named Arabjur, a nephew of Ayuki Khan, set out for Tibet on a Mongol-style pilgrimage—that is, with his mother, other members of his family, lamas, followers, yurts, and herds—a Torgut band measured, in the nomad style, as forty-seven "tents," perhaps two hundred or so people. This occurred during a lull in the almost incessant warfare that characterized most of the territory that had to be traversed.

The route followed by the pilgrims took them through their original

homeland in northern Xinjiang, occupied at the time by some temporarily unhostile Mongols under the domination of the Dzungars, and then
into the westernmost part of the province of Gansu. From there they
most likely followed the preferred route of pilgrims that started from a
town with the typically Chinese frontier name of Anxi, "Pacify the West."
That route went through a semidesert plain at an elevation of nine thousand feet west of the lake known to the Mongols as Koko Nor, or Blue

Lake, and to the Chinese as Qinghai, or Blue Sea. To gain added merit, some of the pilgrims crawled the whole distance to Lhasa, like human inchworms, prostrating themselves times without number on rough ground that lacerated their knees and elbows and hands.

The pilgrims spent five years in Lhasa before starting back on the return trip to the Volga. They took a different route back, going east of Koko Nor and then along the Gansu Corridor to the area of Suzhou on the upper reaches of the Black River. There the pilgrims discovered that further progress was blocked by the renewal of hostilities in Xinjiang.

Arabjur left his stranded followers and galloped off to Peking to submit himself to the Manchu emperor and to seek help for his people. He was welcomed as a prodigal son. His followers were allowed to stay where they were while further moves were contemplated by the various parties concerned.

Diplomatic negotiations, like pilgrimages, were leisurely affairs in those days. In 1709 Arabjur's uncle, Ayuki, sent a delegation of twenty of his followers to Peking via Siberia and Outer Mongolia with the avowed aim of looking into the possibility of getting Arabjur to return to the Volga via the same route. They made the round trip in three years. It took another three years, from 1712 to 1715, for a Manchu delegation that included four of Arabjur's men to return the visit, following the same trans-Siberian route to bypass the fighting in Xinjiang.

These missions did not succeed in their ostensible objective of seeing to the return of Arabjur, as Ayuki said it was better for him to remain where he was. In actual fact, the return of a minor prince and his followers was not the primary concern of the missions at all, but it provided a convenient screen for matters of greater importance. Both parties, the Manchus and the Torguts, were mainly interested in sounding each other out about the possibility of cooperation against the Russians. The Manchus had the additional objective of scouting the territory to the north of them where the Russians were pushing eastward through Siberia on a trek that was to take them all the way to the Pacific Ocean.

The emperor was much pleased with the success of the mission and heaped high honors on the official who led it. But Arabjur and his people remained stranded in the Suzhou area. There he died.

This region in western Gansu was uncomfortably close to the embattled province of Xinjiang, still dominated by the hostile Dzungar tribe. Arabjur's son and successor, like his father before him, journeyed to Peking in the hope of arousing the emperor's interest in the plight of his beleaguered people. He was successful. In 1729 the emperor made him a

Beile, a prince of the third rank, organized his people into a "banner," and granted them the land along the lower course of the Black River, from Maomu to the twin lakes in the north, a safer haven shielded on both sides by great stretches of black gobi. Here at last their long pilgrimage came to an end.

Dorji was a descendent of that Torgut band that had settled in the area two centuries before. The absent prince, journeying, like his ancestor Arabjur, on a pilgrimage to Tibet, was a descendent, many generations removed, of the original Beile whose people, thanks to the Manchu emperor, finally came to rest in this distant oasis after wanderings of thirty years and almost five thousand miles.

For Dorji and other Black River Torguts, the past was kept alive in their memory by the tales handed down by successive generations. And that doubtless accounts for the nostalgia that Ma Hetian found for the Manchus who had enabled them to live out their lives there.

Besides settling the grateful and loyal Torguts on the Black River, the Manchus took other actions to improve their position on their western frontier, that springboard from which nomad tribes throughout China's long history repeatedly pushed east to topple regimes in control of the Middle Kingdom. Concentrating attention on the powerful Dzungars, who had earlier penetrated into territory inside the Great Wall, getting within a hundred miles of Peking before being pushed back, they skillfully played off this tribe against other Mongols and against the Muslims, especially those located in the southern part of Xinjiang. "The result," said one account, "was a war of extermination."

After that war had gone on for some time, the Manchus marched into the province with a subject army of Chinese conscripts and an allied force of Outer Mongols and completed the job of annihilation. By 1755, nine-tenths of the Dzungars and their allies, some six hundred thousand people, had been wiped out. Northern Xinjiang became a depopulated wasteland.

While all this was going on in the original homeland of the Torguts, those who had relocated along the Volga River were becoming increasingly restive as the Russians exerted greater and greater pressure on their way of life. Their leaders were turning into vassals of the tsar instead of subjects of the Dalai Lama. Their religion was threatened by Russian missionaries seeking to convert the Torguts to Christianity and by hostile Muslims who barred their access to holy Lhasa. Their lands were being surrounded by a ring of fortresses and opened up to Russian colonization. And—ultimate indignity—they themselves were threatened with confinement to fixed dwellings instead of being able to range freely over the steppes.

Only people accustomed to roaming so freely, to conducting mass pilgrimages over long distances, would have dared to think of removing all these threats to their way of life simply by removing themselves to another place, a far-distant land, their old homeland in northern Xinjiang. This would involve, first of all, escaping from the clutches of the tsarist government, which would no more acquiesce in losing population than misers would in losing any of their hoard. Then the Torguts would have to travel thousands of miles through terrain in places so bad as to be unpopulated, in other places good enough to be populated but in the hands of hostile elements like the Muslims.

The plans for this massive breakaway from Russian control had to be made in the utmost secrecy. Only the Great Khan, Ubashi, four of the major princes, and the Grand Lama were fully cognizant of their plans, as they quietly began to make preparations. Russian suspicions that something odd was going on among the Torguts were lulled by their contributing a cavalry unit of thirty thousand men to a major campaign against Turkey in 1768–1769, in which they acquitted themselves so brilliantly that they were able to claim a much needed supply of arms as their share of the booty from the defeated enemy.

The Torguts sent emissaries to Lhasa to seek the Dalai Lama's help by using his oracular powers to determine an auspicious time for their escape. All would go well, they were assured, if the flight started in a Year of the Tiger or a Year of the Hare. According to the Buddhist calendar, 1770 was a Tiger Year and 1771 a Hare Year. Ubashi and his Grand Lama decided that the winter of 1770–1771 would be especially favorable, as it would straddle the two most auspicious years. More precisely, they settled on January 5, 1771, as Departure Day.

Before dawn on that fateful day the Torguts took by surprise a Russian squadron that had been sent to check up on them. They captured or killed the entire squadron along with a detachment sent to support it. Then, mounted couriers sped throughout the Torgut encampments to shout the warning that the Kirghiz and other foes had launched an all-out attack against their land. Everyone would have to take themselves and whatever possessions they could carry to a safer sanctuary behind the Emba River, some three hundred miles to the east.

There was not a word of truth in all this. There was no Kirghiz attack, no safe sanctuary, no intention to stop short of the real objective, their old homeland in far-off Xinjiang. The lies succeeded in galvanizing the people to uproot themselves. But even for a people accustomed to seasonal migrations and mass pilgrimages, this wholesale exodus, hastily launched in the middle of a bitterly cold winter, presented logistical problems that boggle the mind. Some sources estimate the number of people involved in the exodus at four hundred thousand. Their yurts, dismantled and loaded on carts or sleighs or camels, numbered in the tens of thousands. Their animals numbered around six million—nearly five million cattle and sheep, eight hundred thousand horses and camels, over a hundred thousand dogs.

For once I shared Martin's enthusiasm as he depicted this exodus as essentially a military exercise in mass mobilization of people traditionally divided along tribal-military lines. We marveled at the organizing ability displayed by these nomads.

Within hours of the initial call to prepare for flight, the most valued belongings were loaded and ready for transport, the animals had been rounded up, and everyone was stationed at an assigned assembly point. At intervals of thirty minutes, contingents of twenty thousand people, women and children, the old and infirm, escorted by mounted warriors, set out across the snow-covered steppe.

As the last contingents got under way, some ten thousand horsemen who had stayed to cover the retreat set fire to the houses and everything else that had been left behind. Ubashi set the example by putting the torch to the timbered buildings that made up the khan's official quarters. Come what may, there would be no turning back, no change of mind for any of the Torguts.

There was only one major hitch in this otherwise brilliantly executed exodus. It involved the seventy thousand Torguts on the west bank of the Volga River. The January date for their departure had been set in part because it was assumed that by that time the river would be frozen hard enough so that those on the west bank could simply cross over on the ice to join the main body on the east bank. They did not do so. Some accounts say that the river failed to freeze over, others that a storm broke up the ice. Whatever the reason, there these Torguts remained, where they are to this day, but now known as the Kalmyk, a name derived from a Turkish word meaning "the remnant."

The four hundred thousand Torguts who fled the east bank of the Volga started the migration as a vast army stretching fifty miles across and forty miles in length. They were organized in columns separated by military corridors. Along these, and on the flanks and front and rear, rode horsemen, to maintain order and guard against possible attacks.

On the first stretch of the journey the Torguts, thanks to the element of surprise, were able to proceed without interference from the Russians or their allies. The Torguts took advantage of this to make rapid marches of over forty miles a day. In one week they reached the Ural River, where they hoped to rest a while before pushing on.

In this region of scanty pastureland that required wide dispersal of the animals, the Torguts encountered their first setback. One of the clans, separated by a distance of eighty miles from the khan's headquarters, which was busy trying to subdue a Russian fortress that lay in their path, was attacked by a force of Kazakhs. The clan was completely annihilated. Nine thousand fighting men were lost.

Instead of a hoped-for rest, the Torguts were compelled to lift the siege of the fortress and make more forced marches that took a heavy toll of animals and humans. They died faster than the proverbial flies, some seven thousand of them, not counting the clan already lost.

Then a blizzard struck, forcing a halt, but also providing a respite from attack by the equally immobilized enemy. The weather proved even more deadly, however, as ten days of savagely gusting winds buried carts and animals and makeshift shelters under a thick, white shroud.

As it became apparent that many of the animals could not survive, the order went out to slaughter as many as possible and to salt whatever meat could not be immediately consumed. While the wind howled and the snow fell, the Torguts gorged themselves in a macabre feast. They ate, drank, and made merry, for they knew that on the morrow many would die.

And so they did. When the march resumed after the storm finally subsided, many of the best fighters fell in a desperate assault against Kazakhs holding a pass through the Ural Mountains that simply had to be forced, for by now the Russians were in hot pursuit, aided by other enemies of the Torguts—the Kazakhs, Kirghiz, Bashkirs, and others.

On the Asian side of the Urals the Torguts spent two months crawling through three hundred miles of country made boglike by unseasonable thaws. Toward the end of March they were beset by small bands of enemies that whittled away at the demoralized marchers by making hit-and-run attacks on stragglers. When they came to drier ground, in late April, the Kirghiz set fire to the grassland, forcing the Torguts to flee south in panic and disorder.

Then they came, in midsummer, to the still drier "hunger-steppe," and thousands more died—some, crazed, of thirst in the desert, others fighting with oasis settlers to get at the limited supply of water.

The Torguts rounded the southern side of Lake Balkash, and after a final climactic battle with the Kazakhs that further decimated them by the tens of thousands, on September 8, 1771, eight months after it started, the death march of three thousand miles came to an end as the survivors, 85,000 out of the original 400,000, staggered across the border into the Manchu-controlled territory of northern Xinjiang and announced to the startled officials there that they had come to throw themselves on the mercy of the emperor.

Some of the emperor's advisers were suspicious of this unannounced influx and counseled against accepting them so as to avoid conflict with Russia. But the emperor, having already depopulated Dzungaria, was anxious to fill up the empty space. The Torguts, he said, were merely returning to their former homeland; they wished only "to return to civilization." He also ordered that, since the refugees were completely destitute, having lost nearly all their animals and other possessions, they should be provided with yurts, cattle, grain, clothing, and other necessities.

Ubashi and his chief lieutenants were summoned to the imperial palace. He was confirmed in his title of khan, and they in that of prince. And the Torguts were given land, ten large districts where their ancestors had once lived in the steppes of northern Xinjiang.

There they remained, but suffering still further decimation in that continually embattled province, for at the time we were at the Black River they numbered only about 10,000, compared to the 400,000 that had started out from the Volga and the 85,000 who had made it back to Xinjiang in 1771.

In contrast, in the same period the Torguts who remained behind on the Volga—that is, the renamed Kalymks—increased from 70,000 to about 130,000 in the 1930s. Some of them did well there. One became a rear admiral in the eighteenth century, another a lieutenant general a century later. Two Kalmyk cavalry regiments entered Paris with the imperial army after the defeat of Napoleon in 1814.

In retrospect, Martin and I felt that the diaspora had not dealt as badly with the little band of Black River Torguts as we had at first assumed. Dorji could at least have the satisfaction of knowing that his "banner" had grown from two hundred to five hundred people. If time had left these Torguts behind, it had at least let them increase in relative peace.

17 / The River That Died of Thirst

✝✝✝✝✝✝✝✝

The death was seasonal, in the spring and summer. Life returned to the river with water in the fall and winter. That was not a natural cycle, but one of human origin, as we saw when we were there. I don't know if the pattern we saw then still holds today, whether the river is still able to revive as it did in the past.

We first encountered the Black River in the summer, when it was dry. Ma Hetian, a Chinese political agent who traveled through Mongolia, saw it in the winter, when it was full of water. He rhapsodized about the economic potential of the area, especially for agriculture, in a book I started to translate while I was at the river and published years later under the title *Chinese Agent in Mongolia.* Ma Hetian was a winter optimist, I, a summer pessimist.

Developments after the Communists came to power in 1949 have introduced new and unexpected factors into the situation. One is the explosive increase in population in the upriver Chinese towns that tap the sources of water leading to the Black River. (Suzhou has grown from less than 10,000 people to over 270,000, and Jiayuguan from thirty families to over 100,000 people.) Another is the construction of that obscure railway along the river.

Perhaps that railway has proved me wrong in my pessimism about the economic potential of the area. But what about the agricultural prospect, and the fate of the Mongols there?

✝✝✝✝✝✝✝✝

"Is that a sketch you're making?" asked Martin, looking over my shoulder. "Or are you just doodling?"

"It's a diagrammatic summary of our trip across the desert," I said. "The

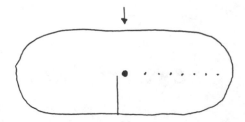

oval is the Gobi Desert. The vertical line is the Black River. The broken linc is our trip. The dot is where we are now. The arrow shows the direction of Genghis Khan's drive south from Outer Mongolia."

"You've got it down to the bare bones all right. And it makes clear why Genghis followed the Black River when he crossed the Gobi to invade China."

Yes, he didn't have much choice. In the twelve hundred miles from the two ends of the oval, only the Black River offered a natural invasion route across the desert. Thrusting up vertically into the heart of the Gobi, it made for easy transit through the bottom half of the north-south distance of seven hundred miles.

"That dot almost scares me," I said. "Here we are, smack in the middle of almost a million square miles of desert, at the end of a lifeline consisting of a river with no water in it."

"Oh, it's not that bad. Didn't you say the men told us that if you dig down two or three feet in the river bottom you're fairly sure to reach water somewhere or other?"

That was true. But the river led a precarious existence. It seemed to be living on borrowed time. There had been a lot more water in the river when Genghis Khan stormed through here than there was now. From our talks with the men at the trading posts, and from the various materials we had brought with us, it was clear that the river was desperately struggling to survive against the onslaughts both of people and of nature.

This was true throughout the whole course of what was actually a rather complex river system. The river originated in two streams that started in the Nan Shan or Southern Mountains, on the border between Gansu and Koko Nor, in the vicinity of two towns that were once major centers on the Silk Road through the Gansu Corridor. One stream started near Ganzhou, the other near Suzhou. After crossing the Corridor in the neighborhood of thesc towns, both streams forced their way through some lower mountain ranges south of Maomu and converged there to form the Black River, so named from the color of the gravel in the surrounding black gobi.

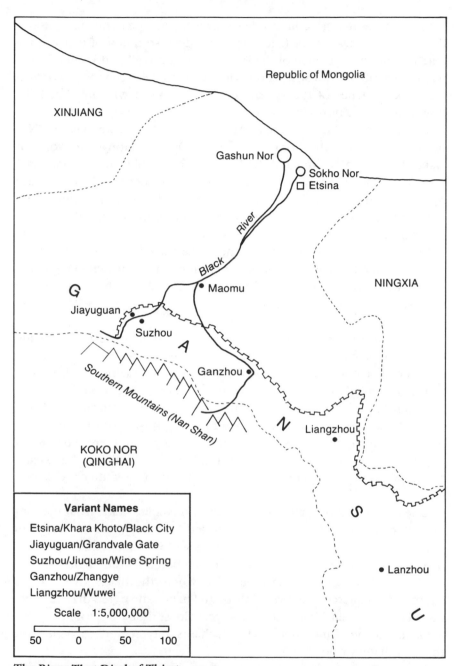

Republic of Mongolia

XINJIANG

Gashun Nor

○ Sokho Nor
□ Etsina

Black River

NINGXIA

Maomu

G

Jiayuguan

Suzhou

A

Ganzhou

Southern Mountains (Nan Shan)

N

Liangzhou

KOKO NOR
(QINGHAI)

S

Variant Names

Etsina/Khara Khoto/Black City
Jiayuguan/Grandvale Gate
Suzhou/Jiuquan/Wine Spring
Ganzhou/Zhangye
Liangzhou/Wuwei

Scale　1:5,000,000

50　　0　　50　　100

• Lanzhou

U

The River That Died of Thirst

In the oases that gave life to these three towns, peasants made use of the water to irrigate their fields. They used up so much of it that none reached the lower course of the Black River until fall and winter. There was no overall plan for sharing this vital resource between the peasants in the upper reaches of the system and the Mongols who inhabited the downstream area north of Maomu.

The intermittent flow of the river ended in two salt lakes, Gashun Nor on the west and Sokho Nor on the east. (*Nor* is the Mongolian word for "lake.") Between Maomu and the lakes the river split into several channels. These were narrowly hemmed in on both sides by black gobi and by sand dunes, which in places even appeared between channels and seemed intent on overwhelming this impudent intruder into the domain of the desert.

We were eager to explore the nearby area of the elongated oasis formed by the Black River. Disappointed in my hope of swimming in the river, I was also almost obsessed with a desire at least to have a dip in the nearest lake, Sokho Nor, which was only a dozen or so miles from where we were encamped.

But any further travel would have to wait for the recovery of our camels from being worked overtime by our unseasonal crossing of the desert. They needed at least two weeks of rest and good grazing. We had been further informed that before putting them out to graze it would be necessary to reduce their blood heat by dosing them with a special medicine. The men at Manager Guo's firm, assuming responsibility for the camels he had supplied, undertook this task for us. They also offered to add our camels to the others they were pasturing in an area with good grass and water. We would be spared the need of having to look after the camels ourselves.

One of the men brought out a bucket of medicine made from the root or stalk of rhubarb that had been pounded into a dry powder and then mixed with water. The result was an orange-colored liquid that smelled as noxious as it looked. Martin said he remembered reading that a special kind of rhubarb grew in the mountains where the Black River had its source. When Marco Polo passed through Suzhou, he noted that throughout all the mountains in that area "the very finest rhubarb is found in very great abundance, and there the merchants buy it and carry it then through all the world."

The camels were made to kneel and were trussed up securely so that their legs were completely immobilized. One of the men seized the jaws of the first camel and forced its head back, mouth wide open and point-

Force feeding medicine to our camels

ing upward, all the while bracing himself against the animal's struggles. The man with the bucket quickly poured a quantity of the medicine into the gaping mouth.

There it stuck. The camel refused to swallow the stuff. The man who had administered the dose backed off a step and, with a well-placed kick at the throat of the beast, caused it to make an involuntary gulp. He then thoughtfully helped the camel wash the taste out of its mouth by pouring a big ladleful of water into it.

I felt a certain sympathy for the camels forced to swallow medicine they found revolting even if it was made of the "very finest" ingredients. Rhubarb, however served, even in pies that others found delicious, always seemed to me not fit for consumption by humans and, I would now add, by animals as well.

While we waited for our camels to recover, Martin and I occupied ourselves in various ways. We scrounged around in an attempt, only partially successful, to vary our monotonous diet. We hobnobbed with the men at the various trading posts and with visitors to our tent. We took walks away from our camp, sometimes together, more often separately, for we —I, in particular—felt a need to escape from being constantly in each other's company.

On one of our walks together something bright red in color caught our attention in an area of dense vegetation. It couldn't be! But it was. A brand new Dodge truck was parked in a grove of poplar trees. Several men lounged outside a nearby tent. We greeted them and exchanged introductions. One of the men was named Liu. From Peking. Very friendly, and quite willing to satisfy our curiosity.

The truck was loaded with two tons of opium. It belonged to a transport company that had seven trucks and forty employees. The sole business of the company was transporting opium from Gansu to the railroad town of Kalgan, about halfway between Guihua and Peking, going by way of the Black River and the Temple of the Larks. The men were waiting for a delivery of several camel-loads of gasoline before starting out across the desert.

The opium quadrupled in value between Gansu and Kalgan. A large part of the difference was taken up by taxes that were levied at both ends and in between. Recently there had been trouble with the princes at the Temple of the Larks over the amount of their cut, but the problem had been straightened out now.

I mentioned the anti-opium campaign under way in Peking. It featured scary billboards showing an emaciated man lying on a pallet, eyes blotto, mouth sucking away at an opium pipe, while an equally emaciated little girl tugged at his ragged clothing, begging him to leave his pipe. The poster was part of a much publicized opium suppression campaign that was earning the government high marks among some foreigners, especially missionaries.

The men laughed. They were happy to pose for a photograph.

In camp, Martin spent a good deal of his time reading. I concentrated my attention on the Chinese book by Ma Hetian that I had brought along because of its title, which translated literally as *A Journal of Investigations in Inner and Outer Mongolia*. The book had been written by a Central Government official who made a vertical crossing of the desert in 1926–1927 on his way to the Soviet Union.

"Was he a Communist?" Martin asked.

"No, definitely not. He was a right-winger. A lot of non-Communists tried to get help from the Soviet Union in that period. Even Chiang Kai-shek, you remember. Ma's book is very critical of the regime in Outer Mongolia as being under Soviet influence."

Martin was quite taken with my summary of the parts dealing with Outer Mongolia. He said the book contained a wealth of firsthand information that shed light on the beginnings of an unparalleled social revolution in that land of mystery.

We were both interested in the author's account of his trip through the

Black River area, as he had probably passed close to our present campsite on his way to Outer Mongolia. As a travel writer he was a bore, however, and he was slipshod in his writing and conventional in his attitudes. He rhapsodized about the economic potential of the area. The Mongols were "primitive herdsmen." He looked forward to a future when "colonists open up this new land." He was almost a caricature of all that was wrong with the mentality of Chinese officials concerned with the frontier people of the country, with the important problem of the relations between the dominant Chinese and the ethnic minorities such as the Mongols, Tibetans, and dozens of other people in China's border areas.

It was useful to have some insight into this mentality. This, and the new information contained in the book, seemed to warrant making it available in English. I decided to take this on as an exercise to improve my ability to handle written Chinese.

The camp-style ivory tower I set up to carry on this work was rather lacking in the usual academic amenities. My desk was a board, the one we used to roll our pasta on, balanced on top of one of our kegs. One of our boxes did service as a chair. I worked away happily, completely absorbed, for hours on end. When there were no interruptions, that is.

One of the nicest things about a real ivory tower is that you can pull up the drawbridge and keep out intruders. Here we were wide open to visitors who probably wouldn't have been able to read a "Do not disturb" sign if we had put one up.

One of our first visitors was a man from a nearby Peking trading post who had a splinter in one finger that had become infected. Unbidden, he gave me his detailed medical history, accompanied by a good deal of miscellaneous chitchat to make this a combined social visit and medical consultation.

I sterilized a sewing needle by passing the end through a flame and prepared to lance the infection. My patient asked for an anesthetic.

"Imagine!" I said to Martin. "This guy wants an anesthetic before I operate on him for the splinter. Who says the Chinese are stoical in enduring pain?"

"Stick him harder," said Martin.

I lanced the infection, dug out the splinter, and applied some iodine and a Band-Aid.

Another man came from the same firm. Toothache. I gave him some aspirins. Zhou complained of his eyes hurting again. Wash with boric acid. Zhou brought in a Mongol who wanted me to visit his wife in a nearby yurt.

"Tell him you don't make house calls," Martin said.

I disclaimed medical competence.

Smiles. Appreciation for my adhering to the ritual expression of modesty.

"No, really. . . ."

More kudos for making my self-depreciation sound so convincing.

"Give up," said Martin.

At first I thought the woman was pregnant. A second glance showed the whole midsection of her body to be grossly enlarged. This had come upon her suddenly after a difficult childbirth about seventeen years before. Elephantiasis? I prescribed a two-week medication of an aspirin a day. By that time I figured we would be beyond the reach of a malpractice charge.

A few days later, in the middle of the night, Martin shook me awake. There was a note almost of panic in his voice.

"I've just been bitten by a scorpion."

This could be serious. Most scorpions are comparatively harmless, but some inject a poison that can be fatal. I asked, rather stupidly, if it hurt.

"Rather," said Martin.

That meant the pain was excruciating.

I woke Zhou and asked him to go over to the trading posts and find out if anyone knew what to do about this. Instead he woke everyone within earshot by simply standing a few paces from the tent and bawling out a question. He reported that an answering yell said the sting was painful but not serious.

I put some iodine on the bite. Then, more to provide a distraction than in hope of its doing any good, I mixed some water and earth into a cool mud pack that I put over the swollen area and held in place with a handkerchief. Martin said it helped ease the pain.

We had other nocturnal visitors. These were vicious midges that swarmed during a period of more than a week when the temperature reached unprecedented heights. It so happened that on one of the hottest of those days Martin was reading Jules Verne's *Five Weeks in a Balloon*. We dissolved into howls of laughter when he read a passage describing the plight of the three "aeronauts" marooned in the Sahara Desert and panting in exhaustion when the temperature soared to 113°. For eleven days we averaged 116°, with a top of 142°, even higher than the 140° claimed by Verne's adventurers.

I stripped down to my shorts. Perspiration streamed down my chest and back, flowed from my forehead into my eyes, and gathered as rapidly as I wiped it off. It dripped down from my chin and the tip of my nose onto the writing board and notepaper until there were so many splotches that I had to give up.

The men at the trading posts advised us to follow their example of reducing body heat by taking a concoction of licorice root boiled in water and sweetened with rock sugar. I don't know whether the medication did us any good, but the rock sugar made wonderful candy.

The heat seemed to affect me more than it did the preternaturally phlegmatic Martin. Perhaps it was just that in this, as in everything else, he kept his feelings in check. A cold fish, to my mind. He paid little heed to what was going on around him. Whenever the mood seized him, he would chatter away at length about Genghis or Napoleon or some other great military leader, impervious to my hints that his heroes were not mine, that his interruptions were interfering with my work.

Camp routine, which should have been simpler now that we were not on the march, turned out instead to be a constant aggravation. I had not realized how much of the routine had been taken care of by Xiao. It was a constant irritant for me to have to prod Zhou into handling his share of our daily tasks, though these were considerably reduced now that the camels were being cared for by others. And I was further annoyed by being constantly interrupted to interpret for Martin despite the fact that by now he had learned enough common phrases in Chinese so that he could handle most routine matters on his own if he had just thought to make the effort to do so.

Martin took no notice as my temper mounted to the point where I exploded. At first he was startled and uncomprehending. Then he countered by citing my unsociableness and hair-trigger temper. We reached the point of discussing the possibility of splitting up and returning separately. Zhou surprised me by vehemently refusing to accompany Martin. Finally we all cooled down and decided to continue together. Martin volunteered to take on some of the routine tasks, such as going to a nearby Mongol yurt for our morning ration of milk. And I was left more in peace to work away at my improvised desk.

Things improved even more later when we were finally able to embark on our exploration of the lake area. We had arrived at the trading posts on July 18. It was now August 2. The camels had had more than two weeks of rest.

Dorji, our Mongol guide, had his own camel. We decided to take only two of ours, the best ones, since there would always be one of us serving as camel puller, leaving only two as possible riders. We also were traveling light, without our tent and the things we would not need until later.

We failed to recognize our camels when they were brought from the grazing area to our camp. One had shed completely and was beginning to acquire a nice even coat of fuzzy tan hair. The other had also shed all its hair but had not yet started on a new coat, so that it looked quite naked. Both had bellies that were beginning to show a gratifyingly taut bulge.

For seven miles our route took us through dense foliage to a slight elevation of black gobi. From there we dropped onto a lower level that apparently at times was at least partially covered by water. It was profusely covered by reeds about two feet high. All around were large bushes, including many tamarisks, most of them dried up, their stumps and bare branches lying in tangled clumps like agonized skeletons in a war-torn landscape. In places there were little green bushes partially covered by sand.

We stopped to fill our casks at one of the little pools of still water that appeared here and there in the otherwise dry bed of the river. The pool was only a few inches deep, so Dorji scooped out the sand at the bottom and, as the water slowly seeped into the depression, took out bowlfuls of the muddy water. These he passed on to Zhou, who in turn poured them into our casks until they were filled.

We continued in a northwesterly direction, guiding ourselves by the major landmark in the area, a huge stone cairn known as Bor Obo. After crossing an area of mud flats, some baked dry and fissured, others still wet and soft, we made camp on a bit of firm ground about a third of a mile from the southwest margin of Sokho Nor, faintly glistening in the dark. The smell from the lake was delightful. Its salty, fishy tang brought back memories of oceans that here one almost forgets could exist, for even in the river oasis the threat of the desert was palpable.

We were disconcerted to find that the water we had scooped from the river bottom was terribly bitter, our worst yet, so bad that it recalled to us Marco Polo's emphatic warning of the "bitter and salt *and evil* water" that one finds in crossing the desert. Vaguely remembering from my high school chemistry that acids neutralize salts, I added some pulverized sour-milk cheese to the tea. It did seem to make the water somewhat more drinkable.

I went to sleep dreaming of the Connecticut shore, as the fragrance from the lake was wafted to us by a breeze that kept the midges at bay and helped the thermometer descend into the lower seventies.

We woke to the sparkling reflection of the rays of the sun rising behind the lake. Several flocks of honking ducks circled about before landing on the water. After breakfast, orienting myself by Bor Obo, about five miles northwest of our camp, I walked toward the lake. Its muddy margin bore the prints of animals that had come here to drink—goats and sheep and camels. The prints of the latter in places were six inches deep.

Salt overlay a considerable part of the lake margin. In places it combined with mud to form a thin covering resembling manila paper, sometimes folded back on itself and looking then even more like paper or like once sodden but now dry cardboard.

I attempted to reach the water by seeking out patches of green marking slightly elevated fingers of land that extended for some distance into the lake. But invariably these ended in muddy barriers that kept me from getting to the water itself. I had to return to camp without my long-sought swim.

To make sure of getting in a good long march, we started out shortly after noon toward the western lake, Gashun Nor. On the way we passed two trading posts staffed by ten men living in yurts and very ragged but cool and comfortable tents. One of the posts was a branch of Manager Guo's firm. Zhou had an animated conversation with the men from his firm, and all of us drank copious amounts of tea made from good, fresh water. The visit was so pleasant that we extended it for some time.

We made another extended stop at a yurt belonging to some friends of Dorji's. They were an older couple and a young girl. We wondered if she was the reason for Dorji's suggestion that we make this social call, or whether he merely wanted to show off his foreign acquaintances. In any case, our hosts all seemed quite happy to welcome us.

The man showed us the two-stringed instrument he had been playing and in response to our questions told us that the body was made of sheepskin, the strings and bow from a horse's tail. The older woman hastened to serve us tea that was made perfect by the unexpected addition of "milk-skin" cheese. The girl, at Dorji's urging, continued what she was doing, which was ironing a colorful red robe with a curious small, flat iron. It was only about half an inch thick, with a long, straight handle. She heated the iron in the fire and pressed it over the cloth against a small board held on one knee. All the while she joined animatedly in the conversation, even looking directly at us when making remarks that, when finally run through the process of double translation, were clearly aimed at Martin and me.

All this was quite different from socializing in a Chinese context. Foreigners seldom got to visit a Chinese home, for they were generally entertained at restaurants in as elaborate a fashion as the host could afford. If they should find themselves in the presence of a gathering that included a young Chinese girl, traditional etiquette required that she sit with downcast eyes and not be so bold as to engage in conversation. Chinese visitors to Mongolia were often shocked at what many interpreted as the loose behavior of the women there.

When we resumed our march we found that this part of the country between the two lakes was unusually rich and fertile in appearance. Tall reeds grew profusely. There were occasional groves of trees, more growing in isolation. Herds of peacefully grazing livestock in big patches of lush meadowland added to a sense of unreality that such bucolic scenes could really exist in the middle of the Gobi Desert.

During our march through here, Zhou and Dorji suddenly took to shouting so fiercely at each other that we expected them to come to blows. Instead they cooled down and soon were again amiably talking to each other as if nothing had happened. Since their dispute, if that's what it was, was carried on in Mongolian, we had no idea what it was all about.

Our aim of making a long march was frustrated by our two extended stops. So, after a day's march of only about a dozen miles, as the coppery sun slid slowly behind the trees, turning the mountains to the north of us first to purple, then to blue, and finally to a dark mass that disappeared from view, we made our tentless camp on a little knoll between two large bushes.

After making our usual camel-dung fire to heat water for tea, we enlivened its silent flames with miniature pyrotechnics by adding some resinous wood from a fallen tree. As we sat around our cheerfully crackling campfire, Zhou and Dorji fell into a bit of friendly rivalry by telling stories for our edification.

Dorji told his stories in Mongolian, for although he spoke Chinese fairly well he did so with a strong accent that made him hard to follow.

That made for rather labored storytelling, especially when Martin interposed questions or comments that had to work their way through our three languages in the opposite direction. But we were all in high spirits and happy to share our feelings of camaraderie.

One of Dorji's contributions was a tale of Genghis Khan's death.

One night Genghis dreamt of deep red blood on pure white snow. It was on the eve of a battle with the last Tangut prince who still dared to defy his power. Genghis asked his wise men what the dream meant. They said the dream was a portent of success on the morrow. The deep red color signified a person of royal blood, the doomed prince, who would bleed from so many wounds that the ground beneath him would turn red. The pure white color signified the snowy cheeks of the prince's daughter. She was known throughout the land of the Tanguts as a maiden of unsurpassed beauty. Many had sought to win her. She had rejected them all. But she could not say no to Genghis.

Of course the battle went as the oracles predicted.

Genghis asked that the maid be brought to his bedchamber. As he was about to have his way with her, she whipped out a tiny stiletto concealed in a hair-ornament and castrated him. Then she escaped and drowned herself in the Yellow River, which ever since has been known to the Mongols as Khatun Gol, the River of the Princess.

Genghis fell into a deathlike sleep. But he did not die. He sleeps only to await the time when Heaven will summon him to lead his people in doing great deeds again.

Another of Dorji's tales was a sort of ghost story.

About two hundred years ago there lived in the region of Gashun Nor two female spirits known as Shulma. They were harpies with enormous breasts that hung down as far as their knees and were thrown over their shoulders when the Shulma took flight. These phantoms terrorized the people by devouring human flesh. To get rid of them the people called on the help of priests from a temple in the nearby mountains of Outer Mongolia. The power of these priests was truly great, for when they chanted their incantations, the Shulma were overcome and fell down dead.

The people buried one of the demons under a huge obo near Gashun Nor. They also heaped stones on the other near Sokho Nor—but apparently not enough, for she rose up from the ground to continue her reign of terror even more vengefully than before. Frantic, the people again called on the help of the priests. This time a veritable mountain of stones was placed over the demon. That great cairn is the landmark known as Bor Obo.

We had that landmark behind us after resuming our march toward Gashun Nor. From the slightly higher ground containing this area of verdant growth we descended into a big depression crossed by several dry river branches leading to the lake. Trees and grass became sparser. Patches of sand and gobi appeared again. To the north loomed the mountains in Outer Mongolia, a barrier to further northward extension of the Black River system.

We approached the lake in the gathering dusk. The ground under foot became softer and more moist, so that walking became possible only by slow and tiring effort. Almost imperceptibly, we sank deeper and deeper into the mud. We failed to realize the gravity of our situation until we noticed the laboring of the camels. They began to sink so deeply into the mud that they were able to extricate themselves only by heaving forward in labored lunges. Their nostrils flared, their mouths gasped for air.

Resting the camels every minute or two, we turned back in search of firmer ground. Dorji, Martin, and I fanned out in front of Zhou and the camels. We called back and forth in the dark, informing each other of the condition of the ground in our individual areas.

Reduced now to steering ourselves by the stars, we laboriously worked our way away from the margin of the lake. Now and then we got onto patches of firm ground. These finally led to what seemed like true terra firma, where reeds and grass grew profusely enough to provide pasture for our camels. The animals were utterly exhausted and continued to pant for breath. We were done in, too.

I had to acknowledge myself frustrated in my attempt to swim in either of the two lakes. This was a trivial pursuit that had been thwarted by the conditions imposed on the river and its terminal lakes by the omnipresent desert. A weightier matter was whether the river itself, and the people dependent on it, would survive the menace of the desert, which not only pressed in more and more closely on both sides but even threatened to overwhelm it completely by intruding among the channels as stretches of gobi and windblown sand dunes. Dorji complained that the upriver use of water by the peasants was narrowing the belt of fertile land and making it increasingly difficult for his people to count on an adequate supply of good pasturage.

The river seemed to have died of thirst when we crossed and recrossed its dry channels. Might there come a time when it would not be able to revive from the seasonal interruptions of its precarious existence?

That question preyed on my mind as we trekked in defeat on the road back to our camp. It also brought to mind how sadly a Chinese poet erred who sought to compare the transientness of things human with the permanence of the natural world. Writing at a time of dynastic collapse, the poet said:

> The state is shattered;
> Mountains and rivers remain.

Alas, it was all too apparent that even rivers can become transient.

18 / Marco Polo's Lost City of Etsina

‡‡‡‡‡‡‡‡

After Marco Polo's mention of Etsina, a city built right in the heart of the Gobi Desert, it was lost to history for over six hundred years. In 1909 the Russian explorer P. K. Kozlov discovered its sand-buried ruins. Martin and I were the last to see it before the whole of the Black River area was sealed off from the outside world.

Since then Chinese archaeologists working in other areas have made a host of spectacular discoveries rivaling in importance those since the middle of the last century that have opened up new worlds in the Mediterranean basin and the Middle East. Many of the discoveries in China came about accidentally in the course of digging into its history-rich soil to lay foundations for new buildings and construct new roads, including thousands of miles of new railroads.

I hope archaeologists accompanied the crews that laid down that obscure railway line along the Black River. If so, I wonder if they found anything that would throw light on the historical gap between Marco Polo's time and ours, and on earlier periods dating back to the second century B.C., when another city was located on or near the site of the ruined city of Etsina that we visited.

‡‡‡‡‡‡‡‡

One reason I was so concerned about the fate of the river and of the people who depended on its life-giving water was knowing what had happened to the once-flourishing city of Etsina that was now only a heap of sand-buried ruins. It was a major center when Marco Polo heard of it while passing through the city of Campchu, his rendering of present-day

Ganzhou, on his journey into China along the Silk Road. Genghis Khan had captured the city in 1227 from the Tanguts, a Tibetan people who two centuries earlier had carved out a kingdom that included the area within the great northern loop of the Yellow River and all the land west of it as far as present-day Xinjiang. His grandson Kublai Khan had made the Tangut kingdom into a province of the Mongol empire. For the duration of Mongol control over China, Etsina remained an important way station between Karakorum, the original center of Mongol power in northern Mongolia, and the Silk Road route into China from the west.

With an amazing accuracy of recollection, at least as far as these specific places and distances are concerned, Marco Polo recorded the following:

> When you leave the city of Campchu you ride for twelve days, and then reach a city called Etsina, which is towards the north on the verge of the Sandy Desert. It belongs to the Province of Tangut. The inhabitants are Idolaters. They possess camels and cattle in abundance. The country produces a number of good falcons, both Sakers and Lanners. The people live by cultivation and their cattle, for they have no trade. At this city you must needs lay in victuals for forty days, because when you quit Etsina, you enter a desert which extends forty days' journey to the north, and on which you meet no habitation nor inn.

Before leaving Peking, Martin and I had read all we could that had been written about Etsina by the Russian discoverer of the city, Colonel P. K. Kozlov, and by other explorers, and we had resolved to visit the site if we could. In discussing the matter with Dorji we were delighted to find that he knew the location and was willing to guide us to it. This would involve only a twenty-four-mile round-trip detour from the line of march we would be taking after resuming our travels.

We did that the very next day after returning from our excursion to the lake area. Dorji led the way on his riding camel, Martin and I rode our two best camels, and Zhou took the first stint as camel puller for our little caravan, which now included all four of our camels. We were traveling much lighter now, making it more likely that our two weakest camels, though only slightly recovered from the desert crossing, would be able to survive the rest of the trip.

Some eight miles into our march alongside the dry bed of the river, we encountered water beginning to push its way along the channel. The advance guard of the stream was little more than a trickle, which at times stalled completely as it seeped into the ground and at times surged ahead in short rushes. When we stopped for the night, without bothering to put up our tent, the river provided nice, fresh water for our tea and added its purling sounds to the rustle of leaves as we drifted off to sleep in our alfresco camp.

In the morning I thought that the river might have risen high enough for me to attempt a swim. Vain hope. The water was nowhere higher than halfway to my knees. After scraping the bottom a few times and stepping into some muddy areas from which I had difficulty extricating myself, I finally gave up and contented myself with a prolonged sitz bath.

When we continued our march, Martin and I arranged with Dorji to mount one of our camels while we took turns riding his so we could experience the difference between his riding camel, a young and spirited male, and our plodding beasts of burden. Unlike our camels, which had a comfortable platform to ride on and were easily controlled by a cord attached to the peg through the nose, Dorji's was provided only with a blanket between the humps in lieu of a real saddle, though it did have stirrups, and was directed only by a headstall, a bitless bridle.

After trying out Dorji's camel for a while, Martin remarked that it was harder to ride because one could not grip with the knees as one can on a horse. Nor did the blanket provide much padding against the sharp ridge of the spine. It was also difficult to control the beast to slow it down from an uncomfortable trot to a comfortable walking pace, as it did not respond readily to an ineffectual bridle that lacked a bit in the mouth or a peg through the nose. Dorji confessed that even he had difficulty because of this, though I suspect he was just saying that to make us feel good.

When my turn came, the camel seemed to sense that it could get away with being even less responsive. It proceeded at its own pace, stopping occasionally to nibble at some choice vegetation, dawdling when the mood seized it, and finally breaking into a brisk trot to catch up with the others. It completely disdained my agonized attempts to reign it in as my crotch bounced up and down on its razor-sharp back.

In one's last moment, according to common belief, one's whole life flashes before one's eyes. Perhaps what I experienced on the camel was my next-to-the-last moment. What flashed before my eyes was a technicolor cartoon of my wildly bouncing body being vertically sliced in two as the camel galloped off into the sunset. Just before the separation became total and the two halves slid down feet-first on either side of the camel, it slowed to a walk on catching up with the others. Then, as when film run in reverse shows swimmers springing backward feet-first from the water to the diving board, my two halves snapped back together again.

Whew! That was close.

After another pleasant overnight stop in a cool grove near the now faster-running stream, the next morning we arranged for Zhou to remain in camp with our two weakest camels and most of our things while Martin, Dorji, and I left right after breakfast on the trip to the ruined city. We traveled light, with just one cask of water, a few blankets, and only enough food for a couple of days.

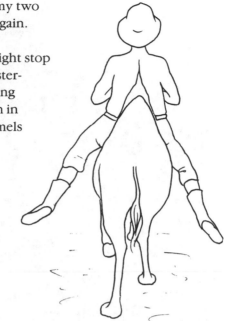

Without Zhou to act as interpreter, talking with Dorji required consid-erable effort. I had to listen hard, and to ask him often to repeat, which he did with unfailing patience and good humor. He was an amiable sort, out-going, and, we felt, rather pleased to be of help to a couple of ignorant but inquisitive foreigners.

Instead of mounting one of our camels I asked Dorji if he would mind my having another go at riding his. He was not only agreeable but even coached me on controlling the beast. This time it maintained a nice steady walk that made for a thoroughly enjoyable ride.

The camel's docility was probably due less to any increased mastery on my part than to the lack of incentive for it to stray from the rest of our lit-tle caravan. For as soon as we left camp and headed east away from the river, we got back into the black gobi that we had traversed in the last days of our desert crossing. In contrast to the abundant growth along the river, the gobi wasteland impressed us as even more desolate and sinister, even more hopelessly arid, than we had remembered it.

I transferred to our own camel while Dorji mounted his at a point about three miles out from the river, where we encountered the first indi-cation that we were approaching the city. This was the much-weathered remains, about twenty-five feet high, of an earth stupa, a kind of Buddhist shrine, generally whitewashed and sometimes ornamented with gilt, that one sees in every temple and at isolated holy spots.

Dorji on his riding camel

Stupas have a practical purpose, serving as repositories of the remains
and relics of holy men. They also have the function of representing the
universe and the tenets of Buddhism by a complicated symbology that
varies somewhat over the huge expanse of that religion extending from
India to Japan. Distinctive features include a bulbous middle, symbolizing
water, above a rectangular base that represents the earth—naturally, as
conceived by Flat-Earthers. Higher conical and other shapes symbolize,
in ascending order, fire, air, moon, sun, and mind or spirit.

A mile farther along we passed a stone marker that Dorji said was an old guidepost. Then we came upon two more severely weathered stupas south of the remains of a square courtyard about twenty-three paces on each side. Inside the enclosure and just beyond the east wall were several partially hollowed out mounds about ten feet high that we were not able to identify. Less than a mile from there we passed another pair of stupas close together.

About seven miles from our starting point we saw in the distance, beyond some intervening sand dunes, the tip of a stupa that Dorji said was on one of the walls of the city. Another two miles brought us to the beginning of a barrier of huge sand hills, many over fifty feet in height, almost completely devoid of growth. We all dismounted in crossing this sandy area, but even so, the camels, and of course we too, had difficulty with the steep slopes because of the insecure footing.

Our progress under the blazing sun was almost Sisyphean, as we slid one step back for every two steps of lunging advance. Sand particles propelled by the strong wind stung our bodies like so many pinpricks. I almost regretted my stubbornness in still going without a shirt so as to soak up more sun. No sooner had we topped one dune and slithered down the other side than we were confronted by still another mountain of sand. It took almost two hours of panting, sweating, mouth-parching toil to cross the two miles of dunes.

From the top of the last ridge of sand we had a panoramic view of the fabled city of many names. Marco Polo knew it as Etsina, a name which is also reflected in the name Etsin Gol, or Etsin River, which the Mongols give to what the Chinese call Hei He, or Black River. The city is Khara Khoto in Mongolian, Hei Cheng in Chinese, or Black City in both languages. Black River, Black City, black gobi—the color was pervasive to the view as well as to the mind.

There on the black plain below us the city's massive walls, incongruous in their futile immensity, vainly sought to shelter the long-dead city from the continuing onslaught of the surrounding gravel desert and wind-blown sand. It taxed the imagination to recall that in that scene of utter desolation and ruin there had once been people who, in Marco Polo's words, lived by cultivation and raised camels and cattle in abundance. And on this point the Venetian was reporting accurately, for in the region around the city, including that on the east away from the river, evidence has been found of extensive agricultural settlement based on a network of irrigation channels.

After sliding down to the plain and stopping for a moment to shake out our sand-filled boots and pockets, we approached the city with a feeling almost of unease that we might be challenged by phantoms from the past. Dorji stayed outside with the camels while Martin and I entered the city through the west barbican. This was a massive protective barrier, as high and thick as the city walls themselves, that so constricted the well-like space before the eighteen-foot gateway as to make it easy for defenders atop the walls to pelt intruders with missiles or burning oil.

Our first impression on glancing into the interior was of scattered heaps of ruins almost without shape, gravel-covered flat areas swept clear of sand, and huge drifts blown over the walls and piled up against them. This cursory glance was all we had time for now, for it was well past the hour for our midday meal, and we were famished and dehydrated.

Interior of the Black City

The mosque outside the Black City

We sought a sheltered place for our camp. There was none in the city because the incessant wind sprayed sand into every nook and corner. Dorji suggested making camp outside the southwest corner of the city in the remains of an intriguing little building with a domelike roof, a gothic arch over the entryway, and a vaulted interior. It was a mosque, Kozlov had thought, perhaps the oldest Mohammedan building in the westernmost portion of China proper. Part of the roof had caved in and there were openings on all four sides of the single twenty-foot-square room, but what remained provided a modicum of protection against the continually raging wind.

While Dorji gathered some stones to build a little fireplace in the center of the room, Martin and I scrounged around for what little dried wood was available in the vicinity. As soon as the fire was going, Dorji sprinkled a little libation into it and murmured some vigorous prayers to appease the ghosts of the city and whatever spirits we might be disturbing in the mosque. Then we boiled water for a simple lunch, consisting only of parched millet and bits of dried cheese in bowl after bowl of hot tea. We downed our lunch as fast as we could so as to get on with our task of exploring the city, somewhat ruefully reminding ourselves that we were nothing more than amateur sightseers, in contrast to the genuine explorers who had preceded us.

Etsina, we knew, had been rather thoroughly investigated and excavated, mainly by Kozlov in 1909, but also by three subsequent explorers,
the last being Sven Hedin just a few years before. Kozlov found and took
back to St. Petersburg an extensive hoard of religious artifacts, stucco and
terracotta figurines, fine glazed pottery, ornaments of various kinds, Buddhist manuscripts and block prints in several languages (Chinese, Turkish, Uighur, Tibetan, and Tangut), works of literature, law, and philoso-
phy, and even Persian manuscripts that included stories of Sinbad.
Obviously, this was no rough frontier town, but a cultural center of some
importance.

Marco Polo may have slipped in saying that the people here had no
trade. Some scholars think Etsina was a major center on the trade route
through the desert, which camel caravans such as those we had encountered en route to the river have plied for thousands of years. It is also sug-
gestive that the excavations in Etsina turned up money from the period of
Mongol domination that included a piece of paper money dated 1260, the
earliest known use of such currency.

But in Marco Polo's time, and for many centuries earlier, this area of
the Black River had also been a major center of military power. Finds by
the Hedin expeditions included thousands of wooden slips inscribed
with Chinese characters that comprised records of an important military
outpost established at or near the site of Etsina in the second century B.C.
to protect China from the incursions of the Huns. Signal towers, the
remains of which we saw later, were built along the whole length of the
Black River to warn of attack from these fearsome nomads. Under the
Mongols and their predecessors, the Tanguts, Etsina was the centerpiece
of this military complex. To the Mongols it was also known as Barshen
Khoto, or Fortress City.

After our quick lunch Martin and I set out together. I took with me a
composite sketch map of the city that I had made months before in the
course of my note-taking about Etsina, knowing that it would be indispensable in orienting myself among the ruins. It made me feel like a tourist setting out, map in hand, to locate places of interest in a strange city.

We first walked completely around the outside of the city. It was
almost a square, about a quarter of a mile on each side, with walls of
stamped clay thirty feet high surmounted by crenelated parapets that
added another six feet. The walls were massive in thickness—thirty-six
feet at the base, twelve feet at the crest.

We entered the city by a small opening cut through the northwest base
that legend says was made by desperate defenders seeking to break out

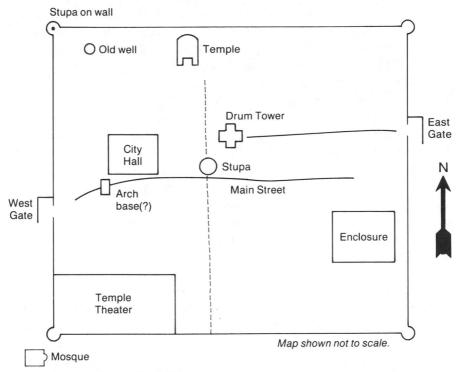

Stupa on wall

Old well

Temple

Drum Tower

East Gate

City Hall

Stupa

Main Street

West Gate

Arch base(?)

N

Enclosure

Temple Theater

Map shown not to scale.

Mosque

Etsina/Khara Khoto/Black City

from enemy encirclement on the eve of the city's final destruction. After we had explored together for a while, I went off on my own while Martin concentrated his attention on the area of the Drum Tower.

My map helped me locate Kozlov's Main Street, stretching from West Gate almost all the way across the city to the opposite wall, which was pierced by the only other entrance to the city, its counterpart, East Gate. But my untrained eye could not distinguish among the structures. Built mostly of stamped clay and timber and showing unmistakable traces of fire, they had long since collapsed into shapeless ruins partially buried in the sand. It was only thanks to my map that it was possible to identify one heap of ruins as the Drum Tower, another as City Hall, still others as a theater and various temples. A slightly elevated heap on Main Street a short distance in from West Gate may have been the base of a ceremonial archway like the one in the northeast section of Peking where I lived. The remains of a stupa could be made out almost smack in the center of the city. Here I picked up several unbaked clay discs stamped with the figure of a seated Buddha. I guessed that pottery fragments scattered among a number of low-lying ruins marked the sites of dwellings of various sizes. Kozlov said there was a well in the northwest corner, where treasure-hunters sought the great wealth supposedly buried there by the city's last ruler, but I was not able to locate it. The only treasures I found as souvenirs of the city were the clay disks and a cracked wooden plate that at one time was probably a nicely lacquered piece.

After poking around the city for a while, I mounted to the top of the wall by a ramp just inside West Gate. Access to the top was also provided by ramps at East Gate and at the northwest and southeast corners. There, on the northwest corner, were the weathered remains of the stupa about thirty feet high that we had sighted from a distance on our approach to Etsina. Near it were three more stupas, all far gone by weathering.

From my windswept vantage point on the top of the wall I got a good view of how the sand was overwhelming the city. The prevailing wind, it was clear, was from the west. In some places on that side of the city the sand was piled up against the outside wall to the very top. There the continual blasting away by wind-driven jets of sand had succeeded in scouring U-shaped breaches to a depth of six feet out of the twelve-foot thick summits and had spilled over to pile up against the interior side of the wall. It was actually possible to enter the city by working one's way up the outside slope of sand and down the inside slope. Much sand had also been blown into the city from the west. Everything with a western exposure showed the effect of sand action. Only the north and south walls lying parallel to the east-west axis were relatively unscathed.

Down in the center of the city Martin was still puttering around near the Drum Tower. It had taken his fancy because in his imagination he saw Genghis Khan standing there on a high balcony to address his mounted warriors massed in the square below. I sat on the edge of the parapet, my legs dangling over it, and hallooed down to him, but the wind tore my voice away from him. He was engrossed in pacing out distances, bending down to examine things on the ground, making entries in a little notebook.

For Martin this visit to Etsina had special meaning, for it was here that Genghis Khan, leading his invasion forces down from the north, had scored a decisive victory that paved the way to his complete conquest of China. We had started out exploring the city together, but our divergent interests soon led us apart, for Martin spoke of little else other than the military significance of everything we saw. Actually, he was not so much talking to me as thinking out loud. And though he did not show much excitement, I knew that he was deeply moved to be, at long last, where the great conqueror himself had been, perhaps even to be, quite literally, treading in the footsteps of Genghis Khan.

As I looked down from the top of the wall, Martin went down on one knee, his back turned to me, in a posture that he might assume in looking at something on the ground but that also reminded me of how Torgut commoners salute their prince. For a moment I fancied he was not examining anything on the ground but had transported himself back to the time of Genghis and was now a warrior reporting to his commander-in-chief. Perhaps he was reliving an earlier incarnation when, as the conqueror's chief military advisor, he had provided the strategy that led to the Khan's victories. All hail to the earlier Martin, l'éminence grise of Genghis Khan, the real key to his success!

The sand that had glared so uncomfortably under the blazing light of day glowed a soft pastel pink at sunset. When full darkness set in, we mounted the wall for a look at the city at night. It lay eerily silent in its dark shroud. I almost imagined we were in a city momentarily suffering a power outage and expecting the lights to come on at any moment. But the silence was too intense, the expectation too obviously false. The Black City was irrevocably dead.

When did it die?

Not, as I had first assumed, when Genghis conquered it in 1227. It lived on for more than a century after that, for among the many dated materials discovered in the city, most of them relating to grain accounts, tax records, criminal affairs, and other mundane matters, there is one dated 1366. That is the last year recorded in documents found there. It probably marks, at least approximately, the time of actual death of the city.

But why did it die? A partial explanation is suggested by that same date.

The Mongols were able to control China for only a short time, as indicated by the conventional dates 1280–1368 for their dynastic reign. In the last years of their rule their Chinese subjects were in open revolt and staged attacks in many different areas. By 1368 the Chinese had succeeded in establishing a new dynasty, the Ming, meaning Bright or Brilliant, which lasted until it was in turn overthrown by the Manchus in 1644.

In 1372 the Ming armies captured the Etsina region from the Mongols. Perhaps they razed the city at that time. The absence of Ming artifacts among the finds dug up there indicates that the area had become practically depopulated toward the end of the fourteenth century.

A major factor in the complete demise of the city and the surrounding

area appears to have been the problem of water. One theory suggests that a general drying up of the area forced the people to abandon it. Another contends that in their attack on the city the Ming forces cut off its water supply by deflecting a nearby branch of the river that was its main source.

As our campfire in the center of the mosque kept the ghosts of the past at bay outside our dilapidated house of prayer, Dorji recounted what the Torguts tell of the city's death.

During the last days of Mongol rule Etsina was commanded by a brave chieftain called Khara Bator, or Black Hero, a name given to him because of his ability to invoke black magic. On hearing that a large force of rebellious Chinese was advancing against the city, he led his warriors out to engage them in open country. But he was defeated and had to withdraw within the walls of his fortress town.

The siege of the city lasted a long time. Unable to take it by force, the Chinese built a dam to cut off its source of water. This was a channel of the Black River that washed up against the wall as a sort of moat whose bed could still be made out. The defenders dug a well in the northwest corner of the city, desperately sinking it down over nine hundred feet, but they failed to find any water.

Khara Bator decided to go down fighting. He gave orders to kill his two wives and his son and daughter lest they be abused by the enemy. And he hid all his treasures, over a million ounces of silver plus untold quantities of gold and many other valuables, in the well before filling it in.

Then, through an opening cut in the north wall, he galloped out at the head of his men to fight his way through the gauntlet of encircling Chinese. One by one his outnumbered warriors fell before the pursuing Chinese. As he fled, fighting all the way, Khara Bator cried out words of black magic. Immediately, all life about him withered and died. Irrigated fields dried up, crops shriveled, trees became skeletons, everything turned black, and sand storms rose to cover the city and the countryside around it.

Dorji's version of sudden death, rather than the scientific theory of slow desiccation, seemed somehow the more believable explanation of Etsina's ruin, as we retraced our steps the next day back to our camp on the river.

It was with not a few pangs of regret that we parted with Dorji. In the brief time we had known him we had developed a high regard for this cheerful, stalwart, devout Mongol. So after a short march together to a point where our paths diverged, we all sat cross-legged on the black gobi to enjoy a last smoke together, telling each other how much we had enjoyed each other's company and hoping one day to meet again.

Then Dorji mounted his camel and headed north, while we turned southward on the second leg of our camel trek that would take us back into Chinese territory and the start of our long journey home.

On Dorji's camel at the Black City

19 / Prisoners of Warlord Little Big Horse

‡ ‡ ‡ ‡ ‡ ‡ ‡ ‡

The Communist victory in 1949 did not mark the end of warlordism or the warlord mentality in China, as many hoped, for centralized reliance on the power of the gun replaced the decentralized militarism of the old-style warlords.

Our exposure to those pustules on the body politic of China first came about thanks—but no thanks—to a pipsqueak warlord, a minor pimple among a rash of military satraps who then controlled all of China's borderlands, and indeed the whole of China, if one includes Chiang Kai-shek as one of that cutthroat gang. He was the youngest of three Muslim warlord brothers surnamed Ma, "Horse." All three—Big Brother, Middle Brother, and Little Brother—were referred to as "Big Horse." Some people distinguished the youngest (he was only in his middle or late twenties) as Little Big Horse.

With the ascendance to power of the Communists, this Muslim Mafia fled with Chiang Kai-shek to Taiwan. Soon afterward Middle Brother was sent to Egypt, with Little Brother tagging along, and later became Taiwan's ambassador to Saudi Arabia. Apparently still up to his old tricks, in 1961 Middle Brother was forced to resign after being charged with "corruption and incompetence."

He and Little Brother continued to live in the Middle East. I doubt if they found the pickings there as good as during their heyday in northwest China.

‡ ‡ ‡ ‡ ‡ ‡ ‡ ‡

Our route south was easy to follow since we were now on what the Chinese called the Great Road. This was actually nothing more than a path that led across the black gobi in generally close proximity to the tree-lined course of the river. In places the road could be clearly made out thanks to the deep ruts made by carts that were also able to negotiate this area. At times, in areas of especially hard-packed soil, it was hard to find our way.

Occasionally the river made a big bend that forced us to choose either to keep close to the stream or to take a shortcut farther out into the gobi across the base of the arc. Sometimes when we took such shortcuts we found ourselves temporarily disoriented or without ready access to water, but these problems were readily solved by simply heading in a westerly direction until we picked up the river again.

There still was not much water in the river, and since there were several channels, we occasionally encountered one that was dry. Unless we were well-enough supplied with water, that meant continuing on until we could replenish our supply. This was just a minor inconvenience calling only for a bit longer march. It was not a life-and-death matter as it had been in crossing the desert.

At one of the channels with only a foot or so of water in it we saw a single Mongol horseman driving a small herd of horses across the stream. They made a noble spectacle as the horses galloped across, heads high, manes streaming back in the wind, hooves splashing water that sparkled in the sun.

It felt good to be on the road again, this time on an experimental schedule of starting off in the cool of morning rather than in the heat of afternoon. The temperature at dawn one day was a cold 47°. But from invigorating coolness the temperature changed slowly to enervating heat. One by one I peeled off windbreaker, sweater, and finally shirt.

We even enjoyed the hard work of loading the camels. This we were able to help with, now that we had learned how by watching Xiao and Zhou and had considerably lighter loads to deal with. Zhou paired off with Martin and me so that we both had only two camels to help load. We never did achieve Zhou's proficiency, and our hands were rubbed raw by the ropes and boxes until they became toughened, but we had the satisfaction of seeing the loads remain solidly in place on our camels.

We were able to ride these a bit more now, though we still preferred to walk, quite apart from the times that we had to do so when it came our turn to be camel puller. My most extended ride was a forced one owing to a sudden bout of illness, my first on the trip.

What hit me is a mystery. I thought then that it might be a touch of the sun, perhaps even sunstroke, but later learned that the symptoms did not jibe. Nor was the weather anywhere near as hot as what we had been through earlier. The midday temperatures were now only a bit over 100° —108° on that particular day—and the nights were becoming cool enough to make for very comfortable sleeping.

In any case, after an extended morning march of twenty miles that was actually no more arduous than usual, though it did take us through the hot noon hour, as soon as we had made camp I flopped down on my sleeping bag in a state approaching complete exhaustion, with shooting pains in the neck, shoulders, lower back, and especially the eyes.

The next day, fortunately as it turned out, we had planned to revert to our previous schedule of late-afternoon marches. I spent the whole morning alternately burning with fever and shivering from cold, fighting off lightning bolts of pain that threatened to split my forehead open and vertiginous nausea that retched my insides out. As the world whirled round and round I clutched my sleeping bag to keep from being hurled off into the void.

By mid-afternoon the pain seemed to be subsiding to a generalized wretchedness, and the dizziness and accompanying nausea were eased by keeping my eyes tightly shut against sunlight that was painful even through closed lids. Martin suggested holding up for a day, but I was unwilling to slow up our progress, so I mounted a camel and rode along with senses dulled by a blanket of misery.

Halfway into our march, as we were crossing a narrow channel of the river with almost two feet of water in it, my camel stumbled and threw me and the whole load into the stream. I quickly dragged everything to dry ground, in time to prevent our things from getting soaked through, but my clothes were thoroughly wet and clung clammily to my body.

The sun and wind dried me out in the second half of our march, but by nightfall the temperature had dropped so much that after making camp it took me more than an hour to stop shivering despite drinking copious bowls of scalding tea and wrapping myself in a blanket and an enormous sheepskin coat.

That dunking in the river was apparently just what the doctor ordered. The next day I was fine, except for sharing Samson's state after his haircut.

In order to avoid as much as possible of the hot sun, we delayed our departure until about six o'clock. We could travel late into the night, as there would be a full moon.

Shortly after darkness set in, a vague shape appeared on the road ahead coming in our direction. Our skittish camels had to be restrained from running off. As we warily advanced we came abreast of a cart pulled by

two oxen with two men walking alongside. We stopped to chat a while and to enjoy a marvelously delicious melon that the carters brought out to share with us.

The men were from Maomu, the first town on our route and our immediate destination. Their cart was an unusual affair with a small body of woven straw and enormous wheels that came up to the top of my head. It carried a load of flour that they hoped to peddle to the Chinese trading posts and infrequent Mongol inhabitants along the river.

"Conditions are safe in the Maomu area," the carters assured us, "but there are rumors that fighting has broken out somewhere south of Gansu."

We were unable to get more information from them.

I had some difficulty in following the men's speech, as did Zhou, for they mumbled as if they had hot potatoes in their mouths. Most of the people in the Maomu area, according to the carters, came from the western part of Gansu. Apparently these people spoke a dialect of Northwestern Mandarin different from Zhou's variety, which I had gotten used to by now.

Their speech was not the only distinctive thing about the people from this part of northwest China. They were also, for the most part, adherents of Islam. As Muslims they were referred to as "Hui" to distinguish them from the non-Muslim "Han" Chinese who comprised over 90 percent of the country's population. As Chinese-speaking Muslims they were referred to as "Han Hui" or "Chinese Muslims" to distinguish them from the Turkish-speaking Muslims of Xinjiang, called "Chantou Hui," or "Turbanned Muslims." And to give them a specific identity they were called "Dungans," a word of uncertain origin.

We knew of the Dungans as having a reputation as fierce fighters who often brawled among themselves as well as with the non-Muslim Chinese. The bloodiest fighting along religious lines occurred about 1870. Millions died on both sides. The result was the partial depopulation of the Northwest and the flight of a considerable number of Dungans across the border into the part of Central Asia controlled by Tsarist Russia.

Our meeting with the two Dungans occurred right after we had passed what seemed to be the dividing line between Mongol grazing land to the north and Chinese settlement to the south. That line was marked by a rather striking hill with an obo on top that stood out prominently from the surrounding gravel plain. It impressed us as a miniature Mount Fuji in the fine proportions of its conical shape. The landmark was Bayan Bogdo, or Rich Lord. We were unable to learn why it was called that, but we knew it to be a place much venerated by the Mongols where important ceremonies were held.

As we advanced south from here, the string of ruined towers that we had passed earlier continued to parallel our route. Some of them, only partially weathered, probably dated from relatively recent times, say around the twelfth century, but others were so worn away as to suggest a much earlier history.

North of Bayan Bogdo we had passed an occasional abandoned Chinese farmstead. South of it we encountered even more evidence that land was being taken out of cultivation owing to the difficulty in securing an adequate supply of water. There were some holdouts, however, and here for the first time we actually saw Chinese working in their irrigated fields, more and more of them the nearer we got to Maomu. At one time, as a stone pillar erected in 1750 proclaimed, that town was supposed to mark the boundary between Chinese and Mongol territories.

We approached the town with no little trepidation, as we were now passing into warlord country that we had no permission to enter. The fortresslike appearance of the town increased our unease. Mud walls thirty feet high, the same as Etsina's, enclosed an area only about a quarter the size of that dead city's. There were two gates to the town, one on the south, the other on the west.

We followed a road lined with poplars to the west gate. It was guarded by two scruffy sentries clad in blue uniforms and armed only with long swords. They stopped us there, took our calling cards in to show to their superiors, and returned shortly to escort us in through the gate. We were told to put up at the only place that could accommodate us, a little caravansary consisting of only a few rooms on one side of a small courtyard.

Immediately after settling in, we proceeded to look around the town and see what we could find to eat, for our inn had no food available for its infrequent guests.

Fair day in Maomu

There were houses for only forty to fifty families, but the population was increased by an influx of peasants from the outlying farms who had come to buy and sell in the lively little market that was being held for two or three days. As an added attraction, a troupe from Suzhou was making its annual visit here to put on an opera performance in the open-air theater.

We joined the big crowd watching the performance. Immediately attention was focused on us rather than on the play. We, too, found the people more interesting than the familiar renditions by gorgeously costumed players who belted out falsetto arias to the accompaniment of ear-splitting cymbals, wooden clappers, and a two-stringed fiddle.

The thing that struck us most was that practically all the women were hobbling around on tiny bound feet. It was a measure of this area's backwardness that even peasant women, whom we thought would be exempted because of the requirements of their work, still conformed to the crippling practice of binding the feet so that the toes were curled under the soles, making them into the supposedly erotic "Golden Lilies" eulogized by an early poet.

We were disappointed not to find much to eat—no restaurants, and only a few things available from street vendors and market stalls. Yet it was an improvement to find more of the delicious local melons, nice hot corn on the cob, long twisted doughnuts, and some sweet cakes.

On returning to the inn we were met by an official who asked for our passports and requested that we present ourselves at the mayor's office the next morning at ten o'clock.

On our arrival there Martin and I were invited to sit on comfortable deck chairs while Zhou stood respectfully behind us. He was all spruced up in his best clothes, a clean white shirt and baggy trousers neatly fastened around the ankles with broad black bands, but the two of us in our worn and grimy outfits hardly lived up to our role in what should have been a sahibs and servant tableau.

This much-feared visit turned out to be a pleasant social call. The mayor, whose jurisdiction encompassed only about a thousand families, sighed sympathetically as he envisaged the hardships we had to endure, including the inadequate accommodations in his town, for which he was most apologetic. In the course of our conversation the mayor asked us whether our travel plans included going to Xinjiang. This apparently weighed heavily on his mind, for he returned to the matter several times.

It was clear why. That province was under the control of the opportunist warlord Sheng Shicai, a native of Manchuria who had risen to power as commander of troops that had been transported from that northeastern area of China across Siberia to Xinjiang after their defeat at the hands of the Japanese invaders. Originally a protégé of Chiang Kai-shek, the power-hungry Sheng turned against his master and allied himself with the Soviet Union as a means to maintain his independence of Nanking.

When the mayor finally accepted our assurances that we had no intention of traveling to Xinjiang, he returned our passports to us and said we were free to continue on our way. As we left, Martin and I heaved great sighs of relief at having made the transition from Mongol to Chinese jurisdiction without the hassles that we had been fearing for months.

In the afternoon we followed up Georg Söderbom's suggestion just before leaving the Temple of the Larks that we look up a friend of his named Du De when we got to Maomu. He turned out to be a sort of country squire who lived in a substantial wall-enclosed villa outside the town. At first he was a bit stiff, but soon loosened up and became quite affable.

One of the things we talked about was the possible existence of a ruined city somewhere in this area north of the Great Wall. We were tremendously excited when he said that yes, he had heard of some sand-buried ruins, and he then proceeded to give us details that dovetailed with those we had obtained from other people we had questioned about the matter. But it was soon apparent to both of us that Du De and our other informants were just relaying hearsay that really applied to Etsina. There was no other ruined city after all. Du De invited us to dinner the next day. He said he would send someone to our inn to escort us to his place.

On returning to town we stopped for a moment to join the peasants in watching the performance that was still in progress. While we were so engaged, the mayor sent down into the crowd to invite us to come up and sit on his special covered porch with him and other notables, which we did with great increment to our face.

The next morning we arranged to have a lot of our clothing washed and repaired. I also doctored a camel that had developed an ugly sore on its back. I dug out the maggots from the sore and filled the hole with shavings from a bar of soap.

In the afternoon we were escorted by Du De's men to his home for dinner. Here we found assembled a dozen other guests, who must have included everyone of importance in Maomu except the mayor himself. Dinner was at the disconcertingly early hour of four o'clock. Coming on top of a lunch that was a bit more substantial that it should have been because everything tasted so good, we had some trouble doing justice to

Doctoring a camel amidst "camel briquets"

Du De's feast. For such it was, an eye-popping, palate-pleasing, stomach-stretching succession of dishes, accompanied by endless toasts of "white-dry," that were urged on us by our host and his guests.

Martin was almost embarrassingly restrained in his sampling of the dishes. To make up for his slighting of our host's largesse, I tried manfully to play the role of the perfect guest. The result was my coming down that night with the most tremendous bellyache in my experience. Martin had no sympathy for my piteous groans of distress. He dismissed my plea of conforming to social custom as mere weak-willed gluttony.

With the loss of our long-cherished hope of finding another dead city, we definitely decided against taking the desert route back outside the Great Wall, opting instead to return via the Silk Road in the Gansu Corridor. That made our next major objective the town of Suzhou, just a few days south of Maomu.

On leaving that pleasant little town, we sometimes followed poplar-lined paths through fields that were or once had been irrigated, for here too we found many abandoned farmsteads among the inhabited dwellings. At times we struck out into the familiar black gobi with its occasional sand dunes.

Far off to the south we saw a curious bank of clouds that seemed suspended on the horizon. It took us a while to realize that we were seeing the snow-capped top of the great Southern Mountains, which formed an almost impassible barrier between the Gansu Corridor and Tibetan-inhabited territory to the south.

Three days of travel brought us to the oasis town called Jinta, or Golden Pagoda, so named because of a conspicuous yellow-painted tower whose dome was said to have been once covered with solid gold. This walled town was a little bigger than Maomu and had a number of permanent stalls and shops.

It also had a pleasant mayor who immediately permitted us to enter when we presented ourselves to the sentry at the gate. He even called on us personally in our caravansary lodgings, where he went through the charade of reproving the innkeeper for giving us such a mean little room —as if there were any better. He also asked a few careful questions about our travel plans, especially whether they included Xinjiang, and after further talk about nothing in particular speeded us on our way.

South of Golden Pagoda we abandoned the sparsely populated cultivated areas and headed for a pass through some hills on the shortest route to Suzhou. After a tiring trek through a bad stretch of terrain called Red Sand Ridge, we crossed over onto the elevated plain on the other side. We stopped there for the night after a march shortened by the threat of rain.

As we were settling in, an old Chinese and a little boy of five or six years emerged from the darkness and hesitatingly squatted down near our campfire. The child seemed cold, tired, and frightened as he huddled close to what I took to be his grandfather.

The man said they were on their way back to Suzhou. He showed us a document containing his name, reason for travel, and duration of trip. It authorized him to make the rounds of peasant farmsteads in the area on

Our caravan crossing the Red Sand Ridge

behalf of a debt-collecting agency, which, he explained, gave him a percentage of whatever he succeeded in getting from accounts that I gathered were badly in arrears.

No one could travel anywhere in the area without obtaining such a document from the head of the Bureau of Public Safety in Suzhou. We also learned that it was to the Bureau Chief, and especially to General Ma Bukang, a Dungan who headed the predominantly Dungan military force here, that we should pay our respects as the persons who held power in the city and all the region around it.

We invited the two to share our supper and to spend the night in our tent. Martin wondered why the child was being taken along on such a tiring trip. There wasn't much doubt in my mind that the reason was to be found in a story about my childhood that was one of my favorites because I was, if not its hero, at least its central figure.

When I was about this child's age, our family's (or rather my mother's) priest came to borrow me one afternoon to take along on an alms-begging trip, reasoning that having a child in tow would soften hearts and open purses. I was brought home well after dark, cold, tired, and bedraggled from the rain. And—this is the part I like best—Pop, who was not a god-fearing man, much less a priest-fearing one, had to be physically restrained from beating up that frightened cleric.

I told the grandfather of the little boy, now deep in the sleep of exhaustion, to place him next to my sleeping bag in the tent. Before turning in myself I brushed my fingertips against the poignant softness of his cheek.

In the morning we all set out together, with the boy riding on my camel, on the fifteen-mile march that finally brought us to Suzhou.

At the north wall of the town our two guests left us to go about their own business. We presented our cards and passports at a sentry post outside the gate. Before long we were permitted to enter through the tunnel-like opening in the city wall but were stopped at a guardhouse just inside the gate and told to wait there.

After a long wait an officer appeared. First he said that the passports were foreign and not Chinese. When I pointed to the Chinese visas stamped inside, he countered by noting that there were none for the province of Gansu. To that I said we had been told that local authorities were the ones to issue these. The officer harrumphed and went off again with our passports, telling us in a polite way that was a veiled command that we were to stay in the city for a few days. We had intended to stop for a couple of days anyway.

We put up at a caravansary with a huge courtyard filled with carts and animals. On one side were a number of dark little cubicles largely taken up by brick-beds so short that I had to lie down diagonally. After the three of us had settled into one of the little rooms, we went out to check on the food situation. Almost all the eating places were run by Dungans,

The drum tower in Suzhou, Marco Polo's Succiu

serving Muslim-style dishes. At what looked like a popular place near the center of town, where an imposing drum tower stood at the crossroads leading north, east, south, and west, we had a great meal of mutton with chopped-up vegetables spiced with hot pepper. Then Martin and I went looking for some American missionaries that we had heard were here, the only foreigners in the area.

We found two families of Seventh-Day Adventists in a compound that was still being put into shape to receive them. Pastor Nils Dahlsten and his wife and two children, together with Brother Phil H. Shigley and his wife, had arrived here less than two months before. We were all delighted to see each other.

At a prolonged dinner to which we were invited, our first Western-style meal in almost three months, the missionaries told us of their plans and brought us up to date on the news. They hoped eventually to work among the Turki Muslims in Xinjiang. Until then they were concentrating attention on the Chinese Muslims, the Dungans, here in western Gansu.

They also told us the latest news. We learned of Italy's attack on Ethiopia, of renewed Nazi persecutions in Germany, and, most immediately disturbing, of the northward thrust of the Communists from their South China base, which was arousing great anxiety as to their ultimate intentions. Were they aiming for North China in order to link up with another group of Communists based there? Or were they going to push west into the Gansu Corridor with the intention of joining the pro-Soviet regime established in Xinjiang by warlord Sheng Shicai?

On the way back in the dark through the ominously quiet streets, we were stopped at intervals by patrols that called out, "Halt!" and only permitted us to go on after we had identified ourselves. At the inn we were told that police from the Bureau of Public Safety had come there three times to demand our passports. I hastened over to headquarters to explain that the military had already taken our papers. We wondered what this lack of coordination between police and military meant. Mere inefficiency? Or conflict of authority?

In the morning we received a visit from a nattily dressed young man whom I had noticed the night before on my visit to police headquarters. He introduced himself as Si Junshan and said he was a student at the Political Academy in Nanking. According to his story, he had started out from Peking in April 1934 and in the subsequent sixteen months had traveled through Tibet, Xinjiang, and, most surprisingly, Outer Mongolia. We were skeptical. After he left, Zhou called him an outright liar and warned us against putting any trust in him.

Our passports were not returned to us that day, or the one following, or the one after that. Our repeated attempts to see either a police or military figure of authority were rebuffed with the laconic excuse that everyone was busy. We were stuck. To test the extent of the restraints on us, we took walks throughout the city, on top of the wall, and through the north gate to the outside. No problems in these excursions.

Four days after our arrival, on returning from one of our walks, we found the alley leading to our inn choked in a cloud of dust made by a cavalcade of carts and animals. The courtyard was a scene of bedlam as troops commandeered all available transport. In the confusion of voices I heard repeated references to fighting just outside of town. In fear of being stranded without transport to flee back into the desert, if that should be necessary, when I heard an officer shout, "Take the camels!" I held on to our animals and protested against their being taken from us.

The troops departed, along with all the carters and camel drivers. Silence descended on the courtyard, now completely empty except for our camels squatting close to the entrance to our cubicle.

The missionaries were as alarmed as we were about the situation. Realizing the importance of the camels for all of us if flight should be necessary, Dahlsten congratulated us on holding on to them, though he cautioned that we had unknowingly run a serious risk in crossing soldiers who rarely brooked opposition from mere civilians, and he suggested moving the camels to the greater safety of his compound. When Martin and I tried to help Zhou lead them out, however, the innkeeper ran to inform the military, who ordered us to make no change.

The next morning the innkeeper demanded a considerable increase in the amount he was charging to have our camels taken out to graze. We refused his demand, saying that our own man usually grazed them and could resume doing so now. With an oily smile, he said the matter would be taken up again later.

After some thought we came up with a plan of action. I sat myself in the doorway to our room with a writing board on my knees. Martin sauntered out, as he often did, by himself. Zhou busied himself checking the camels and after ten minutes or so led them out in the direction of the grazing grounds. Instead, he took them by an indirect route to the mission compound, avoiding the well-patrolled main streets. After a while Martin returned to say the camels were now safely in the mission compound.

In the afternoon the young student named Si came to visit us again. There was no fighting just outside the town, he said. Yesterday's commandeering of transport was due to the movement eastward of a thousand troops, half of the local force, to replace those commanded by two of General Ma's brothers in central and eastern Gansu, who had sent some of their forces still farther east to counter the Communist threat that was still actually far off beyond the southeastern border of the province. Si added the information, without explaining how he had come by it, that wires had been sent to these brothers asking what to do about us.

We were also shown a Lanzhou newspaper, now several weeks old, containing the news that bandits had murdered an English newspaper correspondent in Inner Mongolia and were rumored to have cut off communications with the Temple of the Larks.

Notwithstanding all our worries, this being August 31, my twenty-fourth birthday, at dinnertime I went out with Zhou to get some steamed rolls, a big dish of mutton and eggplant, and some sweet cakes by way of celebration.

The next day we decided to accept Dahlsten's long-standing invitation to move into the mission compound. When we tried to move, however, the innkeeper dashed off to inform the military, and an officer appeared with the order to stay put. Things got worse during the day. We were forbidden to walk on top of the city wall. Then the sentries at the north gate lowered their bayonets and ordered us back when we tried to walk out into the countryside. Apparently we were now under town arrest.

Dahlsten tried to approach the military commander on our behalf but was refused an audience. He could not push very hard for fear of compromising his own delicate position. Our unease was increased by his mention that the troops had not been paid for several months. He said there was danger that the Dungan soldiers, a volatile bunch at best, might break out in open revolt or even cross the thin line into outright banditry.

Late in the morning Si came over with a new story about his situation. He said he was under indefinite detention that had already lasted over three weeks. Perhaps this was another cock-and-bull story, but it added to our anxiety, which increased even more when he said there were rumors that our passports were forged and that we were really Russian Communist spies.

Si's mention of indefinite detention reminded us of Gustav Söderbom's three-year captivity in Xinjiang after running afoul of the warlord there. We were nervously aware that we were up against the kind of arbitrary rule that prevailed in the domain of China's military despots. Dahlsten, too, was becoming more and more anxious about the situation. He and Martin spent many hours together poring over the logisticical problems involved if we should all have to make a run for it back into the desert.

After eight days of frustration and mounting anxiety centered on the fear of being indefinitely stranded if the Communists broke through into the Gansu Corridor before we could get out, we came to the conclusion that there was no alternative but to seek help from our legations. Counting on the lack of coordination among the local powers-that-be, we submitted telegrams at the wire service run by the civilian government.

The day after sending our wires we had a subdued celebration of Martin's twenty-sixth birthday. We waited several more days with increasing impatience and anxiety, wondering if our telegrams had gone through, before replies finally came from our legations. Our identically worded replies said that the authorities had been requested to release us and suggested that we return by the quickest and safest route.

For several days we checked repeatedly at military headquarters, only to receive the familiar response that the officials we wanted to see were not available. Dahlsten reported that the military commander's aide-de-camp, who had received us several times with apparent sympathy, in the course of a visit to the mission dispensary had hinted that the return of our passports would be facilitated if we offered a bribe. We might have been willing to follow that up earlier, but now that our legations had stirred things up, we decided to hold out a bit longer. Sure enough, at long last, two full weeks after reaching here, our passports were returned to us by the aide-de-camp.

We immediately prepared to move over to the mission compound. Since other transport was not available, we hired some men with carrying poles to take our things there. In settling our bill with the innkeeper we told him we would pay only for the first week as we had remained for the second week only at the request of the military, which he had notified of our intended move. He let out a howl of protest, knowing, as we did, that he would receive nothing from that quarter. The inn-

keeper and I proceeded to military headquarters, shouting at each other at the top of our lungs all the way, followed by a crowd of gleeful onlookers. The soldiers were also amused. So was I. Not the innkeeper, though.

After settling in at the mission, we went to call on the aide-de-camp to thank him for his help and to ask for further assistance in facilitating our delayed departure. To our surprise, we were ushered into a huge courtyard where two long rows of soldiers were lined up leading to the steps of a barracks-like building. At the top of the staircase stood the aide-de-camp next to a boyish-looking but obviously superior officer. This could be none other than the redoubtable General Ma Bukang, less formally known as the Dungan warlord Little Big Horse.

We walked down the aisle formed by the soldiers, half expecting them to cross swords over our heads, as they do in movie military weddings, half expecting to be made to run the gauntlet. At the foot of the staircase we stopped and made a bow to the general. From his elevated position he glared down at us and barked out the question why we had dared intrude into his territory. Brushing aside the ritual flowery phrases I had been quickly rehearsing for him, he turned abruptly on his heel and stalked off.

The distance walking back between the two rows of soldiers seemed much longer.

20 / Where the Great
Wall Ends

In recalling my early travels it is fascinating to see how often a minor jigsaw piece of the past acquires greater significance when fitted into a new mosaic of the present.

The fact that during the great Muslim rebellion of the 1870s thousands of Dungan refugees fled from the Gansu Corridor into Russian Central Asia was filed away in my mind as a minor bit of information when I first learned about it long ago. Much later it acquired a completely new significance for me when I came to view it in relation to, of all things, the Chinese system of writing.

Some Chinese and Western scholars have long been battling the nonsense that Chinese characters are pictographic or ideographic and that the language can only be written with the traditional script and not with an alphabetic one. For me, one of the things that helped clinch the claim that Chinese *can* be written alphabetically was my discovery that descendents of those Dungan refugees were actually writing that way. For over half a century the seventy thousand Chinese-speaking Dungans in Russian Central Asia have been publishing newspapers, scholarly works, and all sorts of literature in a simple script based first on the Latin and later on the Russian alphabet.

Those Dungans have reinforced my support of Chinese reformers working for a "two-script system" that calls for supplementing the traditional script with one using our letters in order to achieve mass literacy and make efficient use of modern technology, especially computers.

The loss of face inflicted on us by our Dungan nemesis did not surprise the missionaries.

"He was just retaliating," Dahlsten said, "You embarrassed him by presenting a problem he didn't handle very well and in any case couldn't handle on his own."

For all his being in control of western Gansu, Ma Bukang was too junior to decide anything out of the ordinary by himself. He undoubtedly referred the problem we presented to his older brothers—Ma Buqing (Big Brother), who controlled central Gansu, and Ma Bufang (Middle Brother), who controlled the eastern part of the province. And once our legations got involved, this brought the Central Government into the action. Most likely it persuaded the senior brothers that there was nothing to be gained in making a fuss about a couple of harmless foreigners, and they in turn ordered Little Brother to release us.

This scenario reflected Dahlsten's estimate of the power situation in this area. The three warlord brothers were really independent of Chiang Kai-shek, as witness their opposition to talk of building a railroad through the Corridor, but they were willing to cooperate with him if and when it suited their purposes. Right now everyone was eager for cooperation, at least in military matters, for they all feared the threat posed by the Communists.

I asked Dahlsten how he explained the friendly reception we had received from the mayors in Maomu and Jinta in contrast to the hostile treatment at the hands of Ma Bukang.

"Both of them are civilian bureaucrats appointed by Nanking, but neither one has any real power. Their letting you proceed here carried no weight with Ma Bukang. And while it wouldn't have done you any good anyway, right now Suzhou doesn't even have a mayor you could appeal to. The incumbent has just absconded with the public funds. The head of the Bureau of Public Safety is another Nanking appointee under the general's thumb. He's trying to find a replacement for the mayor."

One thing that helped Ma Bukang and his brothers to maintain their independence from Nanking was the fact that they were Dungans ruling over a largely Dungan population. That did not, however, prevent the Dungans from fighting among themselves as well as fending off the central government.

"In fact," said Dahlsten, "we've barely come out of one of the most awful periods in the history of this province. Some missionaries who lived through the worst of it have left eyewitness accounts of the terrible happenings."

The story began in the late 1920s when a fifteen-year-old Dungan firebrand named Ma Zhongying defied his military superiors and led a band to attack and take a fortified town, thereby earning himself the title of

"Little Commander" and attracting a rabble of like-minded freebooters. In town after town they slaughtered every male over fourteen years of age, impressed younger ones to serve as orderlies, and raped young women and girls.

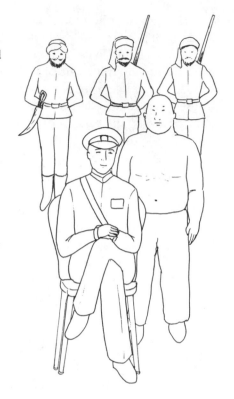

The missionaries who treated Ma Zhongying for an infected gunshot wound described him as "tall, slender, elegant, perfumed, and effeminate." His bodyguard was composed of "fierce, ruthless, bearded, and turbanned men, all typical brigands, heavily armed." He discussed the execution of a man who had displeased him in a peevish tone of voice, "with delicate, languid movements and in nonchalant fashion." But a moment later "his weary tone of voice sharpened in fear, lest the application of a disinfectant should cause a smart to his delicate flesh."

To the terrified peasants in this area he was "General Thunderbolt." For years he savaged the land until he was driven out of Gansu by warlord Ma Bufang and out of Xinjiang by warlord Sheng Shicai. He finally fled across the border into Russian Central Asia in the summer of 1934, disappearing from view but certainly not from memory.

Dahlsten added that the problems we had encountered in our contacts with Ma Bukang and his riffraff soldiery were as nothing compared to what the local population had to put up with all the time. At the worst of times, as when General Thunderbolt was on the rampage, the people feared for their very lives. Even at the best of times they were subject to arbitrary warlord rule against which there was no recourse. These military despots squeezed the people mercilessly and gave little in return, virtually nothing in the way of public services.

It was only thanks to the missionaries that any modern medical attention was available to the people. None of them had been trained as doctors, but all had acquired a good deal of practical experience that was useful in the absence of anything better. Their services were much in demand. Dahlsten said it was their best entree to the people and indeed was the main reason why they were permitted into the area at all. It appeared doubtful to me, though, that they had any greater prospect of success among the Muslims than Gonzell had among the Mongols.

The Dahlstens and Shigleys were committed to staying on to the last, and perhaps even beyond if the Communists should take over, but Martin and I were anxious to get away to the east before we were stranded here. The necessity for haste meant that we had to give up further travel by camel and look into getting bus transportation. That, we now knew, consisted simply of ordinary trucks loaded with goods of which passengers were the top layer. We were informed that there was no regular schedule and that it would be at least September 12, three days from now, before there would be another departure.

That would give us time for a little excursion that both of us were anxious to make. From the very beginning of planning our trip we had included a visit to the western end of the Great Wall as one of the high points of our travels. We particularly relished the distinction of seeing that end of the Wall, in contrast to most visitors to China, who see only the tourist attraction at Badaling near Peking, which can be considered its eastern end, though that is actually a bit farther east on the coast.

"Great Wall" and "end" both require clarification. First the name: what we call "The Great Wall" is known to the Chinese as the Chang Cheng, or Long Wall. Moreover, strictly speaking, there is no such thing as *the* Great Wall. If all Chinese history is considered, there have been many Great Walls. The first was one several hundred miles in length that was built in the seventh century B.C. in North China. It was constructed by the ruler of one of many kingdoms in a time of disunity that culminated in what came to be known as the Warring States Period. Many of the kingdoms built such walls as defenses against their rivals.

The First Emperor of China, who created a unified empire in 221 B.C., linked a number of these walls into a single system the main part of which started in southern Manchuria and ended near Lanzhou. In subsequent periods of China's long history, more walls were built against internal and external enemies. If laid end to end, all these walls would extend more than fifteen thousand miles, the equivalent of about three round-trips between New York and San Francisco.

Only remnants remain of many of these walls. Some barely discernible remains have been found even farther west, actually as far as Jade Gate in the westernmost end of the Gansu Corridor. What is now generally called *the* end of the Great Wall is actually only the end of the two thousand-mile continuous wall that was most recently rebuilt, about six hundred years ago, after the Mongols were expelled, as a defense against further incursions by them or by other nomads in the north.

The place now considered as the end of the Great Wall has a grandiose name and an odious reputation. It was probably some cloistered poet who named it Jiayuguan, or Grandvale Gate. To travelers fearful of that haunted desert to the west it was known as the Gate of the Demons. People living in the area who heard the lamentations of those passing through it into exile called it the Gate of Sighs.

We set out on the twenty-mile trip to this feared world's end of the Chinese with three camels, leaving the weakest one behind. Two of them we prepared for riding astride, borrowing stirrups from Dahlsten for the purpose and folding over a couple of blankets in lieu of a saddle. Our strongest camel took on a ridiculously light load consisting of our bedding rolls and a few other things for what was just an overnight trip.

Our route took us out the south gate and then westward through a suburban belt about five miles wide where the peasant population maintained a system of irrigated fields. This was a lovely stretch with flat-topped mud houses nestled among colorful crops against a backdrop of the towering snow-capped Southern Mountains.

Suzhou and the surrounding region comprised what the local population, which numbered altogether about eighty thousand people, called the Gobi Oasis. The area was somewhat reminiscent of the Denver region at the foot of the snow-capped Rockies. It, too, was on a mile-high plain, which here was high in the southwest, low on the northeast. But in contrast to the fifteen-inch annual rainfall of the American city, Suzhou received only three inches of rain. We were still in desert country.

From the lush farmland we entered abruptly a barren, gobi-like expanse where the usual small gravel was overlaid with larger stones as big as a person's head. Here we encountered a curious optical illusion that made the land seem to slope down from us toward the mountains on the south. It was almost unsettling to be crossing shallow streams that seemed to be flowing uphill away from the mountains.

This was the floodplain of the Great North River, which rises in the Southern Mountains west of Suzhou, flows for some distance at the base of that great range, and near the city abruptly turns north for its run to Maomu, where it helps form the Black River. The course of the river was marked on our left by a line of trees at the foot of the mountains.

From a distance of some eight miles we made out Jiayuguan on what seemed to be a mesa in a narrow gobi pass hemmed in on the south by the white-capped Southern Mountains and on the north by a black-hued parallel range called Horse's Mane Mountains. After ascending a sharply inclined road, we stopped inside a walled suburb where some thirty or forty peasant families, most of the population of the area, lived in dilapidated houses among completely destroyed ones. It was a community so impoverished that the people had hardly enough for themselves, much less for strangers, even paying ones. It took quite a bit of scrounging around among the peasant households before we succeeded in buying some melons and eggs and hard, dry bread for a quick lunch before setting out to look around.

One of the things that struck us first was the existence of a whole complex of walls in varying degrees of preservation, from barely distinguishable sections of the Great Wall to the solid-looking ramparts of the citadel proper. Central to the whole complex was the inner fort itself. This stood in a roughly rectangular space surrounded by a protective outer wall, actually part of the Great Wall, that pressed in close on all sides except the east, where it was removed enough to form an inhabited suburb.

From the northeast corner of the outer enclosure a section of the Great Wall ran up to the barrier of the Horse's Mane Mountains. From the southwest corner another section ran south to the even more formidable barrier of the Southern Mountains. It was here, against the solid barrier of this towering range with its peaks of over seventeen thousand feet, that the Great Wall came to an end after snaking two thousand miles from the sea. The precise end was five miles south of the fort, at the edge of a sheer precipice of two hundred feet cut by the river, which meant that an end run around the wall there was impossible owing to the triple obstacle of the precipice, the river, and the mountains.

In walking around the inner citadel we estimated that it measured only about five hundred feet on each side. Its crenelated walls seemed to be about thirty feet high, fifteen feet thick at the base, only six feet at the top. Barbicans on the east and west sides were surmounted by graceful three-tiered gate-towers with upturned flying eaves that soared sixty feet above the ground and added a majestic touch to the raw power suggested by the walls.

The two entrances to the fort were usually kept locked, but we induced its guardians, a little squad of ten soldiers, to let us in to look around. Most of the buildings in the interior were in ruins. There was an air of abandonment about the whole place.

A young soldier who looked like a teenager detached himself from the rest and urged us to follow him to a spot inside the east bastion.

"Listen!" he said.

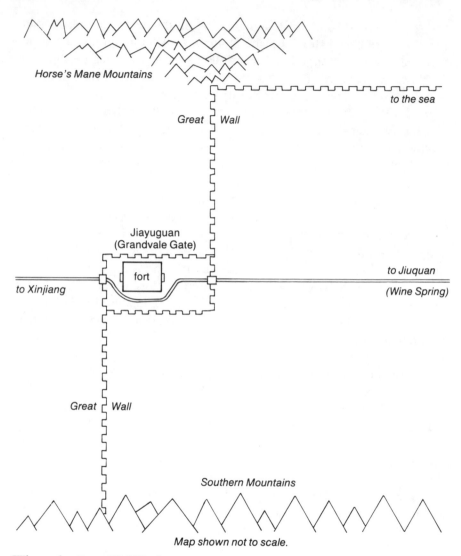

Map shown not to scale.

Where the Great Wall Ends

He picked up a stone and threw it against the brick base of the wall. It fell with a faint sound of stone against stone.

"Did you hear it?" he asked. "Didn't it sound like the cry of a bird?"

Yes, we said, it sounded like the cry of a bird. We asked him why.

This gate, he said, is so impregnable that even birds cannot pass it on their way south in the fall. As cold weather sets in the birds become numbed and fall to the ground near the gate. What one really hears on throwing a stone is the last feeble cry of a dying magpie imploring that the gate be opened so it can fly on to warmer climes.

We walked around the top of the walls and then crossed over by long beams to the barbican on the west side. From there we descended to the road that approached the fort from the east, circled it to the south, and then turned westward through a gate in the western segment of the outer wall. This segment was constructed completely with bricks, since it faced in the direction of potential enemies. Elsewhere the walls were mostly of rammed earth.

Our footsteps echoed with sepulchral hollowness as we walked through the long brick tunnel in this outer wall. At the exit we stopped to look out westward at the black gobi that seemed to stretch endlessly before us. We shared Marco Polo's impression of the area when he passed through it in the year 1273.

"You ride ten days northeast and east," he said, "and in all that way you find no human dwelling, or next to none, so that there is nothing for our book to speak of."

I peered out intently at that expanse of nothingness, evoking the passage of the young Venetian and savoring his surprise when I called out to him, "Ciao, Marco!"

A tablet on the exterior wall proclaimed this to be "First Pass under

Ruined fortress at the end of the Great Wall

Heaven." Before China was opened up to contacts by sea, it was the main point of entry into the Middle Kingdom for foreign envoys, merchants, and travelers. But for Chinese exiled beyond the pale it was a gate of hell where they heaved one last sigh of farewell to their beloved homeland.

The tunnel walls were covered by the graffiti of heartsore Chinese. I made out several verses that wept, some with dry sobs, others with buckets of tears. An inscription by someone of stouter heart, perhaps not an exile at all but a visitor like us, exhorted readers to be strong, to leave behind some record of self after one is gone. The Great Wall remains, went the homily, though its builder, the First Emperor of China, is no longer of this world.

On our way back to the suburb we passed half a dozen soldiers who were having great sport toying with a Muslim of Near Eastern or Central Asian type that foreigners refer to as Turki. The man was weeping, as was a boy of eight or nine, perhaps his grandson, who clung to the long gown of the Turki. He was pleading tearfully with the soldiers to return the fine-looking horse they had taken from him, giving in return a sway-backed nag with a saddle-sore that oozed pus and maggots.

"I think we should return his horse," said one soldier, almost doubling over with mirth at the cleverness of the role he was playing. The good-cop soldier was answered by a bad-cop soldier who said you could tell just by looking at the Turki that he was a horse-thief who actually deserved to be shot on the spot and not just deprived of his stolen goods. There was a general taking of sides in a good-cop–bad-cop charade that went on for some time. Martin and I watched, sickened, raging at this display of rapacity and cruelty and at our inability to do anything about it.

These human wolves were even more wolfish than real wolves. At one point along the way back to Suzhou I happened to be walking absent-mindedly well in the rear of the others when I almost froze at the sight of a wolf walking along parallel to me. It was closer to me than I was to our caravan. I riveted my eyes on it. It contemplated me with a return gaze that seemed wolfish in a frighteningly literal sense. I tried to remember what little I knew about these animals beside the fact that they were inveterate carnivores, and that those in the region of the Southern Mountains were considered especially ferocious, attacking even in broad daylight. But wolves don't often attack humans, I recalled. Was I to be a statistical oddity? Wolves concentrate their attacks on stragglers from a flock, especially sheep. What about a sheepish human straggler? Should I shout for help? No, it would detect fear and be emboldened to attack. Should I make a dash to join the others? No, it could outrun me. Should I? . . .

The wolf turned and sauntered off.

For a week after our return we checked daily at the bus station but were continually put off with the remark that no new information was available as to when a departure might be expected. With time hanging heavy on our hands, we did a lot of walking around town, sometimes together, often separately, as we needed a respite from each other's company.

On one of our walks together we visited the site that gave the town of Suchou its alternate name of Jiuquan, or Wine Spring, which has been used from time to time in the long history of the place. That history goes back to the death of the First Emperor and the establishment of the Han Dynasty in 206 B.C. Only then was the Great Wall extended through the Gansu Corridor as an outer defense barrier running parallel to the inner barrier of the Southern Mountains. Two of the main cities in the area later became the prefectural cities Ganzhou and Suzhou (*zhou* means "prefecture"). These names were telescoped to form the provincial name Gansu.

In the second century B.C., as part of the Han military moves that resulted in the establishment of a fortress town in the Etsina area, the Warrior Emperor sent a general along the Corridor on an expedition against the Huns. There he inflicted a crushing defeat on the nomads. The emperor, so the legend goes, rewarded the general by sending him ten bottles of choice wine from the imperial cellars. Rather than reserve the wine for himself and a few select officers, the general shared it with all his men by poring it into a nearby spring. This unwonted regard for the rank and file so impressed Heaven that it transformed the spring into an endless supply of wine that the whole army could imbibe to its heart's content.

Such was the oft-repeated tale recounting the origin of the name Jiuquan, or Wine Spring, as another name for Suzhou. We made a brief visit to the spring itself, an unprepossessing landmark situated outside the east gate in the rear of several dilapidated and abandoned temples that had been taken over by a horde of poor people and beggars.

At the time of Marco Polo the town was known to him as Succiu, his rendering for Suchou. He mentions it as the first town encountered after ten days of travel through the desert country that he said was not worth writing about. His account reads:

> At the end of these ten days' marches one finds another province which is called Succiu in which are cities and villages enough; and the chief city is also called Succiu. And there are also some Nestorian Christians, and the people of it are idolaters [apparently this means Buddhists]. And they belong to the domain of the Great Khan. This

province forms part of the major province of Tangut. And here there is a great abundance of flocks and of fruits, and they live on the fruit which they get from the land and on their flocks, but at trade they do not work at all. The whole province is healthy and the people are brown.

It seemed to us that since Marco Polo's time things had gone downhill in this area. Brown the people still were, but hardly healthy. Northern Chinese are on the average taller and heavier than those in the south. Not those in Gansu province, however, for owing to poor nutrition they ranked lowest among northerners in this respect. They were further ground down by disease. Intestinal disorders and venereal diseases were rampant. There were people walking about with their faces eaten away by disease. The missionaries were swamped with patients who had no one else to turn to. Raw sewage ran in gutters in the streets. Opium was sold openly by sidewalk vendors who displayed large bowls of the drug, dark red in color, like dried blood. And the worst scourge of all were the parasitic warlords.

No wonder that we saw sections of the city falling down in ruins. Away from the bustling center of town with its imposing pagoda-shaped drum tower there were areas, especially in the northwest and southwest corners of the city, that were depopulated, with tumbledown houses, and even cleared sections turned over to cultivation. We estimated that there were less than ten thousand people in a town that could, and at one time obviously did, hold many more.

In my aimless ramblings throughout this depressing town I had a few experiences of a pleasanter sort. One came about when I barged in on a Chinese funeral.

While walking on the main street near the mission I was intrigued to see a large streamer waving in the breeze in a courtyard near what I took to be a new store that Dahlsten had told us was being opened in the area by one of his Dungan acquaintances. On entering the courtyard for a look around, I was surprised to find a group of professional mourners taking a break from their arduous task of wailing and flailing about in simulated grief. As surrogate family members such mourners could often be seen miming the motions of grief while crying, "Aiya! Aiyou!" to the accompaniment of funeral music more suited to wakening the dead than to speeding souls to the other world.

I started to apologize for my intrusion but was taken in hand by an old codger who insistently urged, "Come, come, come!" as he led me into the group of now happy mourners. Backed up by their boisterous plaudits, he waved a tiny cup of "white dry" before me and invited me to join their merriment. After a feeble attempt at declining the drink, I tossed it off with a loud "I give you a dry cup" to him and his fellow mourners. This elicited a chorus of approval and clamorous invitations to share the dishes and drinks laid out to sustain them in their hired mourning. After many rounds of dry-cupping each other, I left in a glow of good fellowship when it came time for the mourners to resume their doleful duties. There were not many such pleasant interludes to offset our frustrating attempts to get away.

On the nineteenth, as we were sitting down to supper, the aide-de-camp appeared at the mission with the news that Nanking, apparently prodded by our legations, had sent a wire asking why we were not proceeding to Lanzhou. He said arrangements had been made to dispatch us by cart.

By cart! We were furious. It would take weeks to get to Lanzhou by such transportation. Clearly, Little Big Horse was simply trying to get us off his hands by carting us out of town and out of his area of responsibility so he could reply to Nanking that we had left Suzhou. We refused such slow transportation and told the aide-de-camp that since the military was responsible for our enforced stay here, it could also assume responsibility for seeing to it that we proceeded by the "quickest and safest" route that had been specified at the time of our release.

The next day, on checking at the bus station, we found that two trucks had just arrived from Ganzhou and would leave soon on the return trip, though not before the 22d or 23d, as both were in need of repair. One had overturned and suffered considerable damage. Several passengers were hurt in the accident. The injured were being taken to the mission compound in the hope of receiving treatment there. That place soon took on the appearance of an emergency first-aid station. We all pitched in to help set up stools for the injured and tables for the bandages, medicines, and equipment.

It turned out that most of those injured had suffered only contusions and cuts. Among the more seriously injured was a ten-year-old boy who was moaning in pain as he tried to hold stationary his dangling left arm, broken between the wrist and the elbow.

Dahlsten ordered his servants to place several planks on a couple of saw-horses for the boy to lie on. He handed me a bottle and a wad of cotton.

"Here," he said. "Chloroform him."

I was petrified. "Chloroform him! How?"

"Just wet the cotton and hold it to his nose."

"For how long?"

"Until he stops moaning."

I wet the cotton and held it briefly to the boy's nose. He continued to groan.

"Give him some more."

I did. The boy became still. Dahlsten applied himself to the task of setting the arm and encasing it in splints. The boy began to moan again. He frowned. His body twitched.

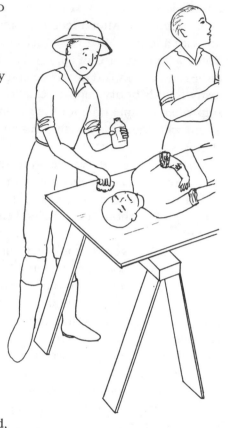

"More," said Dahlsten. "Hold it there longer this time."

The boy stopped moaning and moving. Dahlsten finished his work. The boy remained silent and still.

"Deadly silent," I thought in panic. "Deadly still."

Had I given him a fatal dose? I had never imagined myself praying to hear a child cry in pain. He did, finally, just as I was about to pass out myself.

"Well!" said Martin cheerily. "Think how this will appear on your résumé when you apply for a job: *Other experience:* Summer, 1935, anesthesiologist."

Although we completed our doctoring in short order, the repair of the trucks dragged on for days. In the meantime we busied ourselves making the final preparations for our departure. In the Turki quarter, where most of the men were booted and turbanned and clad in corderoylike coats reaching to the knee or the calf, we finally found a buyer for our camels. A bearded Turki who traced his family back to Bokhara took them after several other prospective buyers refused even to make an offer for what they said were worthless females. For all four we got less than what we had paid for one. Curses on you, Manager Guo!

We did considerably better in selling our tent and other equipment. And we reduced our luggage to a bare minimum by sending many things back to Peking via a company that ran caravans across the desert to the Temple of the Larks and the railhead at Guihua.

The day of our departure came and went, but not the truck. The driver, we were told, was ill, and none other was available. We persuaded the staff to let us trundle the driver off to the mission in an ox-cart. Dahlsten found he was suffering from a painful attack of gonorrhea that would lay him up for several weeks.

Several weeks! We hastened back to the bus station, where in desperation I offered to drive the truck to Ganzhou, and even to Lanzhou if no other driver could be found along the way. My offer was received with even less enthusiasm than it was made.

Then we went to the office of the aide-de-camp to see if we couldn't scare up something there. With great reluctance he finally said that a military truck was scheduled to leave in a few days, and that he might be able to arrange a ride for us. He warned, however, that it was going only as far as Liangzhou, the headquarters of General Ma Buqing, the oldest of the three brothers. This was 160 miles short of Lanzhou. We could only hope that covering that last bit would not be too big a problem.

On September 27, one month and one day after our arrival in the domain of Little Big Horse for what had been intended as a visit of two or three days, we left under military escort, perched with several other passengers on top of a heavily loaded army truck. We waved a fond farewell to the missionaries and an unfond farewell to Suzhou.

Turkis in Suzhou

21 / Trucking along the
Old Silk Road

‡‡‡‡‡‡‡

Recalling my journey through the Gansu Corridor prompts me to express a reservation regarding China's much acclaimed turn toward a market economy. In giving preference to the development of special economic zones in coastal areas with easy access to foreign markets, the new policy abandons any effort to have the economically more favored areas help the economically more backward ones. The result is that the richer areas are getting richer and the poorer areas are getting poorer.

The per capita income of Gansu peasants is less than US$100 a year, the lowest in the country, less than one-tenth as much as that enjoyed by some of the rural population in the coastal areas.

A corollary of the market economy as practiced in China is the callous disregard of the poorest and weakest segments of society, not just in Gansu but throughout the country.

‡‡‡‡‡‡‡

Now that we were actually under way, we had the feeling of starting off on a race with the Communists as to who would be the first to reach a point where either we could leave them behind as we hastened on to Peking or they could block us from further progress to the east. The precise location of the point where their likely northward swath might cross our intended eastward route was uncertain, but it probably lay somewhere between Lanzhou, five hundred miles to the east, and Xi'an, another four to five hundred miles farther east, the junction of the motor route through the Corridor and the rail line leading to Peking.

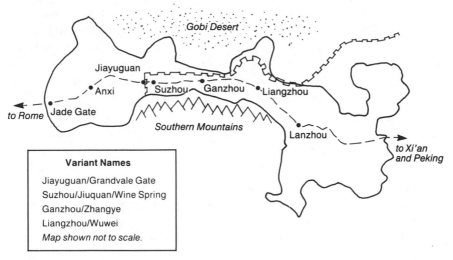

The Silk Road through the Gansu Corridor

Our desire for haste did not prevent us from savoring the fact that in proceeding along this route we were traveling over the fabled Silk Road that at one time led all the way from Xi'an to Rome. Martin was additionally pleased that we were continuing to follow in the footsteps of Genghis Khan in the eastward phase of the campaign that led to the complete conquest of China. He stressed the military origin of the road.

"It really came into being at the time of the Warrior Emperor in the second century B.C. He sent an expeditionary force into the area and extended the Great Wall to the west. His main objective was to beat off nomad invaders like the Huns."

That also made the route safe for trade, a highway linking imperial China with imperial Rome. The land part of the highway extended over six thousand miles from Xi'an in the east to Tyre on the Mediterranean coast. It included the whole length of the Gansu Corridor from the eastern border of the province to the Jade Gate in the west.

Ever ready to display his knowledge of military detail, Martin remarked, "I don't suppose many people know that in 36 B.C. Chinese soldiers confronted Roman legionnaires midway along that route somewhere in the neighborhood of Samarkand."

Over this highway the Chinese had sent camel caravans laden with bolts of silk. For many centuries they alone possessed the jealously guarded secret of how to make this much coveted fabric. Along the way the precious cargo went through many intermediaries as it was bartered against local products that others considered exotic. In Rome it was used to clothe luxury-loving ladies of wealth in gossamer garments that scandalized some of the older fogies, such as the statesman-philosopher Seneca, who grumbled, "I see silken clothes, if one can call them clothes at all, that in no degree afford protection either to the body or to the modesty of the wearer, and clad in which no woman could honestly say she is not naked."

In return for this foremost commodity in China's international trade, the Chinese received such novel and precious things as jade and lapis lazuli, a special breed of Central Asian horses, and new products such as alfalfa and grapes. The Iranian word for grape was borrowed along with the fruit in 126 B.C., a rare case where it is possible to date precisely when a foreign word entered the Chinese language.

Ideas as well as goods traveled in both directions over the Silk Road. Buddhism entered China from India along this route. Later came Islam and various forms of Christianity. Knowledge of printing was carried westward from China long before Gutenberg.

Among the motley cavalcade of merchants and monks, soldiers and civilian emissaries who traveled over the Silk Road, Marco Polo, of course, stands out as preeminent. At a time unique in human history when Europe and Asia were linked in safety by a Pax Mongolica, he was one of the very few who ever traversed the whole length of the road, and the only one who lived to tell the tale of his three-and-a-half-year journey from the Mediterranean Sea to the Mongol capital near Peking.

In evoking these recollections of things past, we felt some diffidence in including ourselves as latecomers in the procession of travelers over the Silk Road. Bowling along in an army truck instead of trekking along with our camels seemed somehow to bring into question our inclusion in that adventuresome band.

However, although our means of transportation would have been unfamiliar to our predecessors, other travel conditions recalled descriptions of what earlier travelers had had to endure. And so, as we journeyed east over the Silk Road, we felt ourselves to be traveling through time that was both past and present.

When we started off we were honored by the company of the aide-de-camp, who stood on the running board until we passed through the south gate, where he got off, saluted, and turned us over to two officers assigned to escort us along the way.

As soon as the truck got outside of town it had to stop every few hundred yards to negotiate the flimsy wooden bridges thrown over innumer-

Our military truck done in by a "bridge"

able irrigation ditches and small river channels. At one of these bridges a plank gave way under the right rear wheel. We all got off, helped remove part of the load, and lent our efforts to lifting the truck up onto a replacement plank.

Whenever possible we got away from the road rutted by carts of different axle lengths and ventured out into the open gobi that alternated with land irrigated by the succession of little streams that ran off the Southern Mountains. We might have made good time here if we hadn't had two flats.

After a full day on the road we had covered only seventy-five miles. As travel was impossible in the dark, we had to stop in a village, where the solitary inn was able to provide only a miserable meal and worse accommodations. The officers and a civilian took one of the two rooms in the inn. The rest of us crowded into the other room.

The second day we had to negotiate long stretches of sand, got stuck five times in a mile of poorly drained roadways near irrigated land, and lost our way repeatedly thanks to a driver whose sense of direction was as deficient as his competence in driving. Under his less than expert guidance the truck bucked and stalled, accelerated and slowed down erratically, veered suddenly this way and that, yawed left and right to the point where we narrowly missed turning over.

Poor Zhou, who had never ridden in a motor vehicle before, was carsick and scared. He was too timid to assert himself when crowded by the other passengers. Sometimes I was able to make a little more room for him by taking advantage of some bumps to elbow the more obnoxious ones aside. Once I had to reach out and pull him back as he was about to fall out when we hit a particularly bad bump.

Darkness was falling as we crossed the Ganzhou River, which flows north from here to its juncture with the Great North River at Maomu. Finally, after a total run for the day of only seventy-five miles, we arrived at the walled city of Ganzhou.

We were not able to leave the next morning because no gas was available. Nothing to do but wait until a supply arrived from Suzhou. Gross inefficiency.

So we had a lot of time to look around. Ganzhou seemed even more squalid than Suzhou. Streets were in even worse condition, with more open sewage. Many buildings were askew or tumbledown because of an earthquake a few years ago. People seemed even more impoverished and in worse health. There were swarms of emaciated beggars and others walking around with immense goiters protruding from their necks and deep hollows where their noses used to be.

It was hard to imagine that seven hundred years ago, when Marco Polo visited it, this human pigsty was "a very great city and noble." Together with his father, Niccolò, and his uncle Maffeo, for some tantalizingly unexplained reason that he dismisses as "business which is not worth mention," Marco stayed in what he called Campchu for one whole year. He wrote about it in these terms:

> Campchu is a city which is in Tangut itself, which is a very great city and noble; and it is the head and rules all the province of Tangut. And the people of that province are idolaters, and there are some of those who worship Mahomet, and again there are some Christians. And they have in this said town three Churches of Christians very large and beautiful. And in that city the idolaters have many beautiful monasteries and very many abbeys according to their usage & customs. And in these monasteries they have a very great quantity & multitude of idols.
>
> Moreover I tell you they have some of them which are ten paces in size, and more and less. And some are of wood and some of earth or pottery and some of stone, & some of bronze, and they are all covered with gold and very well worked and wonderfully. Of these idols some are less large and some small. These great idols are lying down stretched out and several other small idols are standing around those great ones, and it seems that they do there humility and reverence to them like disciples. And the large idols are much more reverenced than the small.

And because I have not told you all the doings of the idolaters I wish to tell you them here. Now you may know that the regulars of the idolaters who keep a rule live more decently than the other idolaters, for they keep themselves from certain things, namely from sensuality and other improprieties, but they hold it not for a great sin. For this is their opinion, that if a woman invites them in love they can lie with her without sin, but if they invite the woman then they reckon it for a sin. But yet I tell you that if they find any man who has lain with a woman unnaturally they condemn him to death.

Among the great recumbent figures mentioned by Marco Polo was the one we saw in the Giant Buddha Temple that is China's largest reclining Buddha, over a hundred feet in length, with an ear measuring more than six feet. But now there was an air of decay about the temples, and no longer were the figures "all covered with gold."

It was sad to reflect that Gansu in the twentieth century was in worse condition than it had been in the thirteenth. At least its cities were surviving, even if in decay, which was more than could be said for the now completely ruined city of Etsina.

We were able to leave the next morning thanks to the arrival of some gasoline from Suzhou. But our hope of an early departure was frustrated by the need to wait while the notables in our company—the driver, the

two officers, and a fat civilian who shared the cab with the driver—recovered from a night on the town. Zhou said the four of them had spent the night a-whoring at the invitation of Fatty. I had wondered about that civilian. Whenever we stopped he was always the center of a fawning cluster of soldiers.

"Is he a government official?" I asked.

"No," said Zhou, "he's traveling courtesy of the military on personal business."

"What business?"

"Buying girls."

At first I thought I hadn't heard right. Zhou went on to explain that Fatty was traveling along the Corridor to buy girls for brothels. Conditions were good for his business, for although it was not a famine year, still, life was so hard that there were some people whose only hope of survival was to sell their sole possession of any value.

Zhou paused for a long moment. Then he added, "We had to sell our daughter in the big famine of a few years ago."

My insides churned. Now I understood Zhou's hesitation when I had asked him, on that long ago day of our start from the Temple of the Larks, whether he had any children. What, according to the manual of good manners, does one say to a fellow human being driven to sell his own flesh and blood so that other members of the family might have a chance to survive?

I could not keep myself from brooding over the macabre statistics that marked the horrendous terminal stage of a Chinese famine. At that time of descent into the bottom pit of hell, I recalled, living human flesh was sold by the pound, whether as food or as slaves. With pork selling at six dollars a pound, strong boys fetched three dollars a pound. Girls old enough for work or for intercourse were two dollars a pound. Infants brought only a dollar a pound. I wondered despairingly how old Zhou's daughter had been.

When we finally got under way we made good progress over gobi country, except for one short stretch where we got so badly stuck that the soldiers commandeered the labor of a dozen nearby peasants to pull us out. Later we were slowed up as the truck seemed to lose much of its power just as we got to some hills. We labored up these in first. At the steepest point we all got down and helped push the truck through a narrow pass.

Along the way we caught occasional glimpses of the Great Wall that ran parallel to our route on the left. In many places the wall was in ruins, but some towers still stood out clearly. Occasionally there were also mountains on our left, some covered with snow, but lower than the Southern Mountains on our right.

Darkness overtook us on the road, but since there were no stopping places in the area we continued to crawl along. Several times we narrowly missed running off the road into a ditch and were only able to stop in time because of our slow pace.

At ten o'clock we finally pulled up to the locked gate of a little walled town with the bumptious name of Yongchang, or Ever-Prosperous.

"Open the gate!" shouted one of our officers.

A sentry atop the gate peered down at us over the parapet.

"Duck if you see him pouring boiling oil on us," said Martin.

A parley took place, with the sentry yelling down to us while our officers shouted back at him.

It was a long time before we were permitted to enter the sleeping town. With dogs barking at our passage, we drove noisily along the dark streets, stopping to hammer loud and long on several doors before we found an inn that could accommodate us.

It took us until noon to cover the remaining forty-five miles to Liangzhou, the headquarters of the oldest of the three Ma brothers. In light of our experience with Little Brother, we approached this walled citadel with no little apprehension.

At the gate our truck was stopped by soldiers who said it would have to wait outside until word was received that it could enter. While waiting, we saw them making a careful check of all incoming and outgoing traffic. They searched everyone, poked long steel rods into filled sacks, and asked carriers of coal to empty one sack chosen at random. We were told that this was aimed at countering Communist activity.

From the gate the truck made its way to the barracks inside the city. After a brief stop there, Martin and I were taken out through the gate again by our two escorting officers and put up at a nearby inn much like the one in Suzhou. We cleaned up a bit and had a hurried, and worried, lunch, for the officers said that as soon as we were finished they had orders to take us to see General Ma.

The meeting was not as we expected it to be.

We were taken back inside the city to a canopied courtyard where a Chinese opera was being performed before an audience of important-looking civilians and soldiers. Our escorting officers introduced us to General Ma Buqing, who offered us his plump hand in a friendly greeting and invited us to take seats right behind him in the second row. With somewhat smug but puzzled satisfaction we sat back in our comfortable chairs, drinking tea and munching nuts and candy conveniently at hand on a little table covered with a white cloth.

Our surreptitious glances crossed with the same from an audience that was as puzzled at our presence as we were. We certainly stuck out in that crowd in our worn and dirty jodhpurs. Our dress-up clothes, such as my nice white ducks, had long since disintegrated, leaving us only with the sturdier garments that we had worn for months. We didn't let our feeling of crashing a party of swells interfere with our enjoyment of the situation. The tea was a delicate jasmine, my favorite. The play was a gorgeously costumed comedy that was easy to follow.

When the performance was over we were all invited to adjourn to another courtyard where tables had been set out with a feast that had a small army of servitors scurrying all over the place to see to it that no plate was empty and no cup unfilled.

We were placed at a table with several important personages, among them General Ma's aide-de-camp. When dinner was over he gave our escort orders to move our things over to the official guesthouse. We were put up in a beautifully appointed room with two servants to wait on us hand and foot. Zhou was taken to the servants' quarters.

"Do you suppose," asked Martin, "that all this is going to end at midnight?"

In the evening we met several other people who were staying in the guest house. One of them was an English-speaking smoothie whose flattery could not hide his condescension. I wondered if my contempt was as transparent. He said there were seven of them, all Central Government officials comprising a high-level delegation of military and civilian personnel on a trip of inspection to Gansu and neighboring provinces.

"Anyone whose performance is unsatisfactory," he assured us, "will be dismissed."

I did not for a moment accept the official's bombast intended for gullible foreigners. I doubted that these high-living junketeers could recognize misrule if they saw it, or would really be concerned if they did, or could really do anything about it in the unlikely event that they wanted to. They lived in the same country but in a different world from that inhabited by peasants driven by desperation to selling their own daughters. And their fiat certainly did not extend to this warlord satrapy.

Perhaps what incensed me most was Mr. Smoothie's attempt to pass himself off as a cultivated scholar-official distinct from the military men who appeared to dominate the delegation. He seemed anxious to present himself as being in the tradition of the Confucian bureaucracy and thus set apart from the illiterate masses, as well as the military roughnecks who made and unmade regimes.

To my mind, the traditional Confucian scholars, and much of the educated elite that comprised their contemporary sucessors, shared an ideology which at best exhibited a paternalistic concern for the people, a sort of intellectual *noblesse oblige,* and at worst represented the civilian counterpart of military despotism. In either case, the elitist mind-set was not so greatly different from the warlord mentality that excluded truly democratic rule by the people as a whole.

In all the high-blown verbiage that was directed at us, it became apparent that the primary aim of the delegation was to work out a joint policy with the local warlords to counter the threat posed by the Communist advance. In the face of that threat, everyone was eager to put on a show of cooperation and civility, a show that even extended to a couple of foreigners who, though otherwise insignificant, might yet have a useful public relations role. Lucky us!

The next morning we were awakened with the sun, as we were to go riding with the visiting delegation. On entering the guesthouse courtyard, we found a grand assembly that included the seven members of the delegation, the mayor standing in for General Ma as our host, ten smartly dressed soldiers, one for each of us as a personal orderly, and twenty horses snorting and pawing the ground in their eagerness to be off.

The soldiers, who included a junior officer as commander, held a horse for each of us as we mounted. The horse assigned to me seemed particularly keyed up. It pranced about impatiently as my orderly fought to hold it still for the several attempts I had to make before finally succeeding in clambering aboard.

Our cavalcade clattered out along streets where everyone hastened to make way for us and paused to watch our imposing spectacle. We rode at a good steady pace to a temple about two miles from the city. It was much damaged by the great earthquake that had recently shaken a large part of central Gansu.

On the way back someone called out, "Let's race!" I had been riding discreetly toward the rear of our cavalcade among the other less than expert equestrians. My horse was made of more mettlesome stuff, however, and without regard for my wishes decided that it could not suffer the ignominy of coming in last. All I could do was to hold on desperately as it broke into a headlong gallop that bounced me wildly up and down and had me looking down in terror at the hard, hard ground speeding away under the pounding hooves of the horses.

At the halfway mark we—that is, the horse and, incidentally, I too—

had caught up with the middle of our
thundering procession. Within sight of
the city we had outdistanced all but
the officer, who was too worked up
to follow the example of the
other soldiers in letting
the civilians get ahead
of them.

The race had a story-
book finish, in which
my horse, with me still
miraculously aboard,
came in first by a nose.
I wanly accepted
everyone's congratula-
tions. Gilding my un-
deserved lily, Martin
remarked what a nice
tale I would have to tell of
winning a race against the
finest of the famous Dungan
cavalry.

After a breakfast that seemed
more like a dinner, as we
were served several elaborate
dishes accompanied even by "white
dry," Martin and I went to a German
Catholic mission which we were told had some
nuns who did dentistry. I went along to interpret for Martin, because the
discussion about his bad filling had to be carried on in Chinese, our only
common language, as we knew no German and the nuns knew no
English. They turned out to be a jolly group much given to joshing.

"That was a pleasant visit," I said to Martin as we left. He mumbled a
reply.

With Martin's problem attended to, we went to call on two priests who
the nuns said had just returned that morning from a two-week tour of
their converts in the countryside. One of the men spoke English. Over a
relaxing glass of wine he sketched in the history of the mission, which
went back to the middle of the last century, and told us of current conditions in the area.

"Bad," he said. "And getting worse."

The province was being impoverished by exorbitant taxes and exactions levied by the warlords and their civilian henchmen. Peasants had no alternative but to replace grain production with the growing of opium as a higher-priced crop that could be exported to other parts of the country, as well as used locally. The vital irrigation network was breaking down. Social services were nonexistent. Yes, it was true that many peasants were driven to selling their own daughters.

"Others are having a hard time as well," said the priest. "It's hard even for foreigners trying to do business here. Ma Buqing has his hand in everything. Too bad you didn't come here an hour earlier. You could have met a young compatriot of ours. He's in casings, represents one of the biggest sausage concerns in Germany. Maybe you'll run into him yet, as he'll be in Liangzhou a few more days. His name is Heinz Nolden. He complained that he can't make separate deals with merchants in the sheep intestines business. Everything has to go through General Ma. That's hard on Heinz, harder still on the merchants, who see most of their profits going to the general."

The priests had only two-week-old information about the Communist situation.

"Of course we're concerned about that threat," they said, "but we have more immediate problems to worry about."

They informed us that there was fairly good bus service between here and Lanzhou. The next bus was due to leave in two or three days. As soon as we returned to the guest house we asked the staff to arrange for three seats to be reserved for us on the earliest departure. Later the tickets were presented to us courtesy of General Ma Buqing.

In the afternoon we were again invited to a performance of opera excerpts and to another feast afterward. During a pause in the performance, the master of ceremonies mounted the stage to call out our names in greeting and to announce that the next item was in our honor. Ma Buqing sent us a handwritten list of plays with an invitation to choose one to be performed. I made a pretense of studying the list, which was written in an indecipherable scrawl worthy of a doctor's prescription, and picked out a title written with a few simple characters that I could make out as meaning "Seven Hundred Miles." It was full of clamorous sound and animated movement but left us still wondering about what it all had to do with the title.

General Ma came over to the guesthouse the next morning to see the delegation off. He dropped in at our quarters to chat for a few moments.

"Tomorrow, at your convenience, please come and visit me, " he said. "Any time will do."

In the afternoon we paid a courtesy call on the mayor. He impressed us as a nincompoop who had been installed by the general as a ceremonial cipher.

Ma Buqing's quarters were a mile from town in a walled enclosure measuring about a third of a mile on each side. Sentries snapped to attention as we walked through the gate. A soldier escorted us across a courtyard and up the steps of a building fronted by a long veranda. There we were met by a junior officer who ushered us into a room where the general was seated at a desk with a telephone and piles of official-looking papers. These were shoved to the sides to make room for a shoebox-size carton of tea leaves, a quantity of tiny boxes a bit bigger than a cigarette package, and sheets of gaily colored paper and a ball of red ribbon.

"This is a very special kind of tea," the general explained. "Very rare. The delegation brought it. These little packages will make fine gifts."

He continued to occupy himself at his task of making small gift packages of tea while engaging us in a soft-spoken conversation, occasionally turning aside to handle matters presented to him by a secretary.

It turned out that the general was a bird-fancier. The veranda was hung with a row of about fifteen cages containing birds from various provinces. Prominent among them were some tiny parrots from an area close to the border with Burma. The general had heard of Mongolian larks and was much interested in what we had to tell about them.

"It's really too bad," I said, "that we didn't know of Your Excellency's interest earlier. We could have brought you a bird from the Temple of the Larks."

I savored the picture of myself mincing across the desert, bird cage held aloft in a hand with extended pinkie, and hoped the general's smile was in appreciation of what I prided myself was a bit of adroit insincerity.

I was no end embarrassed when the general offered to buy me another pair of pants. He also said he would be glad to help us out with money.

"It is most kind of Your Excellency," we said, "but we really have enough money. Please excuse us for wearing such ragged clothing. We had not thought we would be long enough in one place to have some new things made for us."

The general gave us two autographed portraits of himself and also posed for pictures in his flower-filled garden and on the veranda with the bird cages as background.

We were given a lift back into town by the general. As we prepared to enter the car, we tried to defer to him, but misjudged the time to be given to this delicate maneuver of who should go first. The general gave me an impatient shove as if to say: "Enough of this politeness crap! Get a move on!"

We sat with him on the rear seat. Four soldiers joined us inside, two in front and two facing us on jump seats, their rifles across their laps. Five more armed men accompanied us outside, two standing on the left running board, two on the right running board, and one hanging onto the baggage-carrier in the rear. We felt rather apprehensive at being so well protected.

Heinz Nolden was a fellow passenger on the bus that took us to Lanzhou. He arrived with a mountain of luggage that required his buying another ticket. We smugly told him that we had no problem with tickets because we were traveling as guests of the general.

"You got a better deal from him than I did," he said.

It took two days for our bus to cover the 160 miles to Lanzhou. Progress was slow, because much of our route was through mountainous country that had to be negotiated in first or second gear. In places we crawled through sand or soft loess where the road was so worn down by traffic that the banks of earth on either side towered as high as seventy-five feet.

At one point we passed a huge work-gang engaged in repairing the road. Throughout history it had been gangs like this—chiefly peasants, but also including common criminals and those at odds with the powers that be—that built the Great Wall, and died in droves in the process of doing so. To many Chinese the Long Wall was known as the Long Cemetery. As a scholar writing not long after the First Emperor's frenzy of wall-building noted, "Ditches on the roadside were filled with corpses of men who had been forced into the construction of the Long Wall." No doubt some of the press-ganged peasants we saw would also end up in ditches beside the road they were repairing for their warlord masters.

Martin discoursed at length on the logistics of building walls and roads and pyramids and other immense enterprises with conscript labor using primitive tools. That evoked in my mind a composite picture of workers from different countries and different epochs merging into one huge work-gang engaged in the collective effort of building each of these great works. I wondered if my ancestors had been conscripted to work on the Appian Way. And that, in turn, evoked the incongruous feeling that "There but for the grace of God go I."

The loess soil in the area where we encountered the work-gang was

Road gang in the Gansu Corridor

fine for growing things if only water could be obtained for the thirsty plants. Rain was a chancy thing in this area, where only twelve inches fell each year, but even so, many of the mountain slopes were terraced, thanks to the expenditure of prodigious labor. The loess soil was also fine for digging out homes on hillsides but treacherous because of the perennial threat of earthquakes. Over three hundred thousand people had perished a few years before in one such disaster.

The city of Lanzhou stands in such loess country. At an outpost some distance from it a detachment of soldiers stopped the bus. These were troops under the command of Ma Bufang, the Middle Brother in the Gansu triumverate, whose headquarters were actually in the neigboring province of Koko Nor.

"Everyone out!" an officer commanded.

The soldiers ordered the driver and passengers to unload all the luggage. They checked each piece carefully, pawing roughly through everything if the owners were slow to reveal the contents.

Then we crossed the iron bridge that spanned the Yellow River. We were stopped five times to be asked the same old questions before we finally ended up at the bus terminal.

After a great deal of palaver with an official there, Martin and I were taken into what appeared to be a combined military and political office, where our documents were checked once again and we were subjected to a lot of supposedly subtle cross-questioning. Our passports were taken to another room to be given a more careful scrutiny by some unseen official. At long last our papers were returned to us and we were told that we were free to move about as we pleased.

For some unexplained reason, just before we were released we were shown into a room where we saw a young man, dressed in worn Western clothes and generally unkempt in appearance, who told us he was a Czech from Pilsen by the name of Sedláček. He said he had been detained for six months because his passport was not in order. He claimed to have gotten here by traveling clear across Central Asia. We didn't know what to make of this episode.

We put up at a bare, cold inn that boasted a foreign bed too short for me and just barely long enough for Martin. He took it, while Zhou and I made do with planks placed across some benches.

By now it was so late that all the landlord could scare up for us to eat was some bread and tea. We consoled ourselves with the thought that the next day we would be on our own and could call on a missionary named Keble whom Georg Söderbom had long ago suggested we look up if we passed through Lanzhou. He was said to be the most knowledgeable person in the area. So instead of the rumors and alarums that we had encountered so far we could finally find out what the real situation here was.

22 / *By* Titanic II *Down* "China's Sorrow"

‡‡‡‡‡‡‡‡

Our anxious homeward flight along the Gansu Corridor took place in the context of the Long March of the Chinese Communists that started in October 1934 from their base in the southeastern part of the country. We were worried then, a year after the start of the Long March, that our way back might be cut off by fighting thought to be aimed at either pushing into North China or thrusting west through the Corridor. In fact the Communists did both.

The main force under Mao Zedong ended up in the north at the Yan'an base where the groundwork was laid for the eventual takeover of the whole country. Another detachment, commanded by Mao's arch rival for leadership, tried to march west through the Corridor to the safe haven of Xinjiang, which was under Soviet-leaning General Sheng Shicai. It suffered almost total annihilation in savage fighting with the Dungan cavalry of the Muslim warlords.

A few made it to Xinjiang. Most of those, including Mao Zedong's younger brother, were later killed by chameleon warlord Sheng Shicai when he switched back to Nanking in the belief that the Soviet Union was going down under the Nazi onslaught.

Those warlords are gone now (Sheng joined the Ma clan in fleeing with Chiang to Taiwan), and the railroad they opposed then has since been built, all the way from Xi'an through the Corridor to Xinjiang. These developments have irrevocably altered the power relationship between the Northwest borderlands and the Chinese heartland.

‡‡‡‡‡‡‡‡

We found Keble after walking down a narrow lane to the strangely quiet headquarters of the China Inland Mission. As the local secretary of this major missionary organization, Keble ran an operation of considerable magnitude with skill and efficiency that was much praised by foreigners in China and much used by those traveling in the area. He was a genial, outgoing man who seemed to be genuinely pleased to see us and eager to share news and knowledge and to offer help. Of news he had plenty. Unfortunately, it was mostly bad.

The worst was that the road between Lanzhou and Xi'an had just been cut by fighting between Communist troops driving up from the south and Muslim cavalry belonging to the Big Horse warlords—Ma Buqing, his brother Ma Bufang, who controlled the Lanzhou area from his nearby base in Koko Nor, and Ma Hongkui, who ruled over the Ningxia area.

"Lanzhou itself is in no danger of direct assault," Keble assured us. "The Communists don't have the capacity to take large cities. You may be stuck here for weeks, though, maybe months. There's no telling when the area around here will be pacified and the road east opened up again."

The unexpected irruption of the Communists into this area was the culmination of an amazing march of several thousand miles that had started about a year earlier. At that time, as I was rather vaguely aware, they were located far off in the southeastern part of China.

"They used to have pretty secure bases there," put in Martin. "Then Chiang's German advisers developed a blockade strategy that threatened to strangle them. Last I heard, just before we left Peking, some of them had broken free and were somewhere in the southwest."

Keble said that, in zigzagging dashes that disguised their ultimate objective, separate detachments broke out of the blockade and fought their way thousands of miles west and then north along the Tibetan border. It was only in the past week or so that some elements of those forces had penetrated the area to the east of us. So we had lost our race with the Communists. We were just a few days too late to make it out of there by bus.

"There are only two ways to escape now," said Keble. "One is to fly over the fighting. There's a German-Chinese outfit called Eurasia Airline that's flying a lot of people out. But it's swamped with requests for passage. Still, I'm sure arrangements can be made for you to get out in that way."

"What's the alternative?"

"You can go north by raft down the Yellow River to the railhead at Baotou."

It turned out that we had missed a chance to get out that way by an even narrower margin than in the case of the bus. That very morning the

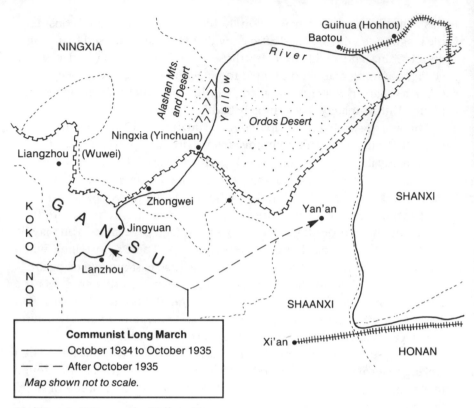

By *Titanic II* Down the Yellow River

last of the women and children of the mission, and most of the men as well, had been evacuated on a large raft that could have taken us, too, if we had arrived at the mission just an hour or so earlier.

I felt like banging my head against the wall in frustration. At the beginning of our travels we had arrived in Guihua too late to join a caravan. Now we had again literally missed the boat.

Well, we had gone off on our own by camel. Could we do the same by raft?

Despite my eagerness to get back to Peking, I felt that the river trip presented itself as a unique oportunity to experience another slice of Chinese life, to learn more about the fabled river that had created both the propitious conditions for the emergence of Chinese civilization and the terrible floods that earned it the name of China's Sorrow.

The Chinese, I knew, traditionally considered floods to be first among the four most dreaded calamities, the others being drought, locusts, and warlords. They feared most the floods of the Yellow River, which in passing through the loose loess soil of China's Northwest picks up enormous amounts of silt, deposits it downstream in beds rising ever higher above the surrounding countryside, and repeatedly breaches the restraining dikes to alter course and inundate immense tracts of China's northern breadbasket.

Martin felt as I did about trying the river trip, especially since we would be going through another part of Mongol-inhabited territory.

"How do we go about arranging for a raft?" we asked.

Keble immediately had a servant run out and fetch a man we later dubbed Admiral Chen. He was a compactly built Chinese of somewhat less than average height whose sober dark clothes and matching skullcap were in keeping with the businesslike manner in which he discussed his business with us. With him there was none of the cloying politeness that often marks interchanges between Chinese and foreigners. He inspired confidence. Keble provided us with a steady stream of information and advice as we negotiated the matter.

We learned that most of the rafts used on the river were made of inflated sheepskins that acted as floats when lashed to a framework of light poles. In the preparation of the floats the sheep were skinned in a special way that minimized the incisions needed to remove the skin from the carcass. The sheepskins were turned inside out, immersed in salt water and a drying oil, and then sewed up and sealed. Inflation was by lung power.

"After they're inflated," Keble cautioned us, "you have to be careful to check them regularly and reinflate them if they're losing air."

Rafts used on the Yellow River ranged in size from small ones of fourteen or fifteen skins capable only of carrying a couple of people in local traffic to immense ones of over six hundred skins that could carry twenty to thirty tons over long distances. The smallest were limited to smooth-flowing sections of the river, as in the vicinity of the city, where it was a common sight to see such rafts floating downstream and being carried upstream. The local people had a saying: "Going downstream, rafts carry people. Going upstream, people carry rafts."

"What size raft do you want?" asked Admiral Chen.

We consulted with Keble. He helped us conclude an agreement with Admiral Chen to provide us a raft of a hundred skins in four days at a price of US$80. This was the smallest raft that could be used with any degree of safety on the river below Lanzhou, where it turns into dangerous rapids as it rushes through mountains north of the city. The price included not just the cost of the raft itself but also the wages of the men who would navigate the craft for us.

Our only additional expenses were for food, cooking equipment, and a couple of mat canopies to provide a bit of shelter. The main item in our food supply was ordinary millet, not the parched variety favored by desert travelers. Cooking would be done on a stove improvised from a five-gallon gasoline can lined with clay and fueled by charcoal briquets. The stove proved to be not very efficient and the charcoal briquets not as good as the nice camel-dung briquets we had used in the desert.

Admiral Chen said that, counting all the twists and turns of the river, he estimated the distance to Baotou to be almost twelve hundred miles, and he assured us that his men would get us there in twelve days. Our agreement stipulated that we would give them M$2 for each day under twelve, and that they would be docked the same amount for each day over that.

While we waited for the raft to be built, Keble sent me to have my innards checked by his colleague Dr. Vaughan Rees in the missionary-run hospital located across the river near a leper colony. The diagnosis was worms and amoebic dysentery. Treatment included a three-day sequence of shots and a stern lecture from Dr. Rees about the danger to foreigners of going native in their eating habits.

Heinz Nolden dropped in to say his company had arranged for him to fly to Xi'an. He wished us luck.

Our completed raft was a 12-by-18-foot affair made up of ninety-six sheepskins, with four more as spares. They were tied to the framework of lashed-together poles in sixteen rows, six to a row, with the long side across the width of the raft. The legs were uppermost, since it was through them that we had to blow in air.

Down the central length of the raft was a six-foot-wide platform made up of tightly interwoven twigs of willow. The areas on both sides of it were left uncovered for ease in checking the inflated skins and blowing them up as needed.

At opposite ends of the matted central platform were the two canopied shelters, each roughly 6 by 6 feet, that were to be our living quarters for the next two weeks. Martin and I occupied one end, Zhou and the crew the other. The space in between was taken up with the stove, miscellaneous equipment, and provisions.

To my landlubber's eye our craft seemed a rather jerry-built piece of nautical construction.

"It's built on the same principle as the *Titanic,*" Keble said.

"Oh, great!"

"But these rafts are actually superior in design," Keble added. "The *Titanic* was built with sixteen watertight compartments. Your raft has ninety-six. The people who designed the *Titanic* made a fatal mistake. They couldn't imagine anything worse than a collision at the juncture of any two compartments, and so they designed it to stay afloat if any two were flooded. What actually happened was that the collision with the iceberg tore a three hundred-foot gash that ripped open the first six watertight compartments." *NOT FACT — ACTUALLY. SUB STD. RIVITING 4'–6' ONLY.*

"That's between a third and a half," Martin said. "No wonder it went down."

"You have no icebergs to worry about," Keble gaily pointed out. "Well, yes, there are rocks in the river, but still and all, I bet your raft will stay afloat even if half of its skins get stove in."

For most of our voyage down the river there would be five of us aboard. At the start, however, we would have two additional men. Admiral Chen said he was going to accompany us with one more man to help us through the worst of the rapids that we would be running into the very first day. After that the crew would consist only of two brothers called Ho the Elder and Ho the Younger.

These were two younger men neatly clad in the same manner as Admiral Chen in what was a Dungan outfit of respectable everyday wear. They were a quiet lot, not exactly reserved but still rather unassuming, as if they knew this to be their proper demeanor.

Admiral Chen and Ho the Elder stepped carefully over the wooden framework to a position on the left front corner of the raft. The other two men positioned themselves at the right rear corner. At these diagonal corners were long flattened poles mounted on spikelike oarlocks.

"They're actually long sweeps that function more like rudders or steering-oars than conventional oars," said Keble. You can't really row in this river. It runs too fast. All you can do is try to take advantage of the different currents to nudge the raft in one direction or another."

We shoved off shortly before noon to the accompaniment of Keble's cheery good wishes. I mentally broke a bottle of "white dry" against the side of the raft and christened it *Titanic II*. The numeral II, I fervently hoped, would represent an advance in seaworthiness over the namesake, not mere succession.

The river was wide only in the immediate vicinity of the city. It soon began to narrow and within less than fifteen miles was sharply constricted into the beginning of a gorge that was heralded by a thunderous

Admiral Chen on *Titanic II*

roar ahead. Our speed suddenly accelerated as the raft was swept down between cliffs rising sharply from the water.

   To our untrained eyes, the river ahead seemed to be a single, massive flow sweeping us steadily downstream. In fact, as we soon discovered, the river was a deadly confusion of currents, and our lives hung on Admiral Chen's mastery of them, his quickness of mind in maneuvering among them, and his crew's fine-tuned teamwork under his direction.

We were immediately plunged into the most dangerous section of the river, a chaotic, churning, swirling, rushing, frenzied bedlam called the Lord's Cauldron. The raft whirled and writhed underfoot like a thing alive, wood ground against wood, ropes screaked in protest under the strain, water leaped over the edges of the raft, wind buffeted the canopies and threatened to tear them away.

Admiral Chen issued rapid-fire commands in banshee screams that could barely be heard above the constant roar of water reverberating against the rock walls. All four men were marvels of strength and dexterity as they whipped the sweeps about in practiced unison while dancing with almost choreographed steps on the slippery footing of the poles.

In our less exposed central location Martin, Zhou, and I crouched down to maintain our balance on the matted platform. Martin snapped picture after picture, as the cliffs rushed up at us and then pivoted away at the last possible moment. I bellowed out the "Volga Boatman" with the bravado of a lone urchin whistling past a graveyard in midnight darkness.

With dizzying speed we swept past cliff after cliff, one undercut to leave a projection called Wolf's Tongue, others where there were heart-stopping moments when the men saved us from smashing into the sheer rock walls by nudging us, just in time, into another current that spun us end around end and even sent us upstream for short distances as the onrushing water careened into the face of the cliff and then reeled back from the shock.

After a brief respite in an open area where we saw immense water-wheels raising water from the river for irrigation, we plunged into the boiling cauldron of the second gorge. In places the churning water formed whirlpools that sometimes stood stationary, sometimes ran downstream with the current. We were caught in one of the stationary whirlpools for an eternity that actually lasted only five or ten minutes. In that time we went round and round several times, while just out of reach the main current rushed headlong downstream. At one point we teetered on the edge of the vortex and seemed about to regain the current, only to slip back into our circular pattern.

Admiral Chen told us later that he was once caught in this very spot for two whole hours while taking a group of missionaries down on a big heavily loaded raft. He said they had managed to get out of it only after the missionaries had offered up prayers.

The two raft episodes reminded me of Edgar Allen Poe's "Descent into the Maelstrom." Perhaps his story explained the difference between our little light raft and the big heavy one of the missionaries. In that account

Approaching the second gorge

of ships and debris being sucked far down into a whirlpool and ground to bits on the rocks at the bottom, only Poe's Norwegian narrator survived the wreck of his ship by lashing himself to an empty watercask that floated at the top of the maelstrom and finally made it back into safer water.

As we were swept downstream it often seemed as if our way was blocked by an impassible barrier of cliffs. We had the illusion of constantly running toward the closed end of a horseshoe. But in its sudden twists and turns the river always found an opening and swept us past jutting masses of stone with such names as Big Screen and Little Screen. The names were at once poetic and apt, for they referred to the "spirit screens," screenlike walls erected just inside the gate of a house to keep out evil spirits that can only travel in straight lines.

Seventy-five miles from Lanzhou and a little past Little Screen, the gorge opened up enough to make room for a few houses on each side of the river at a place called Western Sands Pass. Half a dozen large oxskin rafts that Admiral Chen said carried tobacco, opium, and wool were moored there. It was as if nature had made a convenient stopping place as a reward for those who had made it through the two most dangerous gorges in the river.

Not all were so lucky as to get through safely. As we joined the rafts someone called out the news to Admiral Chen. One of the rafts had run into the rocks at Big Screen. Sixty chests of tobacco went overboard. One man fell into the river and was drowned. His body had not been recovered.

We moored among the commercial behemoths that made our puny raft look like an impertinent intruder. Here we said goodbye to Admiral Chen and thanked him for getting us through the gorges. Along with the rest of his crew he went off to spend the night at an inn that put up some of the men from the rafts, especially those who served as extra hands for the trip through this section of the gorges. After staying overnight they would walk back the much shorter land distance of forty miles to Lanzhou.

We had to wait a long time for our inefficient stove to heat water for tea.

"At least we don't have to worry about dying of thirst," said Martin. "And this river water won't have the taste of sulphur and salt."

Yes, our tea did taste better than what we had had in the desert, though I still would have preferred it Mongol style, with some added "milk-skin" cheese. Our supper was as Spartan as ever, with only a couple of cold steamed rolls in addition to the tea.

On the other rafts the crews were also having supper and relaxing after the day's run. Shadowy figures appeared in the feeble light of lanterns that flickered among the flotilla. A small group of men squatted around a cheerful campfire on the shore. Lively chatter and occasional bursts of laughter came from them and from others on the rafts. From somewhere among them came the plaintive sound of a Chinese flute. A full moon rose over the surrounding hills with majestic slowness and cast a silvery path across the river. The sounds about us gradually subsided.

Martin preferred sleeping on the ground, so I had one of the canopied shelters all to myself. Zhou took the other. A foot below me as I lay snug in my sheepskin sleeping bag the Yellow River lapped softly at the floats that rocked me gently to sleep.

We were off at dawn with Ho the Elder at the front station and Ho the Younger at the one in the rear. Toward the end of the small open area where our stop was located we passed a Buddhist temple perched on a rocky promontory on the left bank. As we drifted by in the early morning haze, the tolling of a mellow-toned bell came to us across the river.

The temple stood at the entrance to our third gorge. Here the rapids were not as swift nor the mountains quite so high. Yet it was a stretch of imposing beauty whose grandeur made us feel like mites on a leaf bobbing along on a mountain torrent. In spite of the cold, we preferred to stand braced against the canopy so that we could take in the view.

The men handled our passage through the gorge without too much difficulty. Beyond it they brought the raft to an open area of hills and cultivated valleys dominated by a walled town with the typical frontier name of Jingyuan, or Subdue Remote Regions. Ho the Elder drew our attention to some caves cut into the hills.

"Bandit hideouts," he said. "Bandits everywhere here."

As it began to grow dark the two men started to look for a good stopping place. They passed several that seemed fine to us.

"Too dangerous," said Ho the Elder. "Bandits."

We pushed on through this area of bandit lairs to the beginning of still another gorge. Here we could not see clearly fifty yards ahead in the gathering gloom.

The men gave us cause to wonder if they knew what they were about when a huge rock loomed up suddenly in our path. Ho the Elder screamed a frantic order and both men dug in furiously with their sweeps to avoid crashing into it. The river rushed the raft past the rock with only inches to spare and then swept us down through a rock-strewn area at such a pace that the men missed a couple of good stopping places because they could not maneuver out of the swift current in time.

Just as the deepening dusk was getting us really worried, the men were able to maneuver into a place they said was safe from bandits. The river was only about a hundred feet wide here and ran swiftly with a constant roar. They tied the raft to an outcropping of rock on a narrow ledge just wide enough to step on but not wide enough to serve as a resting place. So we all had to sleep on board. Martin and I had one canopied area, Zhou and the Ho brothers the other.

Underneath us our fragile craft, in constant motion from the buffeting of the torrent, strained at its mooring like a leashed dog eager to run free. My last thought as I drifted off to sleep was to hope that the raft would not break loose and take us hurtling through the chaos of the pitch-dark gorge.

In the morning we had hardly awakened before the men had the raft under way. They called out a greeting as we passed a big raft that had also sought the safety of the gorge and was getting ready to resume its journey.

In passing through the end of this gorge we rounded a steep, high cliff of sandstone where a huge cave had been carved out by the river to such a depth that the roof seemed about ready to crash down into the water. We were told this was the Cliff of the Goddess of Mercy.

The goddess got us safely through the fifth and last gorge into the beginning of the ever-widening section of the river where the water ran at a slower pace. But then we ran into foul weather. Rain pelted down and wind slowed our progress to such an extent that at times we had to run ashore and wait for a lull in the storm.

Our canopies were not waterproof. Nor had we thought to provide ourselves with enough rainwear and waterproof covering. By late afternoon we were all wet and cold and miserable and ready to join the crews of other rafts that had sought the shelter of inns along the shore of the river.

We were now close to the major walled town of Zhongwei, once a military outpost whose name meant Middle Defense. It was located two miles from the river in an area of intense cultivation made possible by bringing in water from the river. The people here had the saying, "Don't rely on Heaven, rely on the Yellow River."

We heard there were some missionaries in the town, so after leaving Zhou at the inn to look to the drying out of our things, we walked over the muddy road in search of them. To our surprise there was no challenge to us either at the riverfront settlement or on our entry through the gate of the town. We found quite a group of missionaries, who had assembled at this staging point in their flight from the threat of a Communist thrust through here. They were waiting for a raft to evacuate them down the river. We were cordially welcomed by a missionary named Muir who seemed to be the local host.

"Stay for dinner," he urged.

We didn't need much persuasion, though we had really come mainly for news.

"The whole region around here is under the control of Ma Hongkui," said Muir. "He's one of the Muslim warlords, you know, a Dungan. We've been visited recently by some Japanese on a mapmaking expedition."

"Here already?! Last we heard they were just beginning to operate in the area north of Guihua."

"Yes. The Dungans aren't quite sure what stand to take about the Japanese penetration. But for the time being they're working with the Central Government. Right now General Ma is off somewhere fighting the Communists. We don't know exactly where that is, but you know, of course, that they've just cut the Lanzhou–Xi'an route. It's not clear where they're going next."

After having a pleasant dinner with the missionaries and laying in enough provisions to last a few days, we rode back through the cold rain to the inn on horses provided by our hosts. Muir and another missionary accompanied us there. Wrapped in our long sheepskin cloaks, we looked like medieval figures as we rode along the dark streets with Muir in the lead, holding a lantern aloft.

We found the inn crowded with men from the rafts who, like us, were seeking shelter from the miserable weather. One of them, a friend of the Ho brothers, crowded in with the five of us in our small room. This was largely taken up with a brick-bed warmed by a fire under it. Our sheepskin coats were almost wet through, but none of us had any bedding or change of clothes. We all squeezed onto the communal bed wrapped in our dank garments.

At best, sheepskins have a strong odor. When wet and heated, they stink. At first the brick-bed felt nice and warm beneath us as we began to thaw out. Then, as the heat permeated our clothes, they began to steam and smell. Our ever-companionable lice were warmed to the point of flensing us with increased vigor. We steamed slowly throughout the night. By morning we were baked dry.

A few miles below our less than restful stop at the inn we passed several large, flat-bottomed scows with furled sails hanging at their masts. They were being pulled upstream by a long line of untrousered men wading along the shallow edge of the river, their bodies bent over so far that their fingertips were touching the water.

These boats went up and down the river between Zhongwei and Baotou. Going downstream, they floated with the current. Going upstream, they unfurled their sails to take advantage of strong winds blowing down from the north that enabled them to sail against the current. When the wind failed, trackers took over.

The scows carried chiefly opium down to Baotou. As we had learned from the missionaries, this was the main crop in the area, taking up 60 percent of the cultivated land. High taxes and rents forced the peasants to raise opium. Grain that could be grown locally was instead imported from Baotou and brought back on the return trips of the scows.

We were surprised to hear from the Ho brothers that some scows even got beyond Zhongwei, all the way up to Jingyuan. It didn't seem possible that anything could go upstream through the gorges between those towns. But then we remembered the terrible illustrations and descriptions we had seen of 120-ton boats being pulled up through the perilous gorges of the Yangtze River by long lines of harnessed men hunched over with hands almost touching the granite floor of the narrow tracking galleries, only two feet high, cut out of the sheer cliff face.

The memory of those human draft-animals was to imprint itself in my

mind as a metaphor for China straining to pull itself forward against the dead weight of its past.

It took three months for boats to make the trip from Baotou to Jing-yuan, the men said, adding that not many attempted it. None at all tried to go beyond Jingyuan to Lanzhou.

From here on north, the river flowed at a rather sedate pace through land that was largely desert except where water could be brought in for irrigation. In places it cut through loess that had been deposited either by the river itself or by winds blowing in from Mongolia over countless eons of time. Here the river was undercutting steep banks of loess in a process of erosion that was almost frightening.

I had thought that the notorious problem of silt in the Yellow River, which I learned later has thirty-four times that of the Nile and sixty times that of the Mississippi, was due to the gradual absorption of silt into the river as it flowed through loess country. But here we saw the river cutting down huge cliffs of loess that crashed into it in such solid masses as to cause waves we had to avoid by keeping to the other side. It was no ordinary problem of silting that caused the calamities of China's Sorrow.

On our right, after passing a segment of the Great Wall where it came down to the river, we encountered the beginning of the Ordos Desert. (*Ordos,* Mongolian for "camp," is the source of the English "horde.") In places dunes came right down to the water's edge. Far off to the left was the range of mountains called the Alashan, which also gave its name to another big desert on the west bank.

"Some day," said Martin, "I'm going to make a trip to that area to see if they're really building the temple we gave a contribution to back on the Black River."

"Be careful if you go through the Ordos," I said. "Remember what a hellhole Torgny said it was when he traveled there with Lattimore to attend the festival of Genghis."

"I know. Still, I'd like to visit it sometime when they hold that festival. You know Genghis died somewhere near here."

This whole area was of special interest to Martin. Genghis Khan died near Ningxia, across the river from the Ordos, after defeating the last ruler of the Tangut empire, whose capital was in that area. Each year the Mongols hold a great festival at a sanctuary in the Ordos where they say he sleeps in a resplendent casket until the time comes for him to awaken.

This was a terrible place for the dead and a worse place for the living. Much of the Mongol land in the Ordos, poor as it was, had been sold by their princes to the Chinese or forcibly taken from them. It was a dog-eat-dog land. Dispossessed Mongols hovering uncertainly between marginal herding and even more marginal farming. Chinese famine refugees imported as tenants paying up to two-thirds of their crops as rent. Rapacious soldiers drifting in and out of outright banditry. A brutal land and a brutalized people who preyed on each other for want of more rewarding prey or more peaceful alternatives.

"What a difference from the time of Marco Polo!" Martin said.

Yes, the Venetian had a vastly different impression from ours when he traveled from Ganzhou to Ningxia and on east. Along the way he found people who "lived by trade and had crafts of both gold and silk and had an abundance of all kinds of grain." A province where in twenty-five days of travel he found all the land very fertile. Noble cities and villages. The finest musk in the world. Pheasants twice the size of those in Italy.

And beautiful women. Marco was a lusty young man of nineteen or twenty at this stage of his journey. Sandwiched in among details of travel and the lives of the people we find the observation that the women of the area "are very well made in all respects" and "have no hair anywhere on the body except the head."

We didn't see any beautiful women, but then, we didn't have much opportunity to do so, thrown in as we were only with men who plied the river. The Ho brothers were typical of this lot, small, wiry men casually performing prodigious feats in handling rafts but with little in their lives except danger and small rewards.

No wonder that they found solace in the dreamworld of opium. Once we had gotten out of the gorges the men began to take time out by tying up ashore to have a pipe or two, and to sleep off the effects. Here the wind was already slowing our progress. The added time they took out meant further delay. It was in vain that we urged them on and reminded them of the agreement with Admiral Chen to get us to Baotou within twelve days.

In resignation, one day I decided to see what it was like to smoke opium. Ho the Elder prepared a pipe for me. We lay facing each other, propped up on our elbows, with the opium equipment between us. This included a little alcohol lamp, a dish of sticky opium that looked like molasses, a pointed instrument the length of a knitting needle, and a long-stemmed pipe with a tiny porcelain bowl. Ho impaled a bit of opium on the end of the instrument and twirled it over the little flame until it puffed up into a bubble and burst, leaving a dry residue about the

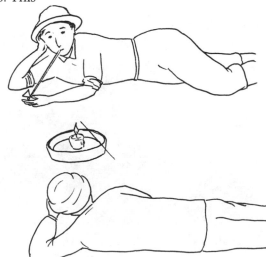

size of a pea. He inserted this into my pipe and instructed me to suck in
the opium in deep breaths.

At this point I saw myself as the emaciated addict on the billboards
prominently displayed in Peking as part of the government's public relations campaign against the drug. So instead of deeply inhaling the smoke
to get it into my lungs, I took it only into my mouth in a few shallow
puffs. I didn't like the stuff anyway. It had a sickly sweet taste and a smell
like hot tar. So I didn't get to dream away the tedium of our slackened
drift down the river.

The wind slowed the progress of our light craft to such an extent that
we were passed by heavier rafts. Once one of the men on a large raft took
pity on us and threw us a rope so we could be towed along. That arrangement ended when the big raft ran aground on a sandbar in the middle of
the river and we cast ourselves loose to continue our slow drift downstream.

At one of our stops Ho the Elder reported the news that three days earlier river pirates from the Ordos had held up three flat-bottomed boats,
killed two men, and made off with M$4,000-worth of goods. He advised
hurrying through here by continuing through the night instead of tying
up to sleep.

In the dark of the moonless night we spoke in whispers as the men
dipped the oars quietly in the water to keep us in the middle of the river.

Our raft near the end of the river trip

We passed the flickering light of campfires on both banks. Occasionally we heard the distant voices of men and saw indistinct figures moving about.

As we progressed north and then east around the great northern bend of the Yellow River, the wind blew colder and harder and slowed our progress still more. It was especially cold at night. Martin and I were more or less comfortable in our sleeping bags, where we sometimes remained for hours even during the daytime as the best way to keep warm. Zhou further pampered us with the luxury of breakfast in bed. The two brothers were more lightly clad and more exposed as they stood by the oars. We invited them to help themselves to our "white dry" to warm themselves during the night. I woke up at one point to hear laughter from the other canopied area. Later I woke again to complete quiet. The men had fallen asleep and the raft was drifting along on its own in the middle of the river. In this area the river was quite wide. There were no campfires on the river banks. I went back to sleep.

At long last, around noon on the fourteenth day after our start, we came within sight of Baotou. But as we were about to approach it, the wind whipped up in sudden fury and blew us across to the other bank. It was maddening to see our goal so close and yet so out of reach.

Along with a number of men from other rafts who were similarly stranded we sought shelter in an inn that evidently catered to carters as well as river people. They were a rough-looking lot who wore dirty towels around their heads as turbans. Most of them seemed to be preoccupied with eating from a huge pot in the middle of the room that was tended by a wizened old man.

Zhou explained the eating arrangement here. Each person gave the old man a quantity of millet and a few coppers to pay for cooking it in the same big pot. Somehow everyone was able to keep track of how much each person had contributed and was entitled to eat. We had Zhou go fetch some of our millet and soon joined the others in wolfing down our share from the common pot.

Just as we were finishing, Ho the Elder rushed in to tell us that a big scow was going to try to cross the river. We dashed down to help throw our things onto it and jostle our way aboard along with innumerable passengers, five donkeys, two horses, two cows, a number of carts, and miscellaneous merchandise.

Several men, including Ho the Elder and other passengers, joined the crew in working the two huge oars. This operation involved not just

drifting with the river but actually rowing across it in the teeth of what was almost a gale. Near the end where we were standing the captain strained at the rudder and bellowed out a raucous cadence of orders to guide the eight men operating each of the oars.

The scow made it, finally, a bit downstream from the city. We followed a tout who urged us to stay in his fancy-sounding Baotou Hotel, where we got a passable room with the luxury of three cots. There we paid off Ho the Elder, giving him a two-day bonus although we were actually two

Journey's end

days late. He was profuse in his thanks and left us with a warm good-bye as he went to join his brother for the eight hundred-mile walk back to Lanzhou.

For our part, we prepared to end our travels with a comfortable train ride back to Peking.

23 / "Two Flat-footed Fools"

‡‡‡‡‡‡‡‡

Not long ago I attended a lecture on the role of chance in everything from the lives of individuals to the workings of the universe. The topic struck home.

It was chance that led me to room next to Winston Pettus in college. It was chance again that brought Martin to Peking just when I was there. And Kay. And George Kennedy. And Owen Lattimore.

And of course it was chance, of the kind that the French call *bonne chance,* meaning "good luck," and not clever planning or forethought on our part, that brought us through the countless occasions in our travels when things might have gone disastrously wrong.

Looking back, I've often wondered whether we were right in entrusting ourselves so much to *bonne chance.* Or were we, as some called us then, just "two flat-footed fools"?

‡‡‡‡‡‡‡‡

We stopped overnight at Guihua to see Georg and Torgny, only to find out from Brita that both were away on business. Torgny had gone up north with Arash to look at some camels. Georg was in Peking.

"Look for him in the Peking Hotel," said Brita. "He makes that his headquarters on trips to the city."

Brita fed us as if she was trying to make up for the lost time since we were here last. She almost made it seem that we had not really left, that we were still impatiently waiting for our camels to be brought to us.

Zhou went off to his own home. He came back in the morning to take us there for a visit. His home was neat and clean, though not much better furnished than the peasant hovels we had met with in our travels. His family consisted only of his wife and mother. The women didn't just outnumber him: both gave the impression of figuratively as well as literally wearing the pants in the family. They were neatly dressed in outfits much like Zhou's, including baggy trousers gathered in tight just above the ankle. His wife was a thin, worn-looking woman taller than Zhou and with unbound feet. His mother was a leathery crone less than five feet tall, who hobbled about on "Golden Lilies."

We apologized to the two for keeping Zhou away from home so much longer than expected. They both made ritual comments about his failure to serve us adequately. We countered with ritual praise. Not entirely ritual, though. We told them, heaping it on to give him greater face, what a help he had been in everything. For the most part we really meant it.

Zhou took us to visit several Mongol temples that we had missed earlier. He also helped me buy a deep-toned camel bell as a memento of our trip. Then we parted. Zhou trudged homeward to resume a life that perhaps, like that of a worn-out camel, would some day be "thrown away" in the desert.

As our train approached Peking, the Gobi and the Corridor and the River seemed to recede farther and farther away in time as well as distance. It hardly seemed real that our trip had lasted almost half a year, from May 15 to October 31, and had covered almost four thousand miles.

"Are you sorry it took so long?" Martin asked.

"In a way, yes. Yet even that frustrating month in Suzhou wasn't a total waste. It sure taught us something about warlordism and how hard it is to get things done in this country. How about you?"

"Well, I've never been in a hurry, you know. I wouldn't have missed any of it. It's all added to my appreciation for Genghis Khan's military achievements. And for that unparalleled Pax Mongolica."

"So you've gotten the background you wanted for the work you plan to do?"

"Definitely. I'm anxious to get on with it. And to do some more traveling in Mongolia. What has all this meant for you?"

"A lot of things. Among others, getting rid of my colds. You know, if people ask me why I made the trip, I suppose I'll really have to start my answer with 'Because I had a cold.' "

"That's silly."

"Not entirely. And of course I got a lot more out of it than just building up my resistance to colds."

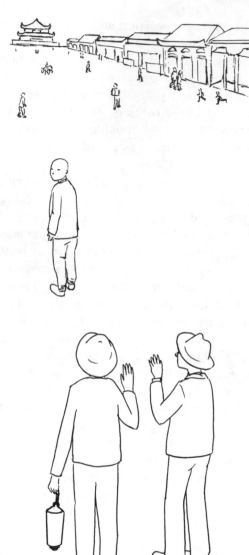

"Such as?"

"New experiences. Some feeling for life at the grassroots level. A keener recognition of the gulf between the rulers and the ruled, between the educated and the uneducated. A sharper perspective on myself. And above all, a purpose."

"A purpose?"

"Yes. Before the trip, I was sort of marking time, unsure what to do with my life. Now I know. I want to direct it first toward learning more, understanding more, about this country, and then toward helping others to understand it. And though I don't know how yet, maybe I'll even be able to contribute a bit toward dealing with some of its problems. Perhaps that's presumptuous. But I'm haunted by Zhou's having had to sell his daughter, by the terrible misery we've seen, by the way people are ground down by those warlord swine and others who lord it over them."

"So what are your immediate plans?"

"Find a place to live. Find a part-time job. Find a teacher to help me with reading. And mend some fences."

Martin looked surprised. "You mean Mr. Pettus?"

"Oh, no. That's over with. It's Kay Wilson. You remember I told you about getting off on the wrong foot with her. When we left she still had me pegged as a bad-tempered bookworm."

"Well, you are pretty short-tempered at times, you know. Especially if you're interrupted at your work."

"I think I was making some progress before we left. But I don't know how things stand now."

I soon found out. We went directly from the train station to the hotel in the hope of arriving there in time for a late lunch. The hotel staff wasn't sure we looked respectable enough to be admitted. No wonder. I was still wearing my battered sun helmet and my lice-ridden sheepskin coat, and Martin didn't look much more prepossessing. A waiter sent to check out the dining room reported that it was empty except for two people who had finished eating and were just sitting there talking. He was told to take us to the other end of the room.

As we trailed after the waiter Martin said, "This feels like those times when people were warned of approaching lepers by cries of 'Unclean! Unclean!' "

For half a second I thought that was what was being called out as we entered the dining room. Instead it was cries of welcome from the two diners. They were Georg Söderbom and Kay Wilson.

While we ate they filled us in on the news.

"I did a little traveling in Mongolia this summer too," said Kay. "Georg arranged for me to visit Duke Larson's ranch with several of my friends. We rode horses and camels, watched wrestling and horse-racing, and ate around a big fire where they cooked a whole ox. It was great fun."

"You've seen some things we haven't," I said.

"We were just talking about arranging for another group of Kay's friends to visit the ranch," said Georg. "This is the third. Larson should start giving her a commission. The two of you have helped to spark interest in Mongolia. You're famous, you know."

"Some people would say notorious," said Kay.

"Well, anyway, there's been a lot of publicity about you. The news accounts sure had it garbled. Even the *New York Times* got things wrong by relying on the wire services. They said Lanzhou was a Communist stronghold, and that you were being detained for your own protection from proceeding there by the 'provincial authorities.' "

"Ah, yes, those dear warlords. Sounds like a garbled version of Nanking's sanitizing them as solicitous provincial authorities."

"People here are divided about you," Kay said. The *Chronicle* referred to you as students at the College of Chinese Studies. Mr. Pettus denied you were students at his school, said you were just 'two flat-footed fools.' "

"That's a libel," I muttered. "We're not flat-footed."

"Kay and I wrote a letter to the editor in reply," said Georg. "So did several other people. We said you were like a couple of Columbuses."

"To change the subject," Kay said, "I have a message to you from Hal Hansen. He said if I ran across you to tell you he thought you'd be looking for somewhere to live and is holding a place for you in the house he found recently."

"Terrific. Do you have any details?"

"Yes. It's a five-room furnished house with three servants. One's a cook. He's prepared to serve both Chinese and foreign food. Each of you pays US$17 a month."

"Fantastic! Are you sure? I know the cost of living is low—but that low?"

"Yes. I checked it carefully with Hal. Maybe one reason is that the place belongs to a Christian lady, a Mrs. Yang, who Hal says has a soft heart for struggling young foreigners she considers sympathetic to China."

"Do you know where it is?"

"Near the Temple of the Goddess of Mercy, at a place called Huang Tu Da Yuanr."

"Yellow Earth Great Courtyard. I like that."

"Hal said you can move in right away. They'll be expecting you."

"The Goddess sure must be looking out for me."

After moving in with Hal I often had the place all to myself, as he went out a lot in connection with his work. He was free-lancing, setting himself topics to look into, writing them up, and then peddling them to various publications. He was turning himself into a first-rate reporter.

I settled into a pleasant routine of improving my reading by a program that included working on my translation of *Chinese Agent in Mongolia.* On one of the few occasions when we had any further contact with each other, Martin introduced me to Owen Lattimore, the leading specialist on Mongolia, to help me deal with a lot of Mongolian terms and references I couldn't handle by myself or with the aid of a teacher I hired.

And I saw more of Kay. We occasionally went dancing at the Peking Hotel—in the ballroom in cold weather, on the roof when it was warm enough. One could spend the whole evening nursing a single drink. We traveled around largely by bicycle. Once, on a more important date, I called for her in a horse-drawn cart that the Chinese sometimes used to transport brides-to-be for their weddings.

Kay invited me to her place one evening to meet her cousin Jean Wilson Kennedy and husband, George. Jean was also born in India. George, another missionary offspring, was born in Shanghai and grew up speaking Shanghainese as a second native language, and then also Standard Chinese, giving him command of two of what the Chinese miscall dialects but are really separate languages, as distinct as French and Italian.

George was a short, intense man who discussed scholarly matters with a marvelous combination of profound knowledge and informal style free of the usual academic jargon. A recent Ph.D. graduate from a German university that was a leading center of sinology, he said he was starting up a new Chinese language program at Yale under a grant from the Rockefeller Foundation. His visit to China was aimed at acquiring books and other materials for his program.

"My prize acquisition" he said, "is a font of Chinese type."

I had to confess my ignorance of what that meant.

"Well, for English you need type for twenty-six letters, double that for caps and small letters, plus numerals and a few other symbols. There are no typesetting machines for Chinese. Printing establishments have to stock type not for twenty-six letters but for seventy-five hundred different characters."

"That many!"

"English type can be contained in a single tray. My Chinese type, which I plan to use to prepare some language-teaching materials, will take up the whole of a big room in the basement of the graduate school in Harkness Hall. You need to have good legs to be a typesetter in Chinese. All day long you have to walk back and forth, back and forth among the racks of type trays to pick out each piece you want for whatever you're setting up."

"Sounds inefficient."

"It is. The Chinese writing system is one of China's biggest problems."

"The Chinese don't seem to think so."

"You're right, they don't. That's part of the problem. A *big* part of the problem. They have all sorts of myths about their language and their writing system. So do westerners. The writing system is undemocratic, too difficult for mass literacy, *real* literacy. And it's very inefficient, unsuited to modern technology, such as touch-typing on a typewriter keyboard."

"Hmm."

"I hope everything I've bought here will arrive in New Haven in time to start up in the fall of 1936. That's when our program is slated to begin. We'll be looking for students then."

Hmm again.

In the summer of 1936 Kay went off to India to teach for a year in the school that her parents had founded there. I went back to Yale to start a program of graduate study. Before parting we agreed to meet in New Haven after she had fulfilled her commitment in India.

We looked forward to ringing my camel bell together to remind us of our travels in Mongolia.

About the Author

John DeFrancis, emeritus professor of Chinese at the University of Hawaii, spent three years studying and traveling in China after graduating from Yale University in 1933. He returned to the United States to earn his M.A. and Ph.D. degrees from Columbia University and embarked on a teaching career at several institutions. He is the author of scores of articles and two dozen books, among which are a widely used series of language texts for teaching spoken and written Chinese and the revisionist *The Chinese Language: Fact and Fantasy* and *Visible Speech: The Diverse Oneness of Writing Systems*. His works on Asian sociolinguistics also include *Nationalism and Language Reform in China* and *Colonialism and Language Policy in Viet Nam*. His miscellaneous works range from *Chinese-English Glossary of the Mathematical Sciences* to *Things Japanese in Hawaii*. He is currently involved in a project to compile a ground-breaking alphabetically based computerized Chinese-English dictionary.

Production Notes

Composition and paging were done on the
Quadex Composing System and typesetting
on the Compugraphic 8400 by the design
and production staff of University of
Hawaii Press.

The text typeface is Garamond and the
display typeface is Schneidler.

Offset presswork and binding were done by
The Maple-Vail Book Manufacturing Group.
Text paper is Writers RR Offset, basis 50.